LOG BOOK

A Pilot's Life

CROCKER SNOW

Edited by Pam Gleason ◆ *A Roger Warner Book*

BRASSEY'S
Washington • London

A Roger Warner book production
Text and pictures edited by Pam Gleason
Cover and book design by Jeanine Black
Photo imaging by Georgia Flood

Brassey's Editorial Offices:
22883 Quicksilver Drive
Dulles, Virginia 20166

Brassey's Order Department:
P.O. Box 960
Herndon, Virginia 20172

Brassey's books are available at special discounts for bulk purchases for sales promotions, premiums, fund-raising, or educational use.

Library of Congress Cataloging-in-Publication Data
Snow, Crocker.
    Log book : a pilot's life / by Crocker Snow.
       p.   cm.
    Includes index.
    ISBN 1-57488-175-2
    1. Snow, Crocker. 2. Air pilots—Biography.   I. Title.
TL540.S656A3 1998
629.13'092—dc21
[B]
                                         97-49925
                                          CIP

10 9 8 7 6 5 4 3 2 1

Printed in the United States of America

ACKNOWLEDGMENTS

The author would like to thank all the people who helped make this book a reality. I am particularly grateful to those who generously shared their unique photographs. These include:

The Cabot Corporation for the picture of Godfrey Cabot on page 16.

Pansy Prince Haley for her photograph of her father, Gordon Prince, on page 22.

Mrs. Olive Watson for her husband Tom's photographs of his trip to Moscow with General Follett Bradley on pages 176 and 184.

Henry A. Liese of Yardley, PA, for rare photographs from his collection, the largest and most complete photographic record of the history of aviation on Long Island. Pages 51, 64 and 101.

Mal Warenoff, President of Aerial Photos International

William Taylor, Chief Executive Officer of the *Boston Globe*

The Boston Public Library

The Society for The Preservation of New England Antiquities

World Wide Photos and the Associated Press

Massachusetts Institute of Technology

I am also grateful to everyone who assisted me in locating these images, especially the ever-helpful John Booras.

Finally, I would like to thank all the people who read earlier drafts of *Log Book* and helped me to shape the manuscript over the years, including my son Crocker Snow, Jr., and Kathey Fitzgerald. Special thanks go to my wife, Janice, for her patience and support.

PREFACE

This is my story, from the pilot's cockpit, of the development of private, commercial, and military aviation. It begins with the 1910 Harvard Boston Aero Meet (when I was a 5-year-old spectator), and continues through World War II and into the jet age.

It is called *Log Book* because it is built around the record of my 15,000 plus hours as a pilot of 140 different makes and models of airplanes, from barnstorming World War I Jennies to the B-29s that crushed Japan. It describes little-known or remembered aviation events in the mostly-peaceful days between the two world wars. It also covers many World War II military activities, highly classified at the time, that have had scant publicity since. Everything described in this book is something with which I was involved.

Friends and family have long urged me to write a book about my flying life. In fact, in selecting pictures for this story, I recently came across a note, written in 1934 and sent to me by the publisher at a long-defunct Boston house. The letter read: "It occurs to me that in the course of your experience you may have prepared a manuscript that should be published in book form. I certainly hope that such is the case and that I may have the pleasure of hearing from you in the near future."

Only a little more than a half a century later, here it is.

Crocker Snow at the East Boston airport, circa 1928.

TABLE OF CONTENTS

CHAPTER 1

SOLO

DATE	TYPE	DURATION	PURPOSE
10/29/26	OX-5 Travel Air	20 minutes	First solo

The first thing that struck me was the void in front. Where always before there had been Billings' experienced hands to direct me, I saw nothing but the front windshield, the whirling propeller, and the open sky. My concern quickly turned to exhilaration, then to complete confidence. The air seemed more buoyant; the plane climbed more easily than ever before. Of course, it was lighter with only one aboard. Dead ahead I saw the golden dome of the Massachusetts State House atop Beacon Hill, the old-world brownstones of Boston's Back Bay, and the thriving waterfront, all dominated by the 500-foot tall Custom House tower.

The cinder-covered East Boston landing field had been smoothed by a pair of draft horses pulling a wooden drag. The weather was clear with the wind light from the west. Today was to be my fifth flying lesson. I had already had an hour and 50 minutes of instruction in air work and landings.

The Travel Air was a three-place open-cockpit biplane, its two short wings tied together with struts and wires for strength and low cost. The forward cockpit had a pair of seats for passengers or instructor, with a single cockpit behind for pilot or student. This fore-and-aft arrangement allowed the instructor to use hand signals without diverting the student's attention from his reference for level flight, the horizon. Today, computer-controlled optical devices called "heads up displays" create a similar effect.

The engine, like many automobile engines, was a water cooled V-8 that drove a two-bladed wooden propeller at a maximum of about 1200 rotations per minute. The instrument panel was Spartan; an ignition switch, a magnetic compass, an oil pressure gauge, an altimeter and an airspeed indicator. The fuel gauge was on the gas tank ahead of the front windshield.

(left) My favorite seat has always been in the cockpit of a plane.

As was common at the time, the plane had no brakes. The landing gear, called conventional then and tail-dragger today, consisted of two wheels ahead of the center of gravity and a wooden tail skid tipped with the metal Stellite. At slow speeds, the tail dragged on the ground, providing the only braking—enough to stop on gravel or grass surfaces when the plane was idling.

On the ground, one steered the plane by blowing just the right amount of air from the propeller over the rudder on the tail. Using the correct proportions of throttle and rudder while taxiing was quite tricky. Too much power often caused a ground-loop when the tail tried to get ahead of the wings. In mild form, this was embarrassing. In severe cases, a lower wingtip could hit the ground.

After taking a pre-flight walk-around inspection with my instructor, Ben Billings of the Boston Airport Corporation, we hoisted ourselves aboard. When Ben was satisfied that everything was in order he called "switch off." The assigned ground crew repeated "switch off," rotated the prop until one blade was at the 10 o'clock position, and called "contact." Turning the magneto switch to "on," Ben repeated "contact," and the line man, placing his hands two-thirds of the way down the blade, snapped the prop through compression, swung himself out of the way, and the motor surged to life.

When our engine was warmed up and running properly, Ben gave the thumbs-up signal. The ground crew pulled away the wheel chocks, and we rolled forward. We taxied onto the

(above) During the 1920s, the Boston Airport Corporation, where I took flying lessons, was the largest commercial concern at the cinder-covered East Boston airport.

4

field, took off, and did a few touch-and-go landings. Then Billings signaled me to stop. Instead of the usual pointer or comment, he climbed out, patted my shoulder, and said, "Let's see what you can do by yourself."

Bearing in mind the adage that the runway behind you is of no use on takeoff, I turned 180 degrees and taxied gingerly to the downwind end of the field. Looking around and seeing no traffic, I turned into the wind, opened the throttle wide, pushed the stick forward to lift the tail off the ground, and soon was airborne.

The first thing that struck me was the void in front. Where always before there had been Billings' experienced hands to direct me, I saw nothing but the front windshield, the whirling propeller, and the open sky. My concern quickly turned to exhilaration, then to complete confidence. The air seemed more buoyant; the plane climbed more easily than ever before. Of course, it was lighter with only one aboard.

Dead ahead I saw the golden dome of the Massachusetts State House atop Beacon Hill, the old-world brownstones of Boston's Back Bay, and the thriving waterfront, all dominated by the 500-foot tall Custom House tower—quite a contrast to the swarming city of today, with skyscrapers of dubious architecture dwarfing all else and a waterfront encrusted with hotels, condominiums and office buildings. Taking advantage of my sole control of the plane, I flew an extended traffic pattern over Boston. I even spotted the house where I was born, on the stone wall bank of the Charles River Basin.

Returning to East Boston, I knew that landing would be the most complicated part of my flight. I would have to watch for

---

(above) The Boston skyline was dominated by the 500-foot tall Custom House Tower. The airport on Jeffries Point is at the top of this photo.

other planes, scan my instruments, pick a touchdown point, then maneuver to line up for a final approach into the wind. I would then descend, gradually reducing throttle and airspeed, until I was just high enough above the ground to flare out, raise the plane's nose by easing back on the stick, stall the wings, and allow the main wheels and tail-skid to settle gently to the ground together. This was called a three-point landing. It is out of style today because most aircraft have their main wheels behind the center of gravity, with a steerable nose wheel up front. Touchdown is made on the two main wheels, while the nose wheel descends gently to the ground during the landing run. Planes with this tricycle configuration are safer and more stable than those with tail-dragger landing gear, which were prone to ground loops.

Fortunately, my first solo landing was a successful three-point, justifying my instructor's confidence in letting me go it alone after two hours of instruction instead of the eight- to nine-hour norm. For me, a 21-year-old first year law student at Harvard, this solo was the climax of 16 years of intermittent preparation.

I was first exposed to airplanes in 1910. From September 3 to 13 of that year, the Harvard Boston Aero Meet attracted my

HARVARD-·BOSTON· AERO MEET

Harvard Aero Field · Atlantic Mass. · Sept. 3rd to 13th 1910

family to the Harvard Aero Field in Atlantic, Massachusetts. I was only 5 years old at the time so my recollections are hazy. I do remember sitting in a crowded wooden grandstand with the family chauffeur, Foley, watching a red triplane make many unsuccessful efforts to get off the ground, before it ended up in a cloud of dust. This earthbound machine was designed, built and operated by A.V. Roe, an Englishman who would go on to create the Avro training plane in which I was to have my first flight twelve years later.

The noise and excitement of the successful flights was memorable. Some demonstrations involved dropping objects that emitted a puff of white smoke when they hit the ground. A few pilots delighted in passing as low and close to the grandstand as they could. These antics soon persuaded Foley that we would be safer in the open, with more room to maneuver or duck if need be.

Years later, I learned this meet had been a significant affair. It was organized by A. Lawrence Rotch, Harvard Professor of Meteorology and guiding spirit of the meet's sponsor, The Harvard Aeronautical Society. President Taft was there, as was his Secretary of the Navy, George von L. Meyer, who came to observe attempts to drop dummy bombs on a mock battleship. The Russian ambassador, Baron Rosen, joined him, demonstrat-

(right) John F. "Honey Fitz" Fitzgerald enjoying his ride with English aviator Claude Grahame-White at the 1910 Harvard Boston Aero Meet.

ing an early interest in military air power. John F. "Honey Fitz" Fitzgerald, mayor of Boston, bummed a ride with the star of the show, English aviator Claude Grahame-White, billed by the *Boston Globe* as "an extremely handsome young man of 31, a graduate of Bleriot's flying school at Pau, a splendid horseman, a good rider to the hounds and a crack automobilist."

Grahame-White won the top prize, $10,000 offered by General Charles Taylor, founder of the *Boston Globe*, for the fastest flight from the field at Squantum over Dorchester Bay to Boston Light, back to Squantum and around the Light again, a distance of 33 miles over water. This took 34 minutes, 1 and $1/5$ seconds, at an average ground speed of 58 miles per hour. Grahame-White also won the bomb-dropping contest with such precision that meet chairman Adams D. Claflin reported that the demonstration "proved conclusively that the aeroplane must be seriously considered in any future wars as the accuracy with which dummy bombs were dropped was a great surprise to all the military officers present."

Grahame-White made extra money by taking people at the meet on 15-minute plane hops for five hundred 1910 dollars. A dozen years later, the going price for such a ride had dropped to 5 dollars.

After this air meet, my next exposure to aeronautics was through dart and glider contests with my two older brothers. The darts, made of sheets of letter-sized paper, first folded lengthwise down the middle, and then with three overlapping diagonal folds

(left) Claude Grahame-White in his Farman biplane, silhouetted against the sky.

on each side, resembled today's supersonic fighter planes in shape and maneuverability. By bending the trailing edges of the tail up (simulating the action of elevators on a plane) we could make our darts do loops. When one edge was bent up and the other down (like moving a plane's control stick to one side) the dart would do a series of rolls. We also cut gliders with wings and V-tails from folded pieces of stiff paper.

Our family summer cottage had a large hall with a balcony along one side. We would launch our entries with no forward thrust from the railing of the balcony. The glider that hit highest on the far wall was the winner. From these games, I learned about the effect on performance and stability of shifting the center of gravity by sticking pins in the right places, improving the glide angle by putting camber in the wings and providing lateral stability with dihedral angle. My brothers and I rivaled each other, but I rarely won the contest.

World War I came when I was 9 years old. Like most Americans, I was enthralled by the skill, daring and gallantry of the early fighter pilots. It didn't seem to make much difference which side they were on. Our heros included volunteers in the Lafayette Escadrille, founded by Bostonian Norman Prince, who recruited Americans to fly with the French. French aces Fonck, Nungesser, and Guynemer; Germans such as von Richthofen and Immelmann; the Canadian pilot Billy Bishop—all got equal billing in the papers. We read that troops in the trenches were apt to cheer the winner of aerial combats over their heads, regardless of nationality.

Soon the war became more personal. In February, 1917, my next older brother, Kick, a 17-year-old Harvard freshman and the most adventurous in our family, volunteered to drive ambulances for the American Field Service in France. On April 6, 1917, when the United States declared war on the Central Powers, my oldest brother Bill, a Harvard junior, enlisted in a Navy pilot's course at Massachusetts Institute of Technology, and went on to Pensacola, Florida as a Naval Air Cadet to train under Lieutenant Commander Richard Evelyn Byrd. In November 1917, he won his wings as Naval Aviator Number 328, and was commissioned an ensign.

In August, Kick returned from France where he and six other members of Section 13, American Field Service, received the French War Medal for valor under fire. They had earned this honor after the differential on Kick's ambulance failed while the group was driving through an area under sporadic

---

(above) My oldest brother Bill won his wings as Naval Aviator Number 328 in 1917. During World War I, he flew anti-submarine patrol off the French and English coasts.

German gunfire. The other ambulances in the convoy stopped to help. Spotting a wrecked ambulance nearby, the men transplanted its rear end to Kick's vehicle. In their haste, they installed the new rear end the wrong way around, so that when Kick started up, he went backward, and could only go forward in reverse speed. The whole convoy stuck together and made it back to the field hospital unharmed.

Intrigued by what he had seen of the war in Europe, Kick spent several months trying to enlist in some branch of American military aviation, but since he was under age, had no luck. The following spring, he went to Canada, where they were not so fussy, enlisted in the Royal Flying Corps, and won his wings just as the war ended. By contrast, Bill flew anti-submarine patrol off the French and English coasts. He piloted a lumbering biplane flying boat, the HS-2L, powered by two 400 horsepower V-12 water-cooled Liberty engines. After the war, these engines, modified for marine use, were widely used to power innocent-looking fishing boats for rumrunning.

While Bill and Kick were getting their first tastes of flying, I discovered a book called *The Aeroplane Speaks* in my Middlesex School library. Written by H. Barber, Captain, Royal Flying Corps, and published in 1917, this book offered the clearest and most understandable exposition of how and why an airplane flies that I had seen, and I studied it with more diligence than I

(left) A German World War I plane goes down after a dogfight. We read that troops in the trenches cheered the winners of aerial combats, regardless of nationality.

did my prescribed reading. The fundamentals of airplane design and operation have changed little since then. For example:

> "And I," said the Propeller, "I screw through the air and produce the thrust. I thrust the aeroplane through the air and overcome the drift; and the lift increases with the speed and when it equals the weight of gravity then—there you are—flight! And nothing mysterious about it at all."

In later years, remembering Captain Barber's book, I realized that machines, from autos to Xeroxes, really did have voices. These could be squeaks, grinding noises, or rattles. Usually the machines were begging for lubrication, without which they would overheat and fail. Other times they would rattle to say a nut was coming loose and was about to let an important part fall off. I learned to listen to these voices, and it paid off.

The war ended with both brothers home and safe. Afterwards, military surplus could be had for very little. Curtiss OX-5 airplane engines, designed for U.S. training planes, cost $50 each, unused and still in their crates. They were intended for Curtiss JN-4s, known as Jennies, which could be obtained new for a few hundred dollars. Kick, who decided not to con-tinue at Harvard, bought an English Avro biplane, the standard Royal Flying Corps trainer. In due course, the crates arrived at a small grass landing field in nearby Weston, Massachusetts. An old potting shed soon became the assembly plant for the plane that would give me my first experience in airplane mechanics and later in actual flight.

The field was operated by the Skywriting Corporation of America which, like other aviation enterprises, was trying to capitalize on the post-war plethora of surplus planes and pilots. Cigarettes had become a staple of life for troops in the trenches, and American Tobacco Company hired Skywriting Corporation to persuade the civilian population that smoking Lucky Strikes was the thing to do. They used English SE-5s, World War I pursuit planes with engine exhausts modified to emit white smoke. A dashing young Englishman named Leslie Robert Gresham Tait-Cox was their chief pilot.

Remembering Claude Grahame-White's popularity at the Harvard Boston Aero Meet, I concluded that the best guarantee for making it with the ladies was to be an English pilot with a hyphenated surname.

I learned later, to my delight, that just being a pilot was enough.

CHAPTER 2

FIRST FLIGHTS

DATE	TYPE	DURATION	PURPOSE	PILOT	PASSENGER
10/17/22	Avro	25 minutes	Test hop	Kitchell Snow	Crocker Snow

The plane rose beneath us, and suddenly we were airborne, sailing effortlessly over the trees at the end of the field, watching the houses shrink and the landscape expand as we climbed. It was all that I had ever dreamed of—the freedom, the solitude and the boundless possibility of the open skies. We could go anywhere. Kick even let me try the controls. I enjoyed tilting the sky and the ground just by moving the joy stick.

In 1922, I graduated from Middlesex School in historic Concord, Massachusetts, where the Revolutionary War started and Transcendental poets made their homes. During my five years there, besides a reasonable academic record and a passing knowledge of several scholastic sports, I acquired something of a reputation as an automotive mechanic.

Without the approval of the authorities, I maintained and operated four motorcycles. The first was an Excelsior that had neither clutch nor starter, only a compression-release lever on the handlebar. To start, one released the compression, pushed the machine as fast as one could, let go of the handle, and vaulted into the saddle without delay. If it was really cold, I found that pouring boiling water on the intake manifold helped get the process going. Later, I had a 4-cylinder Henderson, followed by an Indian and a Harley Davidson. At school, we also had a small boat used by the crew coach, a launch with a 3-cylinder, 2-cycle power plant. I was the only person around who could start this and keep it running. Engines were something I understood.

Meanwhile, my brother Kick, now Lieutenant Kitchell Snow, joined the initial pilot cadre of the 101st Observation Squadron of the Air National Guard. Federally recognized in November 1921, the 101st set up shop at the inadequate

(right) My brother Kick (on the right) with his Air National Guard friend Caldwell Phillips.

National Guard Muster Field in Framingham, Massachusetts. When not occupied there, Kick was busy putting together his Avro airplane in nearby Weston. In the fall of 1922, he asked if I would like to check up on the airplane and its engine, admitting that he and his National Guard helpers were not sure they had everything right. I had just entered my freshman year at Harvard where the curriculum was not as demanding as it is today. (There were other differences: it cost my father $700 a year for my tuition.) I jumped at the chance.

The Avro was an open cockpit biplane with struts and wires between the wings and a tail skid for brakes. The engine, a Gnome-Le Rhone monosoupap (single valve), was different from anything I had ever worked on—an air-cooled radial with the propeller fastened to the crankcase. The engine rotated about its crankshaft, which was bolted to the fuselage. The resulting massive flywheel acted as a gyroscope, so that the plane tended to dive when turning to port, and to climb when turning to starboard. Centrifugal force kept the engine's combustion chambers oversupplied with lubricating oil. Ordinary mineral oil burns, and the thick carbon residue would soon have fouled the spark plugs, so we used castor oil, which does not burn. The hot oil spewed from exhaust ports on the ends of

the whirling cylinders, where it was supposed to be gathered in a collector ring under the belly of the plane. Some of it usually missed this ring and ended up all over anyone or anything in the slipstream. Hot castor oil has a distinctive and pleasant odor, but it is also very sticky. In later years, I suppose to evoke the memory of my earliest flights, I used castor oil in a Bugatti I road-raced.

There was no carburetor on the Avro, and thus no throttle. Except for the slight effect of a mixture control, one regulated engine speed with a "blip switch" on top of the joy stick. Intermittently depressing this had the same effect as turning a car's ignition on and off in the event of a stuck open throttle. The only way the pilot could idle his engine was with the blip switch, causing the characteristic *brrp, brrp, brrp,* sound heard during warm-up and taxiing of many World War I pursuit planes.

By mid-October, Kick was satisfied that the Avro was ready for a test hop. It was a perfect day at Weston; the weather was clear, with a light wind and a blue sky. The engine checked out well on the ground. Even the date was auspicious—it was Tuesday, October 17, and I was 17 at the time. Since I had helped with the final mechanical adjustments of the plane, Kick invited,

(above) Captain Joe Willis and Major Charles Wooley, commanding officer of the 101st Observation Squadron of the Air National Guard.

in fact urged me to come along on the first flight. I hardly needed urging.

We climbed aboard, Kick taking his place in front, me seated behind him. The engine started right away, and after a brief warm-up, Kick raised his left thumb. On this signal, our ground crew pulled the wheel chocks: because of the high idling speeds of the rotary engine, two people were needed to remove the chocks from either side of the plane at exactly the same time. Kick lifted his right thumb from the blip switch, and we were off, rolling over the rough grass, and then, like magic, lifting into the air.

My first flight was all I had dreamed of: sailing effortlessly over the trees at the end of the field; watching the houses shrink and the landscape expand as we climbed; best of all, understanding what was going on and being part of the action. It was incredible— the freedom, the solitude, and the boundless possibility of the open skies. We could go anywhere. Kick even let me try the controls. I enjoyed tilting the sky and the ground just by moving the joy stick.

After 20 wonderful minutes, the stick shook—my brother giving me the universal signal: "I'm taking over." I relinquished the controls, and we headed back to the field. Kick side-slipped over the trees to a perfect three-point landing. My first flight was over, but the exhilaration of flying would stay with me forever. Driving my car (a Locomobile Phaeton) back to Cambridge in a state of euphoria, I fantasized pulling back on the steering wheel and soaring over the earthbound traffic in front of me.

During the twenties, aviation in Massachusetts was slowly gaining status. Officers of the 101st Squadron were lobbying for a better base of operations; one that could serve as a commercial aerodrome for Boston as well as a military base. Instead of working in suburban Framingham, they wanted to be headquartered at an airfield in Boston. Leaders in the airfield for Boston campaign included the 101st's first Squadron Commander, World War I ace Captain Joe Knowles, soon to be succeeded by Captain Charles Wooley and operations officer Louis Boutwell (both to serve with distinction in World War II), as well as three members of the famous Lafayette Escadrille, who would later become my chief flying benefactors. These were Gardiner Fiske, Walter "Pop" Muther, head of the 101st photo lab, and Gordon Prince,

(above) My brother Kick in front of his Avro at Weston. I helped with the final mechanical adjustments of the plane and accompanied Kick on its virgin flight.

who was also an able horseman and steeplechase rider.

The 101st Squadron had the unqualified support of the Boston Chamber of Commerce, whose Postal Committee was trying to obtain airmail for Boston. Other prominent businessmen and aviation enthusiasts joined the search for a suitable location. Porter "Pat" Adams, chairman of the Municipal Air Board, was among the most enterprising and influential of these men. Jeffries Point in East Boston was eventually selected as the best potential site. "Its principal advantage," Pat noted, "was its almost indefinite capability of enlargement through the filling in of the adjoining flats."

Pat's long range vision was remarkable. The land and flats involved were owned by the state, and the legislature soon passed a bill instructing the Department of Public Works "to lay out and construct an aircraft landing field near Jeffries Point in East Boston, to accommodate military, naval, and air mail airplanes, and commercial and civilian flyers." It appropriated $35,000 for the purpose, with the provision that if this amount was insufficient, the project could proceed only if persons or corporations other than the Commonwealth put up the difference. Governor Channing Cox signed the bill into law on May 12, 1922, and the additional financing was soon accomplished. The city of Boston,

then as now seldom able to make ends meet, contributed $4,000. The Chamber of Commerce raised an additional $13,000.

The East Boston airport got its biggest boost from Godfrey Lowell Cabot, whose family connections are immortalized in the jingle, "Here's to good old Boston, the home of the bean and the cod; where Cabots speak only to Lowells, and Lowells speak only to God." Boston's earliest, most durable and forward-looking aviation pioneer, Godfrey Cabot was among the largest private contributors to the Chamber of Commerce fund. In 1905, he had been one of the founding members of the National Aeronautics Association, dedicated to making America first in the air. In 1915 he became president of the Aero Club of New England (ACONE), which had been established in 1902 by the same Professor Rotch who started the Harvard Aeronautical Society in 1909 and put on Boston's first air show in 1910. Today the ACONE is the oldest aviation organization in continuous operation in the U.S., and except for the FAI (the French *Fédération Aeronautique Intérnationale*), the oldest in the world.

In the early days, aviation in Massachusetts united people of very different backgrounds and philosophies. In the twenties, for example, Godfrey Cabot served on the Boston Chamber of

(left) **Godfrey Cabot was among the most influential Bostonians behind the airport for Boston campaign.**

(above) **Porter "Pat" Adams, chairman of the Municipal Air Board, deserves much of the credit for developing the East Boston airport site.**

Commerce's Aviation Committee. An archetypical, stiff, conservative Bostonian, Godfrey was a true Puritan who never smoked or drank. In fact, he headed the Watch and Ward Society, which consisted mainly of militant Bostonian women who liked to bust bottles in bars. Serving alongside him was John F. "Honey Fitz" Fitzgerald, a gregarious Irishman who sang barbershop ballads at committee meetings. Godfrey and Honey Fitz became great friends, both of them aviation enthusiasts who imparted this fervor to their descendants; Honey Fitz to his grandson, who became U.S. President John F. Kennedy; and Godfrey to his son Tom Cabot, a military pilot in World War I who would later play many important roles in aviation.

As first built, East Boston's new airport had two 1,500-foot cinder runways. These were laid out in the shape of a "T," with turning circles at each end, so that, from the air, they resembled dumbbells. Built in 1923 for $58,000, this field has become Boston's Logan International Airport, more conveniently located to the center of the city than any comparable airport in the country.

While Massachusetts' aviation future was being constructed in East Boston, Kick was building flying time in his Avro, as well as in the two-place, 180 horsepower Hispano Suiza-powered Curtiss JN-4s (a.k.a. "Hisso Jennies") kept at the State Muster Field in Framingham. At the time, there were only 10 nonmilitary pilots licensed to fly in Massachusetts. Since the federal government had not as yet exercised jurisdiction over airspace, nor over private or commercial planes or pilots, the sky was essentially the limit. Pilots could fly just about any-where, and as long as they did not crash or run out of fuel and land in someone's back yard, no one complained.

Kick, in common with other pilots operating out of Weston and Framingham, tried to make a little money by barnstorming. This activity consisted mostly of identifying satisfactory open spaces near cities, towns, and villages, then buzzing the community and doing stunts to attract attention. Then the pilot would land, and offer the crowds that invariably appeared 15-minute rides for 5 dollars per passenger. Kick always carried two "barkers" who doubled as ticket salesmen and as crew to start and handle the plane on the ground. I do not know how much money Kick made from this business, but it certainly earned him a reputation.

Although my thoughts were often with Kick and his plane, academic and extracurricular activities at Harvard kept me from tagging along after him. I joined the ROTC in my freshman year and signed up for field artillery, which kept me occupied by equestrian rather than aviation activities. At the time, all the heavy equipment used in the battlefield, from cannons to caissons, was pulled by horses. Our horses ("remounts") lived at nearby Soldier's Field on the banks of the Charles River, and we devoted much time to riding and caring for them. Since I had considerable equestrian experience growing up, I had an edge over many of my fellow officers in training, especially in our first mounted exercise—we were turned loose on horses with no saddles, with only halters and lead ropes to guide them. The last person left on his horse was to be the winner of the contest. The free-for-all that ensued was really a lot of fun.

As classes wound down in the spring, I enlisted as a private in the 101st Squadron, both to be closer to my brother and to learn more about aviation. Since flying enthusiast Pop Muther was in charge of the photo lab, Kick suggested that I sign up to work in photography, reasoning that this would give me the best chance to go along on a few rides, and even do some flying myself.

Kick was not a daredevil, but the freedom he gained by flying allowed him to embody a kind of individuality that more earthbound young men could never hope to attain. With his Avro, he felt that he could fly anywhere, and he did. At the time, everyone connected to aviation was excited about the East Boston airfield project. The field was scheduled for a grand opening on June 5, 1923. Never one to be left behind, Kick jumped the gun and flew his Avro in from Weston, touching down on the cinders in the afternoon of June 4, making him the first to land at East Boston and then the first to take off.

(above) One of the earliest known aerial shots of the airport at East Boston, taken in 1923. Two of the four military hangars have been completed. This small, cinder-covered landing field would eventually become Logan Airport.

My family officially lived in Boston, but our summer home in Buzzards Bay on Cape Cod, staffed year round, was a popular place on weekends and during school vacations. Nearby was the General Charles H. Taylor family compound, Taylor's Point, with its own six hole golf course. Kick asked for and obtained permission to use the longest fairway as a landing field, and he often flew down to "The Bay," setting his Avro expertly on the turf. Over the summer months, we expected to make good use of the plane and of our own, private, neighborhood air strip.

My second flight, and my first cross-country as Kick's copilot, was from Taylor's Point to East Boston, on a crystal-clear day in late June 1923. Passing over the cranberry bogs and Henry David Thoreau's proverbial 356 lakes and ponds of Plymouth County, we saw all of Cape Cod curling like a giant arm into the glittering ocean. Straight ahead a dirty gray smudge loomed on the horizon. As we reached it, we lost most of our forward visibility. A circle of visible terrain a mile or two in diameter moved along directly below us. This was my first taste from the air of urban smog, probably caused by coal furnaces and kerosene lamps.

On Tuesday, July 24, 1923, I was enjoying my summer vacation at the Bay with my mother and my 12-year-old younger brother. My father and oldest brother Bill, who commuted by a private Boston-Cape Cod train called *The Dude*, were at work in Boston. It had been a perfect summer day.

(above) A crowd gathers around Lieutenant Moffat in the first plane to make an official landing at the East Boston airport on June 5, 1923. My brother Kick had actually landed there (unofficially) the day before, thus winning a bet he had with his Air National Guard friends.

At dinnertime, the phone rang. It was my brother Bill. He was in tears. Kick had been in an accident. He was killed attempting to land in East Boston with a dead motor. The first to land at the field, the first to take off from it, Kick was the Boston airport's first fatality.

I was stunned, and only later fully comprehended what had happened. One of Kick's helpers in assembling the Avro, Air National Guard Sergeant Ernie Noyes, wanted to give his young son a ride. Kick obliged, loading the two passengers into the rear cockpit. Just after an over-water takeoff to the east, the engine quit. Kick turned back instead of putting down in the waters of Boston Harbor, presumably because he feared his young passenger couldn't swim. They didn't quite make the landing field, but cracked up on the adjacent mud flats. Sergeant Noyes and his son were unharmed, but Kick died on impact. The accident illustrated what has now become flying dogma: in the event of complete power failure immediately after takeoff, the odds favor a controlled crash straight ahead rather than any attempt at a power-off, low altitude, 180-degree turn back to the airport. It also proved that the safest place in a crash is the rear of the plane.

This family tragedy hit me especially hard. The Avro project had brought Kick and me very close. We often discussed his decision to make aviation his career, convinced that it had exciting possibilities in sport and commerce. Two of his friends, Toby and Dan Freeman, used to visit us at Buzzards Bay. They

(above) Our family's summer cottage on Buzzards Bay.

talked about a far-out idea they were working on with a Yalie named Juan Terry Trippe, a worldwide passenger and mail service with flying boats, and they hoped Kick would join them. Their idea later became Pan American Airlines.

Kick was my earliest hero in aviation. Although his death was devastating, it did not dampen my love for flying. After the accident, my parents were unhappy about my continuing in the 101st Squadron, until I explained that my duties in the photo lab were entirely on the ground. What I did not tell them was that I was flying unofficially. In fact, I chiseled a ride whenever I could, receiving plenty of informal dual instruction in Jennies along the way. Former pursuit pilots Pop Muther and Gordon Prince were my mentors. Under their tutelage, I learned the elements of landings, takeoffs, and simple aerobatic maneuvers such as loops, snap rolls, and controlled tailspins. I learned about side-slipping and fish-tailing to land short over high obstacles, and discovered the importance of a tension-relieving light hand on the stick. I learned about northerly

turning errors, when magnetic compasses show a southern turn when you are actually turning north—these compasses were not much use except when you were flying straight and level. Since there were no gyroscopic instruments then, we had to rely on seeing the horizon and on the seat of our pants for maneuvering.

I learned, most of all, that flying was what I wanted to do. Every aspect of it fascinated me, from the mechanics of the engines, to the construction of the planes, to the subtle touch and timing needed to perform a roll, or land safely on a short field. Kick had been my inspiration, and even after his death, he continued to make me want to learn more about flight, to investigate the possibilities he surely would have explored himself had he lived.

After the accident, I had a recurring dream of Kick in his helmet and goggles, flying his open-cockpit Avro and turning to look back at me with a smile, as he disappeared, climbing through wispy clouds. I felt he was encouraging me to follow him.

I did.

(left) Gordon Prince, Air National Guard pilot and former member of the Lafayette Escadrille, gave me some of my first informal flying instruction. **(above)** Kick flies his Avro away from the field at Weston.

CHAPTER 3

FLYING FOR FAME AND FORTUNE

DATE	TYPE	DURATION	PURPOSE	PILOT	PASSENGER
5/8/27	OX-5 Travel Air	15 minutes	Photographs	Crocker Snow	Dick Sears

We took off over Boston Harbor, immediately losing ourselves in dense fog. Somewhere in the gloom, the French team of Nungesser and Coli was, we thought, flying toward us on the way from Paris to New York. The visibility was near zero. If the Frenchmen were out there, we figured we had a better chance of hitting them than photographing them, so we turned back, found the airport without incident, and landed without pictures.

In the spring of my junior year at Harvard, some friends and I got together to revive the Harvard Aeronautical Society. The official purpose of the first incarnation of this society was "to promote the advance of aerial navigation . . . to render easily accessible to Harvard Students such information regarding aeronautics as it behooves an educated man to know; and to provide an opportunity for those who desire to experiment in this rapidly developing branch of science."

The original Harvard Aeronautical Society, in addition to putting on the Harvard Boston Aero Meet, gave lectures in sciences related to aviation, and showed films about flying. Using nearby Soldier's Field on the banks of the Charles, members constructed and flew an award winning glider in 1910 before building their first self-powered plane. According to the original constitution, any "present or former member of Harvard University is eligible to membership." The membership roster was impressive, with 400 active participants in the first year. However, the society did not survive World War I.

In its new incarnation, the Harvard Flying Club, as we renamed it, was run by students, with more emphasis on flying

(left) **The first members of the Harvard Flying Club when we revived it in 1925. Front row: me, Freddy Ames, Murry Fairbank. Second row: Bob Ayer, August Pabst, Bill Bowers, Oakes Spaulding, and Frank Sproul.**

than research. Two of our charter members were licensed pilots: Augie Pabst of beer fame, and Freddy Ames, heir to a fortune made in railroads, shovels and plows. Freddy Ames even had his own plane. I became secretary of the club, officially incorporated November 1925, my senior year.

In June 1926, I graduated from Harvard and at the same time received my commission as a second lieutenant in the U.S. Army Field Artillery Reserve. However, I had resigned my commission in the Air National Guard earlier "for academic reasons." This meant that the Harvard Flying Club was my only connection to aviation.

In the fall, I entered Harvard Law School, following in my father's and my brother Bill's footsteps. This was the era of legendary professors Bull Warren, who taught property, and Dean Roscoe Pound, who taught criminal law. Most other law schools required students to memorize written statutes and codes. Harvard Law differed in that its curriculum was based on English Common Law. We had to study and interpret past court cases from which the law derived. From this, we learned to analyze and predict—skills immensely valuable for a pilot.

Although the course of instruction was stimulating, my heart was not in it. Just before our first exams, Dean Pound advised us all to relax. He said a very few of us would make Law Review, and have our pick of the finest law firms in the country; many of us would earn good marks, and get fine jobs as lawyers; and if we didn't make the grade, not to worry. We would probably go into business and hire our more legally-talented colleagues. This put my mind at ease.

(above) We towed the fuselage of the Harvard Flying Club's plane to Cambridge for complete overhaul.

That fall, I set out to get my own flying credentials. Although I had had plenty of dual instruction in Air National Guard Jennies, I had never received official teaching. Between classes, therefore, I went to the Boston Airport Corporation, which had a flight school at East Boston, and soloed after only a few hours instruction. Four years of sub rosa flying with the Air National Guard certainly gave me a head start!

In November 1926, Freddy Ames loaned the Harvard Flying Club $2,000 to buy a somewhat worn OX-5 Travel Air from the Boston Airport Corporation. We disassembled the plane and towed the fuselage on the back of Freddy's car to the Gordon McKay Laboratory in Cambridge for engine and cockpit work. We then carted the wings to my family's stable-cum-garage fronting on Cummington Street, about half a mile from where we lived on Bay State Road. Fortunately, neither my father nor mother had any occasion to visit this building, which contained an apartment on the second floor occupied by the family chauffeurs. I hadn't yet told my parents about my flying.

Club members undertook to overhaul the engine and re-upholster the cockpit. My job, with plenty of help from Maxfield

Parrish, Jr. (who had inherited some of his famous father's facility with fabric and paint), was to recover the wings. This meant fitting linen cloth over the bared ribs and spars, and then brushing on several coats of airplane dope. As the dope's solvent evaporated, the fabric shrank, ending up drum-tight and smooth. The process generated a peculiarly pungent odor, not unpleasant for an hour or so (especially with doors and windows open) but after a while it got to you. The morning after we applied the last coat of dope, one of the chauffeurs turned up dizzy from breathing the fumes all night.

I could think of no plausible coverup, and so told my parents about the plane and my continued dedication to aviation. This abruptly, and without the fuss I had anticipated, ended the need for further deception. To my surprise, the family readily accepted my flying, and from then on, were highly supportive. My parents were open-minded, forward-thinking people. My mother, née Lilian Townsend, was an expert horsewoman and cosmopolite of French, German and English extraction, with, she liked to say "a touch of American Indian." My father, Fred Snow, was a partner in the venerable law firm of Gaston, Snow and Saltonstall. My mother once joked that the firm was successful because Billy

(above) The club plane's wings went to my family's garage in Boston.
Along with club member Maxfield Parrish, Jr., I had the job of recovering them with linen cloth.

Gaston, who had been Governor of Massachusetts, brought in all the pols; Dicky Saltonstall, member of one of the oldest and richest families in Boston, brought in all the swells; and Pa did all the work.

That winter, while trying to master the law and finish my part of the club plane, I had 19 dual-instruction flights in Travel Airs and Jennies at the Boston Airport Corporation, including aerobatics and short and cross-wind landings. I gained enough expertise so that on February 5, 1927, I passed my flight test and received Massachusetts pilot's license Number 5. Although the first comprehensive federal air law, the Air Commerce Act of 1926, had been enacted nearly a year earlier, its regulatory functions were slow-developing. It was not until December 15, 1928, that I got my first federal ticket: Transport Pilot's License Number 1196. Two years later, on June 7, 1930, I obtained an international sport flying license from the FAI, so that whatever flights I made would count for flying records then being established. I still have this license. It bears my picture as a young man with a moustache—and the signa-

ture of Orville Wright, who was then chairman of the contest committee.

As spring approached, we finished refurbishing the club Travel Air and put it back together. On March 10, 1927, I test-hopped it successfully from the airport. My log book then exploded with 163 flights in the next seven months. It soon became clear that my first year at law school would be my last. Flying, which had been my passion, was to become my occupation.

I started my career by teaching fellow Harvard Club members to fly. Since I did not yet have a federal pilot's license, most of these lessons violated at least one provision of federal aviation law. Lucky for me, the law was not yet being enforced. My first pupil was Reginald Langhorne (Peter) Brooks, nephew of Lady Astor, and member of New York society. Peter later became an enthusiastic sport and stunt pilot and a founder of The Long Island Aviation Country Club in Hicksville, New York.

By May 1927, I had amassed 60 hours of pilot time. Now I made my first flight for pay. Although I didn't know it at the time, my business opportunity stemmed from a 1919 prize of

---

(above) My first international sport flying license, issued in 1930, was signed by Orville Wright.

$25,000 offered by New York hotel owner Raymond Orteig for the first heavier-than-air non-stop flight between New York and Paris. No one had come close to winning the prize, although several pilots had made successful transatlantic flights by landing to fuel up on the way across. A few pilots had attempted the non-stop voyage, eager both for the money and the glory.

Early in the morning of May 8, 1927, World War I ace Captain Charles Nungesser and his copilot Captain François Coli took off from LeBourget airport in Paris, pointing their plane towards New York. The morning of the ninth, the plane was reported over Newfoundland. Pathé News, the leading world-wide motion picture news service, hired me to fly their photographer, Dick Sears, to intercept them and take pictures as they passed Boston. I think I was chosen because the weather was terrible for flying, and I was known for my willingness to go up in any plane under almost any conditions—a reputation that later caused me trouble as a flying instructor, since I was sometimes accused of setting a bad example.

News reports, relayed by phone to East Boston, came from observers first in Nova Scotia, then in northern Maine, that the Nungesser flight had passed by, heading southwest. It was a wet day with a heavy blanket of fog over the ocean, but we strapped Pathé's cumbersome wooden tripod to the lower left wing of the Travel Air, mounted the heavy, hand-cranked, 35mm camera, and stood by. Further reports suggested the flight was following the coastline, enabling us to compute an estimated time for it to pass Boston. Shortly before that time, we took off, heading east into the gloom.

My log book records a flight of 15 minutes, reaching a maximum altitude of 50 feet. The visibility was near zero. We concluded that the chances of photographing anything were equally low, and that there was a greater probability that we would collide with the flying Frenchmen than capture them on film. We aborted our mission.

The French press at first reported that Nungesser and Coli had landed safely in New York. But they had not. Aviation authorities and the press ultimately concluded that none of the sightings were authentic, and that the plane had gone down somewhere in the Atlantic.

The hero of transatlantic flight, Charles Augustus "Slim" Lindbergh, stepped forward to claim the Orteig prize a few weeks later. He was then a 24-year-old air mail pilot little known outside the aviation fraternity. According to his posthumous *Autobiography of Values*, during his lonesome night flights, he imagined a world in which airplanes would conquer time and space, opening the world to commerce. He hoped to use the $25,000 prize to start his own aviation business.

Most transatlantic hopefuls were outfitting themselves with multi-engine planes to increase their odds of completing the flight. However, Lindbergh, a 2,000-hour pilot, knew that none of the available multi-engine planes could do more than stretch their glide if an engine failed over the ocean. The more engines, he reasoned, the more chances of an engine failure. With this argument, plus a promise to name his plane *The Spirit of St. Louis*, Lindbergh persuaded a group of St. Louis businessmen to raise $13,000 in the spring of 1927. Within a few months, Ryan

Airlines built a Wright Whirlwind-powered high wing monoplane with the necessary range for $10,580.

Meanwhile that spring, two planes cracked up preparing for the flight. Commander Richard Byrd (who had flown over the North Pole on May 8, 1926) was testing one, the Fokker *America*. One crew member was seriously injured. In the other accident, that of the twin-engine Keystone *American Legion*, both pilot and copilot were killed. Press coverage of the competition to conquer the ocean was front page news and public interest was intense.

The story of Lindbergh's takeoff into history is now legendary. On May 21, 1927, at 7:52 a.m., Slim Lindbergh staggered off a soggy grass strip in New York, with Lloyds of London betting 10 to 3 that he would never be heard from again. Thirty-three and one half hours later, he landed at LeBourget airport in Paris to the thunderous applause of the civilized world.

When the news arrived in Boston, church bells rang, vessels in the harbor tied down the cords of their steam whistles, and fireboats wove curtains of spray into the air. Lindbergh's dramatic flight, added to his appealing personality, made him an instant international hero, and persuaded governments and the public that air transportation was here to stay. Lindbergh's achievement did more than any single flight before or since to encourage the development of air transportation world-wide.

By the time of Lindbergh's flight, East Boston had a thriving business in air mail. In December 1925, the Post Office Department granted its first air mail contract, CAM-1 between Boston and New York, to Colonial Air Transport. The mail was collected at day's end, and loaded into Colonial's Pitcairn Mailwings, which took off from Boston every evening. Their path to New York was marked by high-powered rotating searchlights, seen by the pilot as a bright flash each 10-second sweep. Lighted airports and emergency fields had similar beacons with a green flash between sweeps. Besides these beacons, air mail pilots might be greeted along their routes by automobile spotlights or flashlights as they passed over the heads of the interested public. Pilots often rewarded such communications with blinking landing or wingtip lights.

Carrying air mail was a sensible commercial enterprise based on aviation's growth. However, not all pilots had such commonplace ideas, and East Boston was home to a wide variety of money-making schemes and schemers. Most memorable were the aeronautical entrepreneurs with business plans that were variously bold, bizarre and bewitching. For instance, pilot Tommy Croce was primarily a barnstormer, but he was also a self-anointed flying ear specialist. He carried hard-of-hearing patients to 8 or 10 thousand feet and then brought them down fast enough to pop their eardrums. This was almost always painful. Sometimes it seemed to help. At that time, most popular medicines, like castor oil or tincture of iodine, either tasted awful or hurt, which may be why Croce's patients thought his treatments were beneficial.

Like the rest of us, Tom Croce gave flying lessons, and did passenger hops. Croce's original fleet consisted of a Canadian OX-5 Jenny, known as a "Canuck," and a Curtiss Oriole, a three-place biplane of similar size and performance. After messing up the Oriole's fuselage and the Jenny's wings in accidents, he used his own engineering and design to marry the good wings and fuselage together, and called it a "Canoriole." He used this cross-breed for quite a while, until one day he landed in a soft field while barnstorming. As his plane came to a sudden stop, the top wings and center section connecting them fell forward into the whirling prop. His wing bracing design had worked when the forces on it were front to back, but not so well in reverse.

Tom Croce was not the only one to employ questionable methods of airplane repair and mechanics. Eddie O'Toole was a tall Irishman with wire-rimmed glasses and a little black mustache. He ran the only airplane and engine shop at the airport and would take on almost any job. His pet remark, when going over a list of problems with a customer was "no strain comes there." He would then proceed to fix the problem, whatever it was, with hay-bailing wire, "a hay wire" job.

On a higher level, Ted Kenyon and his wife "Teddy" had a Travel Air with a hole in the bottom of the front cockpit designed for an 8" by 10" Fairchild automatic aerial mapping camera. They flew for a Philadelphia concern that provided the camera, processed the film, and made mosaic maps.

In addition to these commercial enterprises, the almost constant flights of Air Reserve and Air National Guard planes ensured that there was always plenty of action at the airport. There were also frequent transient military flights, many involved with Massachusetts Institute of Technology's pioneering aeronautical research.

(right) Aerial photographers such as Frank Hartley, shown here, did a good business at East Boston during the twenties and thirties.

By my spring term at law school, I had built up considerable time in the 90 horsepower Harvard Flying Club Travel Air. Unfortunately, this flying was entirely at my own expense. I could only watch enviously as my friends, who were still in the Air Guard, flew hither and yon in their 180 horsepower Hisso Jennies, and actually got paid for it. Needless to say, I regretted resigning my ANG commission, and was itching to get in on the government-underwritten flying deal.

My role-model was now MIT graduate student Lieutenant Jimmy Doolittle. He was doing a thesis on control at slow flight, and liked testing his theories in the air. A narrow gauge railroad connecting with the South Ferry ran from East Boston to Lynn, crossing the marshes west of the airport on a strip of elevated fill. Jimmy would orbit in his Jenny, waiting for a train to leave the ferry terminal. When he spotted one, he would fly down to it, hover a few feet above its roof, and bank from one side to the other. I don't know what train operators thought of being used this way, but Jimmy appeared to be enjoying himself. As summer drew near, I started working on a way to join him.

Army and Air Guard pilots had to be commissioned officers with at least a Junior Airplane Pilot (JAP) rating. There were, however, provisions in the regulations permitting direct commissions for qualified citizens. One of the requirements for this was a JAP rating. Since only commissioned officers could take a JAP test, this road proved a dead end. Fortunately, I had retained my ROTC commission in the Cavalry Reserve.

(left) By the end of July 1927, I had become a commissioned officer in the Army Air Corps Reserve.

Without much difficulty, I transferred into the Army Air Corps Reserve, and from there to the Air Guard. On July 30, 1927, I took and passed a JAP flight test. Three days later I made my first military solo cross country, to Washington and back, via Mitchell Field on Long Island, Miller Field on Staten Island, the Naval Aircraft Factory in Philadelphia, Logan Field in Baltimore, and Bolling Field in Washington.

The only aids to air navigation at that time were Rand McNally road maps and railroad tracks—our "iron compass." There were also occasional air markers painted on rooftops, and, when we were really lost, we would search for place names at railroad stations. There were, of course, no television towers; not even FM radio antennae and microwave dishes on hills. Consequently, most cross country flights, even with cloudless skies, were at low altitudes so we could follow our navigational aids. When the weather was bad, we generally had to fly under it, since instrument flying was still in its infancy.

The south coast of Long Island and the shores of New Jersey were mostly salt marsh, and the green and blue bays and estuaries teemed with wildfowl that startled into flight at the approach of my low flying plane. On this (for me) pioneering flight, the weather was clear and bright, and I well remember the special, new thrill of being alone in the air, free to do as I pleased, while actually going someplace. Passing over the landscape, I was moved both by its untouched beauty and by that same sense of freedom I discovered on my first flight with Kick.

Shortly after my first cross country solo, Captain Luis Boutwell, the Air Guard squadron's operations officer, told me that he had just received orders to ground all Jennies on August 31, remove the engines and instruments, and make a bonfire of the rest. The aging, mostly wooden Jenny was being replaced by the modern, welded-steel-tubing PT-1 Primary Trainer. Captain Boutwell offered me my own private Jenny, and gave me a packet of blank government requisitions for gas.

"If the engine coughs once," he said, "Bail out and come back to pick up another one."

My log lists 47 flights in my doomed Jenny between August 4 and August 30. Fifteen were cross-country, several to Taylor's Point. During the same 26 days, I checked out in the squadron's newly assigned PT-1, and made twelve PT-1 flights. Next, I checked out in a DeHavilland DH-4B (known as the "Flying Coffin" because the gas tank was between the engine and the pilot's cockpit) and made five flights in it. Then, I took friends up three times in an OX-5 Waco and once in an OX-6 Travel Air. Finally, I added a Stinson Detroiter to my trophies. I was consuming lots of petrol, filling many pages in my log, and gaining intense and irreplaceable experience.

My frenetic flying continued for the rest of the year and led to my first full-time job offer. With no Army Jennies left after August, most of my flying was in the National Guard's new PT-1 and the Harvard Flying Club's Travel Air, but I was always ready to fly anything else. An entrepreneurial friend, Matt Luce, acquired an English Martinsyde, which was a lumbering, wood, wire and fabric biplane, powered by a Rolls Royce engine. I test hopped it for him, and then he asked me if I would like to fly it commercially.

This was during Prohibition, the infamous Volstead Act sneaked through the legislature while millions of young Americans were overseas, saving the world for democracy. When the soldiers came home from Europe, they added to the pent-up demand for something better than moonshine and bathtub gin, creating a thriving, illicit business supplying Belgian alcohols, French wines and English whiskeys and gins. The wholesale part of the enterprise, rumrunning, involved loading cargo ships at the French islands of St. Pierre and Miquelon, off the coast of Newfoundland, and transferring the contraband to small boats in international waters. Because of its long, irregular shoreline and plenitude of hidden, private landing docks, New England was the beneficiary of most of this business. The smuggled beverages were then loaded into waiting planes and spirited off to the heartland.

Tringaly's Boatyard at Jeffries Point, right next to the airport, converted small boats into specialized rumrunning vehicles. They started with surplus Navy vessels or offshore fishing boats, typically powered by one conventional marine engine—the 100 horsepower, 4-cylinder Van Blerks, for instance. With this engine, the boats would putt-putt along at an innocent 10 knots while entering or leaving port. At Tringaly's Boatyard, however, they would gain an additional pair of converted, 12-cylinder, 400 horsepower Liberty airplane engines, enabling them to outrun the U.S. Coast Guard on the open seas.

Since airplanes were often chartered to rendezvous with waiting cargo ships, those of us flying out of Boston knew many of the rumrunners. We learned that their operations were often financed by syndicates that included the most proper Bostonians. My job offer, which involved taking unspecified items from Boston to various locations, paid a bit too well. I suspected that the Martinsyde was to carry cargo somewhat more volatile than the mail.

Like most Americans I had no scruples about breaking an unpopular law as a consumer, but it wasn't my first choice as a profession. I turned down the job. When the 1933 repeal of the Eighteenth Amendment ruined the rumrunning business, several successful rumrunning pilots became famous in racing and long distance flying, no doubt benefitting from their long experience flying from the law.

(left) I had my own personal Air National Guard "Hisso Jenny" for the month of August, 1927.

35

CHAPTER 4

SKYWAYS TAKES OFF

DATE	TYPE	DURATION	PASSENGER	PILOT
7/12/28	Stearman C-3B	12 hours, 45 minutes	Bart Bacon	Crocker Snow

I took off from the Stearman factory in Wichita, Kansas, and headed towards St. Louis, my first stop on the route to Boston. Cruising over farm country, I navigated by dead reckoning, using various cues to verify my position. Section lines running north-south and east-west were a good check on my compass, and the cows, turning their behinds to the wind, showed me which direction it was blowing. Usually as I flew over cattle on their ranges, they barely budged. On this day, however, as I skimmed along at my customary low altitude, the cows scattered, startled by the noise of the plane. This meant I had strayed from my path: cows living on a direct course between cities were accustomed to airplanes.

By the end of 1927, aviation was experiencing an incredible surge of popularity and public interest. Continued improvements in airplane technology, as well as such feats as Lindbergh's successful transatlantic flight, made flying seem a glamorous and commercially viable activity. Lindbergh followed his flight with a nationwide tour to promote aeronautics, financed by multi-millionaire Harry Guggenheim. Airplane sales and investments soared, while entrepreneurs designed new planes for sportsmen, corporations and the infant passenger airlines.

Flying in Boston was also taking off. Since I did not return for my second year of law school, I was free to pursue aviation as a commercial venture. Not long after I turned down Matt Luce's rumrunning proposition, my friend Ted Kenyon approached me with a much more interesting one. He and Andy Ivanoff, a Russian MIT student, were forming a company to compete with the Boston Airport Corporation, the largest business at the airport. The plan was to give lessons, carry passengers, and sell airplanes. This was the height of the Roaring Twenties, when the economy seemed destined to grow to the sky. Andy had made

(right) The Skyways hangar. We had distributorships for Bellanca, Moth and Stearman airplanes.

Society for the Preservation of New England Antiquities: T.F. Hartley Collection

enough money in the stock market to buy himself a Kreider Reisner Challenger (a three-place open cockpit biplane). Ted Kenyon had his photographically-equipped Travel Air. I had my love for flying. We were ready to go.

On March 19, 1928, we incorporated Skyways with the three of us as directors and officers. Ted and Andy sold their airplanes to the company for $3,000 worth of stock each. With no plane to contribute, I agreed to fly for the company at $5 an hour for 600 hours to be paid in an equal amount of stock. This wage was good for the time: by comparison, we paid our mechanics 80 cents an hour, and thought they were handsomely recompensed.

We operated out of the airport, but our first office was downtown, on the mezzanine floor of the Copley Plaza Hotel. In those days, pilots wore riding boots, breeches, and white, parachute silk scarves, distinguishing us from more ordinarily-clad businessmen and hotel guests, and ensuring that everyone who saw us knew about our flying. Ted Kenyon's wife, Teddy, was also a pilot, and quite a photogenic one in her boots and breeches. When she passed through the lobby, it didn't hurt our PR any.

The riding boots were not, by the way, entirely cosmetic. Boston airport was still a cinder covered landing area, so ordinary shoes or sneakers would quickly have been filled with soot. In addition to the standard, equestrian-inspired uniform, early pilots also wore a watch facing inwards on the left wrist, and small silver-and-blue "QB" wings in the left lapel. The former enabled a pilot to see the watch face without removing his hand from the throttle, which was always on the left side of the cockpit. The latter identified the wearer to others of this select society as a Quiet Birdman who, over-nighting in a strange city, could be trusted with the name of one's personal bootlegger. A QB pin was said to be the only decoration that Lindbergh wore.

Soon after Skyways incorporated, a most interesting job came our way. On April 13, 1928, two Germans and an Irishman—Baron Guenther von Huenefeld, Captain Herman Koehl, and Major James Fitzmaurice—made the first successful east to west non-stop crossing of the Atlantic. This was the eighth attempt to fly from Europe to the Americas. Soon after crossing the ocean, however, the trio ran out of fuel and crash-landed their Junkers *Bremen* on Greenley Island, a dot in the mouth of Canada's St. Lawrence River. An air rescue head-quarters was set up on frozen Lake St. Agnes, 75 miles northeast of Quebec near the north shore of the St. Lawrence. This encampment, 700 miles from Greenley Island, was located about as far from civilization as any of the news crews wanted to travel.

Pathé News, still looking heavenward for a leg up on its competition, hired L & H Aircraft of Hartford, Connecticut to

(above) Pilots often wore a QB pin to identify them as "Quiet Birdmen" who could be entrusted with the name of one's personal bootlegger.

(right) Here I am in front of a Skyways Stearman.

fly two plane-loads of cameramen and reporters to cover the rescue operations. L & H had a pair of Fairchild FC-2 high wing monoplanes, powered by the new Wright Whirlwind engine, but only one pilot qualified for the flight. Dick Sears of Pathé, who a year before tried to intercept Nungesser and Coli with me, recommended that I fly the second Fairchild. I enthusiasti-

cally accepted the job for Skyways and went to Hartford to join the convoy.

Dick, his cameras and tripods, and several other Pathé newsmen, were aboard as we took off from the city early in the morning. My instructions were to follow the leader, Osie Mather, chief pilot for L & H, which left me plenty of opportu-

(above) A regular crew of photographers hung around the airport and helped keep aviation exploits in the news. Dick Sears, who accompanied me to Quebec, is on the far right.

nity to enjoy the scenery, since he would do the serious navigating. We followed the Connecticut River north to the Canadian border, skimming along as though suspended between the snow-covered White Mountains to starboard and the Green Mountains to port. When we entered Canada, we flew low over flat farmland, broken up into long, narrow rectangles extending lengthwise at right angles from the highways in patterns reminiscent of rural France.

As we passed the northeastern outskirts of Quebec, Osie started circling, then headed northwest into the wind to make a nice landing down a snow covered farmer's field. Since I had no way to find out what was amiss, there was nothing to do but follow him in. I landed as short as I could and stopped well behind him, braked by several inches of wet snow.

His trouble, it turned out, was a gas gauge reading zero.

We had both started with full tanks, and mine still read a quarter full, enough to take our plane to its destination. Osie didn't know whether he had sprung a leak, burned more gas than I had, or had a faulty gauge. He suggested I go on ahead while he checked.

Our planes had narrow tires on large wheels; today's balloon tires had not yet been invented. Even so, taxiing back to the downwind end of the field was such slow going in the wet snow that I wasn't sure we could take off in the space available. Our solution was for all eight of us to tramp up and down my landing tracks, compressing the snow into some semblance of a hard-packed runway. We then planted a stake where Osie and I agreed I had to be off the ground or abort. Bundling back into the plane, we gave it the old college try. With the throttle wide open and the stick forward enough to lift the tail skid out of the snow, it seemed forever before we had gained enough speed to ease the stick back. We were still on the ground and rapidly approaching our marker stake when we hit a solid bump, bouncing us into the air just in time, and off we flew.

The balance of the flight felt much like my first solo. I was alone now in the driver's seat over sparsely-settled, snow-covered foreign country, without much knowledge of where I was going. Frequent snow showers cut the visibility to near zero and made the flight even more exciting. As we soared along, I wondered if my passengers realized how little experience I really had.

Fortunately we made it to Lake St. Agnes without further incident. The encampment was easy to spot, with four or five airplanes already on the ice. After we touched down, we were greeted by a motley crew that emerged from what resembled a fishing camp. I recognized two of them. One was Bob Fogg, New Hampshire's favorite airman, who had his headquarters at the Weirs on Lake Winnipesaukee. In the summer he carried the mail all over New Hampshire's largest lake with his three-place Waco open biplane on floats. In the winter, he switched the floats for skis.

The other familiar face was Howard "Goofy" Stark, with his Stinson Detroiter. The Detroiter had a four-place heated cabin, and was one of the first planes ever equipped with an electric starter and wheel brakes. Perhaps because of these amenities, Goofy had arrived at the lake dressed in a Palm Beach suit and sporting a straw hat. He made quite a contrast to the other flyers, who wore leather jackets or fur-lined flying suits. But then, Goofy Stark almost always stood out.

Goofy was, in fact, one of the most colorful characters I knew. He had first been exposed to airplanes as chauffeur for General John F. O'Ryan, President of Colonial Air Transport. While wintering with his boss in Florida, Goofy took flying lessons. On his first solo, instead of doing a little spin and returning to the airport, he headed south over the water and went all the way to Cuba. We first met when Goofy landed his Stinson at Boston, overshot the landing area and stood his plane on its nose in the mud. When the tail was pulled down, the first six inches of the aluminum propeller tips were found to have been curled back. Unperturbed, Goofy simply borrowed a hacksaw, cut an equal amount off each blade, and went on his merry way. Later, he became one of the first practitioners of blind, or instrument flight, and developed the "1-2-3," or "needle, ball and airspeed" system pilots used in darkness and bad weather until Sperry gave us the gyroscopic artificial horizon and directional gyro.

AIRPLANE REACHES BREMEN

MONTREAL, April 233 (UP)— The Ford relief plane sponsored by the North American Newspaper Alliance and the New York World landed on Greenly Island today after a 460 mile flight from Seven Islands, Que. A Canadian Marconi company message received here said the plane landed at 11.40 a. m.

The plane, which left Detroit last week, was loaded with supplies and repairs for the monoplane Bremen, stranded on Greenly Island after a flight from Dublin, Ireland.

In the relief plane were Capt. James Fitzmaurice, the Irish member of the Bremen's German-Irish trans-Atlantic crew, pilot, Ernest Koeppen, mechanic and a representative of the flight's sponsors.

The Marconi company had word from its Quebec operator first and this was immediately followed by a flash from its Clarke City operator, announcing their safe landing.

Under plans made before departure of the plane, Koeppen will immediately set to work to repair the Bremen, whose pilots Baron Von Huenefeld, Capt. Herman Koehl and Fitzmaurice landed on Greenly Island more than a week ago.

Other members of our party included noted Canadian bush pilots Humphrey (Hump) Madden and Duke Schiller, along with newsreel crews sent by Hearst, MGM, and The March of Time. Duke was scheduled to leave early the next morning for Greenley Island, estimating that he would be back with the *Bremen*'s crew in two days. Meanwhile, the rest of us would sit at the camp and wait. Our brother Canadians grumbled in a friendly way about how we Americans ("freeloading Prohibitionists from south of the border") were depleting the camp's supply of liquor, and something had to be done about it. As the most recent addition to the problem, it was suggested that I might go pick up a load in Quebec.

"I would be glad to make the trip myself," said Bob Fogg, "But my Waco can't carry nearly as much as your plane." Bob also suggested that, since I would be going back to Connecticut, I might pick up an extra half dozen cases of Johnnie Walker Black Label Scotch. "It's Governor Trumbull's favorite," he said.

No neophyte in this kind of business, Bob advised me to

(above) The fate of the *Bremen* fliers was well-covered in the press.
(right) Duke Schiller, on the left, with the crew of the *Bremen* at Lake St. Agnes after their rescue.
Later, the *Bremen* fliers would be fêted both in Boston and in New York.

land on Quebec's Plains of Abraham, which just happened to have a conveniently located government liquor store.

I explained that, although I had no objection to going, I was working for L & H Aircraft, which owned the Fairchild, so their chief pilot would have to approve before I made any extracurricular excursions. Osie didn't turn up until the next morning, but he was all for it. I duly recruited Dick Sears as cargo loader and headed towards Quebec.

The Plains of Abraham was (and is) a public park bounded by the edge of a sheer cliff rising from the north bank of the Saint Lawrence River. It was here in 1759 that English General James Wolfe defeated the French, ensuring British control of Canada. In 1928, the park was an open area surrounded on three sides by buildings. I wasn't convinced at first that the space was adequate for a loaded takeoff, since the longest dimension was along the river, with apartment houses at the west end. However, the unobstructed cliff edge looked like an ace in the hole, so we landed into a light west wind, found the liquor store easily, loaded up the plane, and were ready to go.

Before attempting to take off, however, I paced the available distance, east to west, estimated the height of the obstructions, and worried. The takeoff run would be short, and if we couldn't get off the ground, the plane and all its precious cargo (myself and Dick included) were likely to crash into a building. After some contemplation, I decided that the best bet would be to aim for the southern end of the building line where it ended at the cliff. If there was any doubt about making it into the air, I could turn to port and miss the buildings. I was sure we would at least have flying speed by then.

In the event, I was right. Near the end of the take-off run, a few hundred feet short of the buildings, I played my ace, making a slight left turn. We settled a few feet as we went over the cliff, picked up enough airspeed to avoid a stall, and were on our way. I breathed a sigh of relief.

Not long after I returned to Lake St. Agnes, Duke ferried in the transatlantic flyers. The victorious men stepped out of the rescuing airplane, and it seemed only minutes before the newsreel people had finished their interviews and pictures. Then, almost immediately, they began clamoring to get the exposed films back to wherever they were processed.

We had already gassed up from what looked like 55 gallon drums. When I examined them more closely, however, I saw they were labeled 44 gallons. This confused my fuel consumption calculations until someone explained that Canada used Imperial gallons, one fifth bigger than U.S. gallons. I adjusted my calculations accordingly—if I hadn't, we might have been in trouble. If it took 44 Imperial gallons to fill my tanks after a three hour flight from the U.S. to Canada, and I had thought it had taken only 44 U.S. gallons, I would have counted on having one fifth more fuel than I had. This could mean the difference between 36 minutes of flying time and dry tanks.

Hartford was our first stop. We flew back much the way we had come, with Osie leading the way over the snow-covered fields, south to where the snow gave way to muted brown, then tan, and finally green spring landscape. We touched down at

Brainard Field and taxied up to L & H's hangar. Before we could do anything, three motorcycle cops surrounded us. I was afraid that our load of whiskey was the object of their attention, but I needn't have worried. The police were there to protect, not confiscate our cargo, ensuring its safe delivery to the governor's mansion. Such was Prohibition in high places. I didn't realize until later that Bob Trumbull was a director of L & H Aircraft in addition to being Governor of Connecticut.

The late twenties were noted for the extreme optimism of the business climate, and Skyways was soon an attractive prospect for investors with spare capital. Our first new money came from my father, enough to buy a Wright Whirlwind-powered Stearman C-3B, as well as to become New England

Stearman distributors. Olcott Payson, of a prominent Maine banking and railroad family, became a stockholder, director, and partner in management. Stephen Paine, founder of Boston's investment banking firm of Paine Webber; and Lester Watson, a Hayden Stone partner, came aboard as investors and directors. Financier Robert Gross of Boston completed the group. In 1932, Gross would pick up the Lockheed Airplane company from the bankrupt Detroit Aircraft Corporation and build it into one of the world's leading aircraft and aerospace manufacturers. With this kind of backing, we were able to add New England distributorships for Bellanca, DeHavilland Moth, and Gross's first aviation venture, the Viking Flying Boat Company, which also produced Kittyhawk planes.

(above) Our Skyways staff in front of a Stearman. Left to right: our linemen Goldie and George Barry, Teddy Kenyon, Ted Kenyon, Crocker Snow and Charlie Emerson.

Originally, our planes were staked out in the open. Later we moved into a tin hangar. With our rapid rise in fortune, it was definitely time to make some improvements. We arranged financing for a brick and mortar hangar to replace the tin one. We built shops and offices at the airport and expanded our base of operations, creating and operating flying fields at North Andover and East Wareham, Massachusetts. Finally, we developed a residential flying school at Marstons Mills on Cape Cod. For this we set up a separate company, the Cape Cod Airport Corporation. Our location was the Bill and Daniel farm, once an Indian campground and later a National Guard muster field. We bought its 160 acres for $16,588.

These were heady times. We sold airplanes as fast as we could get them. Some went to aviation businesses: flying schools, crop dusters, and aerial photographers. Others went to large companies. Most went to private owners for sport and travel.

One day Earl Schaeffer, president of Stearman, called to advise me to pick up as many shares of Stearman stock as I could. It was not listed on any exchange, but I found some for $100 a share. Not long afterwards, Boeing Aircraft Company acquired Stearman, and I had a quick and tidy paper profit. Nothing wrong with insider information back then.

Flying was simple in those days. There was no air traffic control. I often flew from Boston to New York, hedgehopping all the way and landing at North Beach Airport, later to become LaGuardia. Bob Bell of North Beach Air Service was so eager to sell aviation gas he provided customers with free limousine service to the city; about a 20-minute ride. This compared with 15 minutes to downtown Boston from my airport office. My '28 airplane cruised at 120 miles per hour, so I averaged 2 hours downtown to downtown. With today's air and ground congestion, terminal delays and security checks, 500 mile per hour shuttle airspeed hasn't significantly reduced passenger time between the centers of these two cities.

One of my favorite chores was ferrying new Stearmans from the Wichita, Kansas factory to Boston. Much of the route west of the Alleghenies was open country consisting mainly of dairy and beef farms. Because airports with adequate service facilities were apt to be found near large cities, most air traffic between the midwest and the northeast went via St. Louis, Cleveland and Buffalo to Boston, a 1500-mile trip.

I navigated by dead reckoning. Section lines running north-south and east-west were a good check on my compass, and I soon learned that cattle stand with their behinds to strong winds. One thing surprised me at first. Sometimes, as I flew over them at my usual low altitude, the cattle would scatter, and other times they would hardly look up. It finally dawned on me that cows on the direct course between cities were accustomed to airplane noise. Scared cows were thus an early warning that I was off the beaten track.

By 1928, there were four established aviation operations at Boston besides the Army Air Corps Reserve and the Air National Guard: Colonial Air Transport, later to become American Airways; Curtiss-Wright Flying Service; Boston Airport Corporation; and Skyways. Curtiss-Wright and Skyways competed toe to toe. Curtiss-Wright was much bigger, with branches all over the east and connections with both the Curtiss Airplane and Wright Engine companies.

As 1928 passed into history, there were 132 American companies producing aircraft and accessories for sport, private flying and commercial air transport markets. Airmail was booming. The year 1929 also brought a plethora of new aviation ventures, mergers and corporate consolidations, both national and local. In January, Curtiss-Wright bought the Boston Airport Corporation, of which my Harvard Flying Club friend Freddy Ames had become a director; Ames formed East Coast Aviation, with temporary repair shops and sales offices at nearby Muller Field in Revere; and Colonial, Curtiss-Wright, East Coast and Skyways signed long term leases for space to build hangars, shops and offices at the airport.

On April 15, 1929, Colonial Air Transport inaugurated the first regularly-scheduled common carrier air passenger service between Boston and New York. Holder of the first airmail contract in Boston, Colonial had moved more slowly into the passenger market. Two years earlier, on April 4, 1927, Colonial had carried its first load of six passengers between Boston and New York, departing Boston for Hadley Field, New Jersey at 6:15 p.m. and landing at just after 9. Mrs. Gardiner Fiske, wife of my 101st Squadron mentor Gardy Fiske, bought ticket #1 for $25.

"It was so cold," she commented afterwards, "We covered ourselves with blankets, and so noisy that we wrote notes instead of trying to talk to one another."

(right) Carrying Bart Bacon, noted World War I pilot, as a passenger, I flew his new Stearman back to Boston from the factory in Wichita, Kansas.

Colonial soon realized that air mail generated no such complaints, required less space, and pound for pound, was much more profitable than passengers. The U.S. Post Office Department paid Colonial $3.00 for each pound of mail carried between Boston and New York. It only cost the sender a 5-cent airmail stamp for each ounce, coming out to $0.80 a pound. This meant that the one-way fare for a 180-pound passenger would have to be raised from $25 to $396 to equal the net take from the same weight of mail! Colonial (and other air mail companies) therefore made little effort to attract passengers. Instead they bought the requisite number of stamps and filled any extra capacity in their planes with promotional material to prospective customers. Some even stuffed envelopes with an ounce of blank paper to mail to themselves. Either way, their net profit was $2.20 for each additional pound they carried. In the first six months of 1929, Colonial transported 171,545 pounds of mail, nine times their payload just a year earlier, earning them over $500,000 from the government. No wonder they preferred to carry mail, even if they had to pay for the stamps!

At this juncture, those airmail companies that were gearing up for passengers deserved some credit for giving up a sure thing for an uncertain vision of the future. Those that turned towards the passenger market had their reasons. There were rumblings in Congress which, a year later culminated in the McNary-Watres Act, substituting a variable rate per mile for airmail and adding a built-in credit for the amount of passenger space provided.

Colonial first used Fokker SuperUniversals for its passenger routes. These planes could carry six people in an enclosed cabin, with the pilot's cockpit up front behind the single Wright J6-9 engine. Colonial's best known pilot, L. Ponton "Bon Bon" d'Arce, would wait for all passengers to be seated. Then, wearing a bowler hat, a navy blue blazer, grey pants, and a swagger-stick, he would strut through the cabin to the cockpit, where he swapped his derby for radio head-phones and a white silk scarf.

In May 1929, Skyways joined the fray by opening a scheduled passenger service between Boston and Whitefield, New Hampshire, a popular resort town. This route was subsidized by the White Mountain Hotel, which welcomed all the skiers, boaters and vacationers we could bring them. Curtiss-Wright also started a regular passenger route, choosing Boston, Cape Cod, Martha's Vineyard and Nantucket. In July, the Airvia Transport Company began a second passenger service to New York, using Savoia Marchetti flying boats, with speed-boat connections from loading barges to the South Station in Boston, and to 42nd Street in New York.

None of us knew what was in store for us just six months later.

(left) Colonial Air inaugurated the first regularly scheduled passenger service between Boston and New York in 1929. The route was soon to become a well-travelled one.

CHAPTER 5

SPORTSMAN PILOTS

DATE	TYPE	FROM	TO	REMARKS	TIME
10/26/31	Stearman C-3B	Miami	Havana	Clear	2:05

As we neared landfall, the shark-infested Caribbean waters turned a brilliant blue green. Just ahead and to port, I spotted Morro Castle, the fort guarding Havana harbor. I headed there while our Pan Am escort kept straight ahead for Campo Columbia. Wanting to give Lilias a bird's eye view of the city, I flew down the Malecon to the Yacht Club, along Avenida Quinta to the Country Club and back over downtown Havana to Campo Columbia. I did not realize that our flight path had taken us directly over the President's palace. Fortunately, the Cuban air force's slow response time gave us a chance to land before the fighters assigned to take us out were airborne.

Back in 1929 everything seemed to be coming up roses. The Dow Jones Industrial Average, flirting with 400, made new highs almost daily. My investment in Stearman, already doubled, almost doubled again when United Aircraft and Transport absorbed Boeing. A few economists, like Roger Babson (founder of Babson College) and Bernard Baruch (famous financier and advisor of presidents) urged caution, but the majority believed that the stock market had reached a new plateau from which the only direction was up.

In this climate, aviation business boomed. Airmail and air passengers were only part of the story. Even more important was the rise of the sportsman pilot. While some flyers aspired to earning a solid living ferrying people and goods from city to city, and others looked to the skies to establish records for speed, distance or altitude, many flew for fun, sport, and personal transportation. Sport pilots who took lessons at Skyways often significantly augmented our income by buying planes from us, which we would then store and maintain.

(right) Sportsman pilots, such as this member of the Long Island Aviation Country Club in Hicksville, New York, contributed significantly to the growth of the aviation business.

Henry A. Liese Collection

Sportsman pilots used commercial airports like Boston's or flew out of private air clubs. On the East Coast, the most important of these was the Long Island Aviation Country Club, founded on March 17, 1929. Located alongside the privately-owned Long Island Motor Parkway in Hicksville, New York, it had its own well-manicured grass landing field,

hangars, a club house, tennis courts, and a swimming pool. More importantly, it had over 300 well-heeled members who enjoyed owning and using sophisticated airplanes. The club's roster included still-familiar names like Auchincloss, Boeing, duPont, Fairchild, Guggenheim, Lindbergh, Rockefeller, Vanderbilt, and Whitney. I was a relatively impecunious charter member.

This club was planned as the first of a countrywide network, whose mission was "To promote social relations . . . to encourage and provide a means for the enjoyment of outdoor and indoor sports, games and pastimes of every kind and nature, and particularly to promote, encourage and develop the sport, science and practical application of aviation and aeronautics." Ambitious plans called for clubhouses to be designed in the shape of airplanes and to provide every amenity one might expect to find at a country club.

"These clubs," read the proposal for the chain, "will be located near the principal cities of the country and, it is expected, will do much towards popularizing aviation among the wealthier classes by providing a congenial atmosphere for their participation in flying as a sport. . . . It will be but a short time before a member can make the 'Aviation Country Club Tour.' He can actually circle the United States in comfortable, easy 'hops' from club to club. He enjoys not merely the courtesies of each flying club, but actually a full and complete membership in every one."

In May, 1929, Skyways opened its Marstons Mills residential flying school, offering courses for private and transport pilot's licenses as well as a special course for sportsman pilots. We used de Havilland Gipsy Moths and Stearman C-3Bs. Students came to fly and engage in other activities that the pleasant vacation community could provide. Facilities around the school offered golf and tennis. The clubhouse was situated on the edge of a lake, excellent for swimming, fishing, and boating. The school also had a motorcycle race track, and, later, an automobile track and a polo field. Our catalogue informed prospective students that "The country surrounding the School

---

(above) My Aviation Country Club membership card from its inaugural year.

is flat, eliminating risk from forced landings. Nowhere else in the East can a flying field be found that offers so many advantages, with no drawbacks."

Private airplane sales were brisk, and we soon had waiting lists for popular models like Bob Gross's new Kittyhawk. In March, we sold one to my lawyer brother Bill. The very next month, I offered to buy it back in return for a brand new one later on, since I had a customer who was so hot for a Kittyhawk he was willing to pay a premium for immediate delivery, even of a slightly used plane. Bill said he wasn't interested. On May 30, however, he called to say he changed his mind and that I could have the plane after all.

"Tell me where it is, and I'll send a pilot to pick it up," I said.

Bill hesitated for a moment before responding.

"You'll have to send a truck," he replied.

Later I learned the whole story of what was probably the funniest aviation mishap of the year. If we had been able to schedule it in advance, it would have served well as a public attraction.

Early in the morning, Bill had driven to Marstons Mills to practice landings with his new toy. When he got there, he found his plane conveniently parked in the mouth of the hangar facing out. The hangar was not far from the access

---

(right) The Skyways residential flying school brochure promised comfortable buildings, "an experienced caterer from Cambridge, Massachusetts," facilities for "every form of summer recreation," and courses for private pilots, sport pilots and those who wished to earn a transport pilot's license to fly for pay.

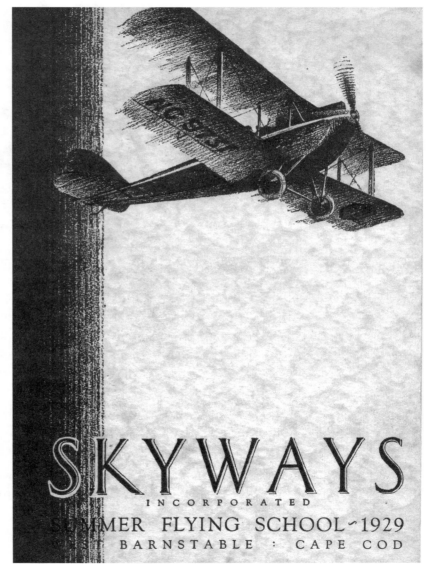

SKYWAYS

INCORPORATED

SUMMER FLYING SCHOOL ~ 1929

BARNSTABLE : CAPE COD

road, Race Lane, from which it was separated by a sturdy rope fence. Across Race Lane stood the resident students' living quarters, where the school's caterer lived. He was a tall, husky young Scandinavian who doubled as an airport line boy.

No one else was out so early, but Bill decided he didn't need help anyway. The Kittyhawk had neither starter nor brakes. However, there were small chocks in front of the two wheels, so Bill cracked the throttle, turned on the ignition switch, went to the front of the plane, and snapped the propeller through. Nothing happened, so he opened the throttle a bit more, and tried again. Still no luck, so he opened the throttle about halfway.

This time the engine took hold with a roar, and, as Bill started to run around the left wing to climb into the cockpit, the plane jumped the chocks and rolled out the hangar door. The line boy, hearing the engine, came out to see what was up.

All Bill could do was hang on the wingtip, keeping his plane circling left until help arrived. He was thrown just before the Scandinavian reached him, however. The plane now headed down the field with Bill and the line boy in hot pursuit. Then, the wayward machine did a 180 and started chasing the two men back towards the clubhouse. By now it had gathered enough speed that it actually began to fly toward them and they were barely able to duck out of the way. Still flying a few feet

(above) My brother Bill's Gipsy Moth with his Packard in the background. Unlike Bill's wayward Kittyhawk, the Moth never tried to fly on its own.

above the ground, but gaining altitude and seeming to make a break for freedom, the plane caught its wheels on the rope fence separating the airport from Race Lane, and nose-dived to the road. Its flying days were over.

During the late twenties, sea-planes and flying boats were common. Since they could land on any sizable body of water, they were useful for flying to destinations without suitable landing fields. Demand was high, and the market seemed ripe for the introduction of another amphibious model that could take advantage of both dry and wet landing areas. Accordingly, my Skyways partner Olcott Payson and I persuaded our fathers to finance the design and manufacture of a two-place, folding-wing amphibious flying boat. Our fathers each put up $20,000 on one condition: that neither Olcott nor I would fly our creation until someone else had flown it at least 50 hours. We were delighted.

Our design team consisted of Bob Ayer, an early member of the Harvard Flying Club, and later chief test pilot for American Airlines; Bob Hall, who became vice president, engineering of Grumman Aircraft Company; and Bob Dexter, brought on board by Hall. The Granville brothers, who had a small airframe repair business at Boston, built our prototype. Later, they would move to Springfield, Massachusetts, where they manufactured airplanes, including the famous GeeBee Racer.

Our factory was the bottom floor of an abandoned shoe plant in East Boston, close to the airport. In under a year, we designed and constructed the Skyways Amphibienne. It was a pusher biplane, with a 145-horsepower Warner Scarab radial air-cooled engine. We incorporated some of the features of our best-selling planes, such as folding wings like those on a Moth, which made the plane easy to store in a small space. The press shared our optimism about the Amphibienne's prospects: a small notice in the "Aviation Week" section of the *Boston Evening Transcript* claimed that our plane was "expected to revolutionize airplane design."

We did our test-flying off the secluded waters of Buttermilk Bay, away from Boston and Marstons Mills onlookers. Olcott and I cheated slightly on our promise to our fathers by doing the original taxi tests. During these, I sometimes got a few feet off the water, so, technically at least, I was flying the plane.

After some discussion about appropriate candidates, we hired Lewis Dabney "Swede" Parker to do the real test flying. His family had a summer home near our Wareham airport, where he had taken flying lessons. Swede was one of the best seat-of-the-pants pilots I ever knew. He had two weaknesses, however: he was impulsive, and he had little interest or experience in instrument flying.

After putting the Amphibienne through her paces, Swede declared himself happy with her normal flight, landing and takeoff characteristics. In order for the plane to be certified, it had to pass engineering and flight tests mandated by the Bureau of Air Commerce. We arranged to have these tests performed at Boston. On May 11, 1930, Bud Rich (Skyways chief of maintenance), Olcott, Swede and I gathered on the beach near the family boat house at the Bay. The Amphibienne was about to embark on her first cross country, 60 miles to East Boston,

where the Bureau of Air Commerce inspector Joe Boudwin was waiting. We insisted that Swede wear a parachute, which he donned before hoisting himself into the cockpit.

Bud, Olcott and I watched nervously as Swede taxied to the extreme northeast end of Buttermilk Bay, an irregular, egg-shaped body of water with its longest dimension lying southwest to northeast. The plane took off easily into the prevailing southwest wind, made a slow climbing turn back over us, and then headed northeast toward Boston. When it reached the far end of the bay at an altitude of about 1,000 feet, we were horrified to see it roll over on its back. As the plane went into a slow, inverted spin, I hollered uselessly for Swede to bail out. He did, landing on the underside of the center section. He then kicked himself away from the still twirling prop, and fell free as the plane righted itself and descended in a lazy spiral into nearby Little Buttermilk Bay.

Swede's chute opened quickly, and he landed on our neighbor Wright Fabian's estate, a peninsula separating Buttermilk and Little Buttermilk Bays. By the time we reached him, he was on the beach, unhurt and folding his chute. When we

asked what had happened, Swede confessed that the plane was handling so well, he had intended to do a half roll followed by the last half of a loop, and buzz us before heading for Boston. Unfortunately, he said, the plane stalled upside-down before he could get the nose down to finish the loop.

Swede was then still a low-time pilot. I always wondered if he had pushed the stick forward to start his dive when the plane was on its back—the right thing to do only when the plane is flying right side up. However, since flying boats were never designed for aerobatics, there may have been nothing he could have done to recover once he started his roll.

Our Amphibienne was washed out, but its Warner Scarab engine was unhurt, and went on to fly again. Since we had only spent half our capital, Olcott and I promptly gave our fathers checks for $10,000. Pa, taking it all in good form, said it was the quickest return he had ever had on an investment.

This was the end of our brief career in aircraft design and manufacture, but the beginning of Swede Parker's as a test pilot. He went on to try out planes professionally for Lockheed, and traveled to Japan in 1939 to train Japanese military pilots. As

(above) **The prototype of our Amphibienne before its final flight.**

(left) **Olcott Payson, my partner in Skyways and the Amphibienne venture, also enjoyed auto racing.**

an individual, he stayed flamboyant to the end. Returning from Japan, he had an argument with Lockheed's chief test pilot and fired several rifle shots into the boss's house. Swede's second wife, Barbara, was a "Wampus" (a young movie star), and a protegée of William Randolph Hearst. Hearst's influence enabled Swede to move to South America and avoid prosecution. In 1950, he disappeared after leaving Gander, Newfoundland to deliver a Superior Oil Company DC-2 to the Middle East. The Canadian government reported two occupants of the missing plane: Swede and a mechanic. No flight plan was filed, and there was no radio contact after takeoff. An extensive air search found nothing. The last time I saw his wife, in 1972, she believed Swede was still alive, and probably a recruit of the French Foreign Legion. It was a pretty fantasy.

On Wednesday, October 30, 1929, most of us were shocked by the newspaper headlines. "STOCKS COLLAPSE IN 16,410,030-SHARE DAY," bannered the *New York Times*. The subhead of the story read, "Bankers Believe Liquidation Now Has Run Its Course and Advise Purchases." But the Dow kept tumbling from its 1929 high of 381, to a year's low of 199; and to an all-time low of 41 three years later. Along the way, the average stockholder (and I was average) lost 90% of the market value of his investments. Speculators who had taken advantage of the 25% margin opportunity were mostly wiped out.

(left) Our show-off test pilot Swede Parker. One of his weaknesses as a pilot was impulsiveness. Our Amphibienne was a casualty.

(right) Most of us were shocked by the sudden tumble of the stock market.

VARIETY

PRICE 25¢.

Published Weekly at 154 West 46th St., New York N. Y., by Variety, Inc. Annual subscription, $10. Single copies, 25 cents.
Entered as second-class matter December 22, 1905, at the Post Office at New York, N. Y., under the act of March 3, 1879.

86 PAGES

VOL. XCVII. No. 3   NEW YORK, WEDNESDAY, OCTOBER 30, 1929

WALL ST. LAYS AN EGG

It was not until 1954 that the Dow Jones recovered its 1929 high. The decade-long, world-wide economic depression that followed the stock market collapse featured bank closings, mortgage foreclosures, business failures, suicides, economic upheavals and widespread unemployment. The only businesses that truly thrived during the first part of the Depression were rumrunning and bootlegging. These enterprises, and the Al Capones they spawned, finally went belly-up in 1933 with the repeal of Prohibition.

By most accounts, both historical and fictional, the Great Depression had equally devastating effects across the board. But such was not really the case. Those with well-paid professions or substantial fixed income or capital did quite well. Due to deflation, their dollars purchased 27% more in 1933 than they had in 1929. Those with cash and the courage to invest in the stock market at or near the bottom did even better. In two years, the Dow multiplied almost five-fold, going from 41 in 1933, to 195 in 1935.

For Skyways, the first post-crash year was a mixed bag. We lost some of our best corporate customers, including United Fruit Company, with its fleet of Bellancas. Perhaps this was a portent—corporate jets are usually the first to go. Sales of airplanes for commercial use were off, as was enrollment in transport pilot's courses. By contrast, sales and service for sport and private flying were hardly affected. Our Cape Cod school weathered the financial storm well, due mainly to the airminded duPont families who summered in nearby Oyster Harbors. Most of them had their own planes in which they commuted to Wilmington, Delaware, and they wanted the best of service, which we were happy to provide.

Shortly after the '29 crash, Chris Herter, editor of *Sportsman Magazine* (and later Massachusetts Governor and Eisenhower's Secretary of State), invited me to write an article on the ease of learning to fly, which I did. After the article came out, some readers wrote to say that I didn't know what I was talking about: learning to fly was far more difficult than I had made it sound. Chris then cooked up a second article. In the magazine, I claimed that the type of person who enjoyed motor-cycling, skiing, or riding horses took to flying quite readily. I offered to solo in one day two volunteers who had never touched the controls of an airplane, but otherwise met my standards.

We received hundreds of enthusiastic applications from everywhere and from all sorts of would-be pilots. We sent the candidates questionnaires, asking such apparently irrelevant questions as "Can you ride a motorcycle?" and "Do you have an ear for music?" We then sorted through the questionnaires and came up with two likely students.

The first was Mrs. William Simms Newlin, an enthusiastic fox hunter and mother of a 2-year-old boy. The second was Harvard student Joseph H. "Sandy" Choate, III, a strapping member of the freshman football team. Both arrived at Marstons Mills on the afternoon of October 11, 1930. Charles Emerson, Skyways' chief Boston pilot, joined me to give them a briefing that afternoon.

We met again at 6 a.m. the next morning to begin our training in earnest. Spectators soon began to arrive. We had two planes warmed up and waiting: a Kittyhawk 90 horsepower biplane for Mrs. Newlin and her instructor Charlie Emerson; and a Whirlwind-powered Stearman for my student, Sandy Choate. We spent the day practicing the elements of banks, glides, and the all-important techniques of taking off and landing. Both Sandy and Mrs. Newlin proved apt students.

With the sun getting low, we took a 20-minute rest stop, during which Charlie and I filled our students with as much knowledge as possible before making a last dual flight. Aside from having trouble with her takeoffs, Mrs. Newlin handled the plane well. Sandy had that thing a good aviator should possess: a combination of courage, daring and confidence. Both students made consistent, safe landings all day.

After Sandy and I made a number of successful takeoffs and landings, we stopped in a far corner of the field. I then stepped out of the cockpit and nodded. He gave the Stearman the gun, made a pretty takeoff and circled around the grounds. Banking beautifully, he came up, banked again, and started his final glide. I held my breath as he came in to land. I could see by the way the ship was flattening out that the first of the double flights would be a success. It was: Sandy touched down with a fine three-point landing.

Our crowd of spectators didn't realize until they saw me walking toward them that Choate had been flying solo. When he got out of the plane, he was greeted with hearty congratulations and photographed repeatedly.

(right) My "solo in a day" student Joseph H. "Sandy" Choate.

Now every eye turned to the far end of the field where the blue Kittyhawk stood motionless in the gathering darkness. Nobody could see more than the bare dim outlines of the ship. We waited a long time, with the light diminishing. Then somebody shouted "Emerson is out!" and the Kittyhawk began to move.

The plane gained speed and the tail started to lift, but then dropped back. Mrs. Newlin's principal difficulty in takeoffs had been to overcome her habit, formed in bicycling and sledding, of turning the foot-controlled rudder bar in the direction in which she wished to steer, which was the reverse of the action in flying. She taxied back to Emerson, apparently for a word or two, and then turned almost toward us. The motor roared, and the Kittyhawk made a splendid take-off, swept up over the road almost to the edge of the lake, banked, and came down the field. Back to the ridge of woods, another bank, then the final glide. Down she swept, straight into whatever wind there was to make a soft, faultless landing, touching down at 5:25. Ten minutes later it would have been too dark to have attempted it.

The "solo in a day" event won us much favorable publicity. From the front page of the October 14, 1930 *Boston Herald*: "COUPLE MAKE SOLO FLIGHTS AFTER ONE DAY'S TEACHING: Young Woman and Youth Astonish Spectators at West Barnstable." From its editorial page: "Crocker Snow and his associates gave a dramatic demonstration Sunday of how much easier it is to operate an airplane than most persons suppose." The *Boston Globe* commented: "Accomplishments like those of Crocker Snow and Lieutenant Charles Emerson in teaching pupils to fly in one good long lesson will do at least as much towards popularizing aviation as half-a-dozen transatlantic flights." On a more sober note, the *Boston Traveller* cautioned that "The two young air students do not know how to fly, and no such impression should be permitted to get abroad."

The publicity boosted our flying school recruitment, and supported our confidence in the durability of sport and social flying. In 1929, U.S. companies produced 6,193 aircraft; in 1930, 3,437; and in 1933, only 1,324. In this vanishing market, many of the manufacturers seemed to feel as we did—that sport flying was their best bet. Their sales brochures bear this out. They included descriptions like these:

- The Ryan *Foursome*. "The new Foursome is designed particularly for the private owner or sportsman who wants the comfort and reliability found in the limousine, private yacht, or Pullman car, combined with the high speed and freedom from transportation schedules that only a privately owned airplane can offer."

- The Laird *Whirlwind*. "A thoroughbred—looks and acts the part. The airplane has made its debut in the field of smart sports. . . . Country estates are now planned with airplane landing facilities, a nation-wide chain of exclusive flying clubs is being sponsored by that select group which always sets the pace."

- The Eastman *Flying Yacht*. "For those who love the stinging spray of mile-a-minute speed across the water, and the joyful indolence of a pine rimmed lake, there awaits a new thrill.

(right) Airplane brochures from the early 1930s emphasized the social aspects of flying.

A S P A R T A N

FOR EVERY PURPOSE

Within a Saturday afternoon cruising range from any metropolitan waterfront lie unfished lakes—duck flats and game areas rarely explored. Where old time transportation has precluded trips of any distance except once a year, now sportsmen can make excursions almost weekly to their favorite camps."

Olcott Payson and I concluded that the best way to promote sport flying was to engage in it, and we had plenty of opportunities. On Friday, July 10, 1931, participants in the Long Island Aviation Country Club's first Invitational Seaplane Cruise assembled at the Seawanhaka Yacht Club on Long Island. The planned itinerary started with lunch and golf at the Timber Point Club in Islip, thence to Watch Hill, Rhode Island, for dinner and dancing at Narragansett's Dunes Club. Similar sports and festivities were planned over the next days for Nantucket, Cotuit, Provincetown, Vineyard Haven, Marion, and Colonel Green's Round Hill Castle at Dartmouth. The cruise was to end at the Montauk Point Yacht Club. The invitation set the tone:

> Evening dress during the Cruise will be informal and consist of white flannel trousers and blue coats. Day dress during Cruise will be optional, and golf suits are suggested. It is suggested that all members and guests include bathing suits, golf clubs and tennis rackets in their wardrobe. Your attention is invited to the fact that professional pilots and mechanics will be permitted in all planes, providing the owner of the plane is present at all times. It is important however, that any professionals taking part in the Cruise appreciate their position, so that no embarrassment will be caused by denying them the privileges of Cruise members.

Olcott went along in his Stearman on floats. I stayed home and tended the store.

Social flying had enough enthusiasts that we almost established an aviation country club in Boston. In the early thirties, Skyways had a 100-acre plot under option in nearby Norwood, where we planned to construct an airfield, club house and other amenities. This project generated considerable enthusiasm among the flying fraternity, with a number of subscribers willing to put up cash. A full-page spread in the March 4, 1931, edition of the *Boston Evening Transcript* was headed "Boston Aviation Moves Forward Towards the Social Graces." There were pictures of the land and of a check signed by Lindbergh, one of our early subscribers, captioned "Even Lindbergh pays his dues."

In the end, however, financing turned out to be a major stumbling block. Besides building the club house, we had to buy the land and build an airport. So far as I know, only three clubs eventually joined Long Island in the proposed aviation club network. These were Westchester at Armonk, New York; New Jersey at Caldwell; and Philadelphia at Wings Field. Long Island was the only club that had to provide its own airport, constructed in 1928 and early 1929. No such favorable economic climate would help us to our goals. On May 23, 1931, about halfway to our financial target, with the stock market still in free fall and no end in sight, we gave up the venture.

Belonging to the Long Island Aviation Country Club kept me in touch with a number of people who held positions of

(left) Participants in the first Invitational Seaplane Cruise sponsored by the Long Island Aviation Country Club in July 1931.

authority in various circles. Fairly early on, I discovered that people one meets early in life have a way of reappearing later, and good friends in the right places can often smooth some very unexpected paths. Friends from Harvard, for instance, would make many of my later experiences possible, and occasionally get me out of trouble. One such time was on my honeymoon in October, 1931. Here is how it happened.

tryside and went to the casino at Marianao, which was reputedly run by the same people who illicitly operated *Bradley's*, an undercover casino in Saratoga Springs and Palm Beach. There I placed my first bet, $5.00, on 3 fives coming up at chuck-luck. They did, at odds of 180 to 1—enough to pay for my whole trip!

In my senior year at Harvard, my classmate, Boyd "Nix" Everett and I had taken a spring vacation to Cuba. On April 7, we checked in at the Sevilla-Biltmore in Havana, and the next day started "doing" the town. We loved the bright white city, especially the Playa Marianao, whose Yacht Club boasted three bars: one on the beach, one in the dining room, and one on the large sunbathing roof. We played golf at the Havana Country Club, with its thatched hut bar between the 9th green and 10th tee, and visited *Sloppy Joe's* bar, which, like Paris' *Café de la Paix*, boasted that if you stayed there long enough you would meet everyone of importance in the world. We also toured the coun-

In early 1931, Nix and I went stag to a deb party at the Longwood Cricket Club. I soon spotted a most attractive girl I had never met. Using a well-worn collegiate gambit, Nix, who didn't know her either, cut in and formally introduced us. Her name was Lilias Moriarty, and she hailed from Newport, Rhode Island. We hit it off immediately, and things happened fast. It was not long before we were engaged.

Lilias learned to fly at Skyways, soloing after only 7 hours of dual instruction in 10 days. This experience must have helped me persuade her that a flying honeymoon to Cuba was a great idea. On October 24, 1931, we were married in Bristol, Rhode Island, at a small ceremony attended by several press photographers. I didn't realize why until later, when I read a clipping

(above) *Sloppy Joe's* bar in Havana, where "if you stay long enough, you will see everyone of importance in the world." I went there with my friend Nix Everett.

from the *Boston Evening Transcript*. It said: "Mrs. Snow was educated in Paris, and in 1928 was selected as 'America's most fascinating Sportswoman' by John Barrymore, F. Scott Fitzgerald and Cornelius Vanderbilt." Lilias hadn't confessed her glamorous past!

We took off from Bristol's small grass field and landed that evening at Wings Field to spend the first night at the Philadelphia Aviation Country Club. The next day, with a howling head wind, it took us a very rough 4 hours, 15 minutes to reach Raleigh-Durham, North Carolina, which we decided was enough for one day. On Friday, with light winds, we reached Havana in 7 hours, 45 minutes, via Savannah, Jacksonville, and Miami. We had arranged for servicing by Pan American at the airline's Miami airport, with its small, picturesque thatched passenger terminal, and in Cuba at Havana's Campo Columbia and Camaguey airports.

Making ready to leave Miami, we met Captain R.O.D. Sullivan, later to become Pan Am's chief pilot. He was scheduled to take off shortly for Havana, on the first leg of a flight to Puerto Rico, and offered to escort us over the water in his big, high-wing Sikorsky amphibious flying boat. We accepted, and agreed to rendezvous with the Pan Am at Key West. We arrived there almost together, then crossed the open ocean at 500 feet, flying literally under the wing of the twin-engine boat, which was well stocked with rubber life-rafts, and had radio contact with the shore. It was a comfortable feeling to be tucked in

(above) The casino at Marianao, one of Cuba's famous attractions.

there, considering what we had heard about the shark-infested Caribbean waters.

As we neared landfall, the water turned a brilliant blue-green. Just ahead and to port, I spotted Morro Castle, the fort guarding the entrance to Havana harbor. I headed there, while the Pan Am kept straight on for Campo Columbia. At the time there was no air traffic control, no radar, no required flight plans, and the only civil aviation radio communications in the area were Pan American's.

Wanting to give Lilias a birds-eye view of the city I had enjoyed so much a few years earlier, I flew her down the Malecon to the Yacht Club, along Avenida Quinta to the Country Club, and back over downtown Havana to Campo Columbia. In the process, I unwittingly passed directly over the President's palace.

Earlier in the year, Cuba's President, Gerardo Machado, had been the target of an abortive revolt, and his enemies had gone underground. Machado was understandably a bit fussy about unidentified low-flying planes passing over his head. Campo Columbia was a military airport. By the time we touched down there, two armed Cuban Boeing PW-8 pursuit planes were warming up, with orders to intercept us. We were immediately surrounded by Cuban soldiers with guns drawn, and I was taken into custody. Meanwhile, a Cuban in civilian clothes consoled my attractive young wife with Spanish charm.

The civilian turned out to be Thorwald Sanchez, of the Bacardi Rum family. His cousins, Carlos, Edward, and Pedro were Harvard classmates of mine. He had hurried over from Pan American's terminal, and was trying to persuade the military that we were okay. He acted worried, but I suspected that he was secretly amused by the whole show. He even offered to take Lilias out to dinner while I straightened things out.

Among the papers I presented to my captors was a telegram from the Cuban Consulate in Boston. It read, "*AUTORIZADO AVIADOR CROCKER SNOW Y UN PASAHERO ATTERIZAR TERRITORIO CUBANO DIA 27 ACTUAL. LORES JEFE DEPARTAMENTO DIRECCION.*" This missive had an impressive impact. We were soon on our way to the brand new, luxurious Nacional Hotel. The next morning an even more useful document was delivered to me: a gracious letter from the Cuban *Secretaria de la Guerra y Marina*. It was an authorization "*para efectar vuelos y aterrizajes en todo el TERRITORIO de la Republica, accompanado de su esposa, en el aeroplano de su propiedad Stearman C-3B, Licencia N.C. 6252.*" Even with my limited Spanish this sounded good. Thorwald confirmed that we now had carte blanche to fly and land anywhere in Cuba, and invited us to visit the Sanchez plantation near Camaguey. He said that small planes had no trouble landing right on the front lawn.

We spent our next few days sightseeing, both from the air and on the ground. Using our authority to the full, we made several local flights carrying Sanchez and other friends. On November 2, we headed for Pan American's Camaguey airport, a 3 hour, 40 minute flight in the rain; fueled; and flew another 40 minutes east to Central Macareno, a Boston-owned sugar plantation in Manopla. A 1,000 foot grass strip had been pre-

pared and marked for us, and we were invited to stay as long as we wanted. Besides cane-growing and sugar-processing activities, the plantation offered attractive guest quarters, a large swimming pool and tennis court, and a private narrow-gauge railroad passing through miles of cane fields and ending at a small port on the south coast. Moored there was a 30-foot cabin cruiser, available to staff and guests.

Except for a few supervisors, none of the scores of native workers on the plantation had ever seen an airplane up close, and they swarmed around us when we landed. Two of them were assigned to guard the plane. I took them, Miguel and Oscar, up for short rides and they became instant celebrities.

We spent five days there enjoying the sunshine and the luxurious accommodations—there was even a forest of marble columns in the bathroom. Then we headed back to Camaguey, refueled, and 15 minutes later landed on the front lawn of Central Senado, the Sanchez plantation. Although we were expected, none of the Sanchez family were home, so we decided to continue on to Havana, a 3-hour flight through numerous showers. We stayed at the Havana Country Club for a few days,

---

(above) Buildings like the President's palace gave Havana a European feel. When we accidentally flew over it on our arrival in Cuba, we alerted the Cuban military. Fortunately, their response time was slow.

socializing and seeing the sights we had missed before. The Cubans we met were delightful and spoke fluent English. The city, with its Teatro Royale and Presidential Palace, seemed very European.

Learning that Pan Am's Captain Sullivan was scheduled to depart Campo Columbia northbound at 9 a.m., November 10, we decided that this would be a good time to start home.

We woke to a grey, rainy, windy day. As we drove to the airport in a taxi, waves broke over the sea wall protecting the Malecon. Our driver explained that the storm was a typical "norther" that would probably last for at least three days. At the airport, Captain Sullivan, right on schedule, told us he would be flying as low as possible, both because of strong headwinds aloft, and to keep out of the clouds. Formation flying on instruments was not practical, and he wanted to be sure we could stay together crossing the water.

"As low as possible" turned out to be skimming the cresting whitecaps, so this time I stayed just above and slightly behind the Sikorsky's right wing—if one of us was to tangle with a rogue wave, the flying boat's keel would be better equipped for the encounter than the Stearman's wheels. Fortunately, we stayed out of the drink, and made it back to Miami without incident. There, Pan Am again filled us with gas and oil, and this time threw in a couple of in-flight lunches. As we left Miami Beach to port, the weather cleared, and we passed many rows of tall parallelograms of rusting structural steel—the skeletons of half-built beach-front hotels, casualties of the real estate boom and bust of the late twenties and early thirties.

Further north, beyond Palm Beach and Jupiter Inlet, we flew along pristine barrier beaches stretching on for miles, backed only by sand dunes, palms, and thick undergrowth. The tide was low, leaving a wide swathe of hard-packed sand between high and low water—an ideal landing strip—so we landed, careful to stay in the middle, clear of the water on the right and soft sand on the left. Lazing in the sun after a skinny-dip, we enjoyed our lunch, watching the sandpipers scurrying back and forth ahead of the curling surf as it washed up tidbits of food for them. Offshore, small formations of pelicans, their slow wing beat interrupted by glides with motionless wings, traded up and down the beach, their long, underslung bills thrust forward, their legs, like the tail-surfaces of our plane, stretched out behind them.

Soon after resuming our flight, we crossed the out-thrust nose of Cape Canaveral, its marshes a haven for thousands

(above) Lilias in the cockpit of the Skyways Kreider-Reisner Challenger at Boston.

of wildfowl, shore birds and herons, startled into flight by the strange bird overhead. After gassing up at Jacksonville, we followed the outer beaches of Georgia's romantic sea islands: Cumberland, Jekyll, St. Simonds, Sapelo and St. Katherines, enthralled by the beauty of unspoiled land and sea. As we left the wild beaches of the deep south and headed for Charleston, South Carolina, I thought what a magic carpet the private airplane had become. Even the pursuit plane episode at Havana had added spice to a wonderful experience.

These romantic musings were soon replaced by concern, as the afternoon sunshine faded, and the blue sky turned a dirty orange-grey. By the time we reached Savannah, visibility had dropped near zero, and there was a smell of wood-smoke in the air. Through the haze, we spotted the bright flash of a rotating beacon followed by three green flashes, the identifier of Savannah airport. Since a beacon on in the daytime signals very poor flying conditions, we landed.

On the ground, we learned that wide-spread forest fires fueled by high southerly winds had blanketed our route with a dense pall of smoke. All northbound flights had been canceled. Since it was late in the day, we followed suit. In the morning, the surface visibility was still low, with the smog extending all the way from Savannah to Raleigh, North Carolina, just over 300 miles ahead. Clear skies were forecast from there to Boston. Our Stearman was equipped with a gyroscopic turn-and-bank indicator, and I had become comfortably proficient in Goofy Stark's 1-2-3 method of instrument flying. We had enough fuel to get well beyond Raleigh, so we decided to give it a try.

After takeoff, we climbed on instruments and broke out clear and visibility unlimited on top of the haze line at 7,000 feet. Our only view of the ground was occasional glimpses, straight down, of the sun reflected off shiny railroad tracks. Nevertheless, we hit Raleigh on the nose in 3 hours, 25 minutes. The visibility had improved, so we landed, gassed up, and were on our way to Philadelphia. It was now plain sailing. Wings Field in 3 hours, then home in 1 hour, 58 minutes.

At the time, any slightly unusual flight was news. The next day's paper credited us with coming through when all other flights were grounded, and with setting a speed record between Philadelphia and Boston. I doubt if either of these credits was justified, but it was a nice punctuation point to a memorable trip.

CHAPTER 6

PRETTY PILOTS

DATE	TYPE	TIME	PURPOSE	PASSENGER	PILOT
5/25/27	OX-5 Travel Air	15 minutes	Dropping posters	Miss Erhart [sic]	Crocker Snow

We reached a maximum altitude of 200 feet in the rain and scattered fog, and flew about for 15 minutes while my passenger tossed out "flyers" advertising a benefit for Denison House, a home for the indigent where she was a social worker. Boston appeared and disappeared below us as we drove through the mists. Perhaps the weather was marginal for flying, but I was always eager to fly, especially if it involved an attractive young lady passenger.

Back when throngs of spectators gathered at the airport to see the planes and catch a glimpse of the pilots, those of us working there came to recognize the regular airplane watchers. Some of these spectators were simply interested in seeing the activity; others went on sightseeing flights whenever they had the time or money; still others would become student pilots. One of our most loyal aviation enthusiasts was a tall, slender woman who was a social worker at Boston's Denison House, a haven for the indigent. We all recognized her beat-up open Kissel touring car, which she brought from downtown Boston to East Boston via the now long-gone South Ferry

which carried cars for a dime and foot passengers for a penny.

Four days after Lindbergh's flight, our Denison House friend approached to ask if I could possibly fly her over the city to drop leaflets advertising a charity fund-raiser. The weather was not so hot. In fact, it was drizzling, with a low ceiling, and most pilots probably wouldn't have gone up. However, I was always ready for any good excuse to fly, especially if it involved an attractive young lady passenger, so I said "Sure." She loaded up her "flyers" and we were off.

My log book records only that my passenger was "Miss Erhart," and that we reached a maximum altitude of 200 feet.

(left) Daisy Kirkpatrick, president of the Ninety-Nines, a club for women pilots, gets into her plane.

Aerial Photography

The next day's paper featured her picture, and a short item that read: "Not only rain fell from the clouds yesterday but also circulars advertising the Cedar Hill Carnival to be held . . . for the benefit of Denison House. Miss Amelia Earhart threw the advertising matter from a plane as she flew over Boston . . . piloted by Crocker Snow, a Harvard student. Miss Earhart is a licensed pilot, but decided that she would not take the 'ship' up alone as she had to throw quite an amount of advertising matter overboard. The rain nearly put a stop to the flight, but it was finally decided to take a short spin through the clouds and this was done, the plane driving through the mists for about 15 minutes."

I never could have guessed that less than a year later my unassuming passenger would be the first woman to cross the Atlantic by air, and henceforth the most famous female pilot in the world. Of course, since Amelia Earhart's historic flight originated in Boston, we did know something was up.

In late May, 1928, a tri-motor Fokker F-7 piloted by Wilmer Stultz, with Lou Gordon as mechanic, arrived at East Boston to have pontoons installed for a transatlantic flight. The plane belonged to a Mrs. Frederic Guest. We understood that she had bought the plane, hired the crew, and aimed to be the first woman to make an Atlantic crossing. I don't think Mrs. Guest ever showed up at Boston, but we noticed Miss Earhart hanging around the Fokker. When she was aboard as the only passenger as it left for Newfoundland on the first leg of its transatlantic voyage, we thought she must be a pretty slick hitchhiker.

(left) When I took Amelia Earhart up in the Harvard Club plane back in 1927, I had no idea she had a pilot's license.

Forty years later, a mutual friend, Alice Mills, put me in touch with Mrs. Guest's daughter, Diana Manning, who told me the full story. Mrs. Guest was from the prominent New York Phipps family. She had quietly planned her great adventure, going first to her friend, Commander Richard Evelyn Byrd, for advice. The Commander recommended the Fokker and suggested Wilmer Stultz as pilot. While the plane was been readied for its flight, the Phipps relatives learned about the project. They raised hell, persuaded Mrs. Guest not to go, and dug up a publicity-hungry actress to make the voyage instead. Mrs. Guest wouldn't buy this plan, and instead, asked publisher George Palmer Putnam to find a more suitable replacement. He suggested Amelia Earhart, whom he later married.

On June 17, 1928, the Fokker *Friendship* departed Trepassey Bay, Newfoundland, with Amelia aboard. When the plane landed at Burry Port, Wales, 20 hours, 40 minutes later, Amelia was immediately dubbed "Lady Lindy" by an adoring press.

Amelia was reportedly discomfited by the extraordinary amount of publicity she received, since she had only been a passenger in the historic flight and was not responsible for its success. In 1932, she made up for this by becoming the first woman to fly solo across the Atlantic. During her career, she set many transoceanic and speed records, became an evangelist for women in aviation, and was by far the best known aviatrix of her time. She even came back to Boston, where she served as a vice president of Boston and Maine Airlines (later to become Northeast), a job she fit into a very busy flying, writing and lecturing schedule.

Amelia's final disappearance over the Pacific in 1937 was one of the period's biggest mysteries. She was trying to complete the final leg of a record-setting flight around the world at its largest distance, the equator, in the Lockheed *Electra* equipped with extra fuel tanks. Accompanied by her navigator, Fred Noonan, she took off from Burbank, California and flew to Florida on May 21, 1937. The pair departed Miami on June 1 for Puerto Rico. In the next two months, they flew over the Atlantic to Senegal; across the African continent; over Arabia; across the Red Sea to Pakistan; and on to Thailand, Singapore, Java, and Australia. From there, the duo pushed on to Lae, Papua New Guinea, where they looked across the Pacific Ocean to Honolulu, Hawaii.

On Friday, July 2, the *Electra* departed Lae, its immediate destination tiny Howland Island, 2,556 miles away, where Amelia planned to stop for refueling. Howland, a desolate dot in the ocean, was just north of the Equator, over halfway to Honolulu and across the international date line. Even with its tremendous overload of fuel, the plane cruised at an average airspeed of 145 miles per hour, and should have been able to reach the island in 18 hours. Amelia had planned to remain in contact with the U.S. Coast Guard Cutter *Itasca*, a ship standing off Howland Island. She made regular calls to the cutter as she approached, noting at 19:12 hours Greenwich Mean Time, that her gas was "running low." Her final transmission came in at 20:14 GMT, 20 hours after takeoff. Then her radio transmissions ceased, and she was never heard from again.

At the time, war in the Pacific was brewing. This led to speculation that Earhart was on a spying mission, and had been forced down and executed by the Japanese, possibly on Saipan, the heart of the heavily defended Mariana island chain, nearly 1,000 miles north of the direct route between Lae and Howland. Neither *Itasca* nor the Howland ground station was able to get a good bearing on the Lockheed's final radio transmissions, although considering the state of the art of the equipment in use, it could not have been far away. With insufficient fuel to have gone back to the Marianas, it seems most probable that the plane ran out of gas, and was ditched over one of the least inhabited parts of the Pacific.

This tragedy could have been avoided. Late in 1936, my friend, Bradford Washburn spent a weekend with Amelia Earhart and George Putnam at their Rye, New York home. The Putnams described Amelia's planned flight to Brad, who was an experienced pilot, explorer, geographer and aerial photographer. They wondered if he might be interested in serving as navigator. When he learned that the trip would include a nearly 3,000 mile over-water leg from Australia to Howland Island, Brad asked what kind of navigation Amelia planned to use.

(left) Amelia Earhart kept her ties to Boston after her historic flight, serving as Vice President of Boston and Maine Airways, later to become Northeast. Here she chats with Northeast founder Laurence Whittemore.

"Dead reckoning," Amelia replied.

Since dead reckoning requires constantly checking the course with visual references to the surface, Brad advised against it. He said the Equatorial Pacific was usually covered in the daytime with a layer of fracto-cumulus clouds. Flying below them, their shadows would look like islands; flying above them, they would obscure most of the view below.

Amelia explained she would have a Coast Guard cutter at Howland with voice radio and radio direction-finding equipment. At the time, this combination only worked on low frequency (usually 278 KC) for short distances, so Brad advised installing high-frequency radio-direction finding equipment instead. This, he explained, would require a trailing antenna on the airplane and knowledge of Morse code, neither of which Amelia had. Amelia said she planned to make an early start in 1937; that there wasn't time to learn Morse code, modify her plane's radio, and install a high-frequency direction finder on Howland. When Brad suggested that she delay her flight, both she and GP explained that this was impossible because it had to be completed in time for a book about it to be available for the 1937 Christmas season. Brad told me he couldn't help comparing this episode with the meticulous preparation of similar oceanic flights by Anne Morrow Lindbergh and her husband.

My contact with Amelia Earhart was limited, but I was involved to a greater extent with several other accomplished early women pilots. Some I encountered in passing, like the brave World War II WASPs, whose light touch enabled them to fly the short-winged B-26, towing targets for B-17 and B-29 gunners to practice shooting. These B-26s had been grounded because they killed so many male pilots. Other female pilots kept popping up professionally and socially. Two of them stand out. Both ultimately played important parts in the Second World War.

My relationship with the first of the pair started in the spring of 1931. One overcast day, my friend Bob Harkness swung by the airport with his younger sister Nancy. She was a rosy-cheeked teenager, appropriately attired in riding breeches and boots. Bob explained that she was a student at Milton Academy and had already taken flying lessons in Houghton, Michigan. He asked if I would give her a check ride and see what I thought. The note in my log book said: "Check-out with 300 foot ceiling. Awful job keeping her from climbing into the soup. She ought to make a good pilot if the conditions under which she learned have any bearing. All dual and 14 hours solo in 10 days. Warner Fleet with prop held together with tacks."

Nancy's passion for flying blossomed, and I often coached her while she was at Milton, and later, when she moved on to Vassar. She became an accomplished, skillful pilot, with a real sense of the air. At some point, I introduced her to the man she would marry. Bob Love was a recent graduate of Massachusetts Institute of Technology, where he had learned to fly. Nancy and Bob hit it off immediately, united, in part, by their mutual enjoyment of flying.

Bob later bought a hangar at Boston and formed Intercity Airlines to fly between Boston, Springfield and Albany, New York. These business ventures gave Nancy many opportunities

Aerial Photography

to build flying time and polish her skills. When war came, Bob, an Army Air Corps Reserve officer, was assigned to the Air Corps Ferrying Command. We had both known the ACFC commanding general, Bob Olds, socially. Bob and Nancy were also on friendly terms with General Swede Norstad, who was very close to the head of the Army Air Corps, General Hap Arnold. These connections gave Nancy a leg-up in her ambition to form a military auxiliary for women pilots.

Two years after I met Nancy, I had a more dramatic encounter. Our airport lunch club was a greasy spoon in the lean-to of one of the original tin hangars. After lunch, a few of us often went behind the hangar to compete in target shooting with my 22-caliber Colt Woodsman. So as to be undisturbed during this pleasant break, I always designated someone to mind the store. On this day, it was Bud Rich, Skyways maintenance chief. Not long after we had started shooting, he arrived at the impromptu range, puffing from his quarter-mile run, to say there was a customer waiting to see me. I asked why he couldn't take care of him.

"It's not a him, it's a her," Bud said. "She's something, and she has a Rolls Royce with a chauffeur."

This image persuaded me. I handed the Colt to one of my companions and accompanied Bud back to the Skyways hangar.

(left) I gave lessons to many women at Skyways, including Nancy Harkness Love, who would found the Women's Auxiliary Ferrying Squadron in World War II.

My customer was an attractive, well-dressed woman in her late twenties. With a forthright voice, she introduced herself as Jacqueline Cochran. She said she was planning to enter the coming World Aerobatic Competition for Women at Roosevelt Field on Long Island; that she wanted to win it; and that I had been recommended as a good instructor in stunt flying. When I asked to see her pilot's license, she showed me a Bureau of Air Commerce Transport Certificate. The number was very low—in the 60s as I recall. The lady must have a friend in court, I thought.

We buckled on our Irving parachutes and climbed aboard a Kinner-powered Kittyhawk. After a session of loops, slow and snap rolls, barrel rolls, hammerhead stalls, Immelman turns and spins, we landed. Miss Cochran had done well, was pleased, and said she wanted to sign up for intensive instruction for the next two months.

"That's fine by me," I replied. "I'm available most of the time, so just call me when you're free."

"No, no," she said, "I live on Long Island, and I want you to come down and stay."

When I demurred, explaining that I had a business in Boston to run, she said, rather archly, I thought, "I'll make it worth your while."

I looked at the Rolls and considered. This was almost an offer I couldn't refuse. But refuse it I did, recommending

(right) I once gave Jackie Cochran a stunt flying lesson. She would later go on to be one of the most accomplished female pilots ever.

instead that she try Casey Jones at Roosevelt Field.

Curious, I called a friend in New York, who told me Jackie was a recently licensed pilot, the protegée of a prosperous Wall Street lawyer named Floyd Odlum. Later, around the time Amelia Earhart was lost, Jackie's name started appearing in the press as she set one new speed record after another. She was the first woman to compete in the prestigious Bendix Transcontinental air race in 1935, and she won the trophy in 1938. In 1953, she became the first woman to break the sound barrier in an F-86 Sabre jet, following in the footsteps of Chuck Yeager.

When World War II came, Nancy and Jackie competed for the top woman's slot in the Army Air Corps. Nancy Love won the first round when General Arnold asked her to organize and

(above) Joan Fay dropped out of Radcliffe to fly with us.
Here, I am helping her fuel up her folding-wing d.H. Moth at a regular automobile gas station.

run the Women's Auxiliary Ferrying Squadron. Jackie won the second round when Arnold designated her to head the Women's Air Force Service Pilots, created to train women pilots, fly tow target missions, and do anything except ferrying. Jackie won the tie-breaker when Nancy's WAFS became the ferrying division of Jackie's WASPs.

After the war, Jackie became President of Washington's National Aeronautic Association, of which I was a board member. She qualified on almost every plane in the United States Air Force stable, and made scores of records. Nancy continued flying, but only for fun. She and Bob always had airplanes: the most exciting must have been their stripped down, two-place World War II P-51 Mustang. The P-51 has been called the "answer to every fighter pilot's dream" and many fliers argue that it was the best, fastest, most maneuverable plane to come out of WWII.

Although Nancy, Jackie and Amelia Earhart were among the most famous and accomplished women pilots of the time, they were not by any means alone. From the beginning of my involvement with aviation, women always flew. One of the earliest in Boston was Harriet Quimby, a newspaper writer who was the first American woman to receive her pilot's license in

1911. She was also among the first to lose her life in a plane crash at the Harvard Boston Aero Meet in 1912.

During the pre-war years, Skyways taught a number of women to fly (in addition to our "solo in a day" student), including my first wife Lilias. One of my favorite young lady pilots was teenaged Alice duPont, whom I soloed at Marstons Mills in a Kittyhawk on July 15, 1930. Quick to learn and enthusiastic, she was ever-ready to join in flying junkets, such as exploring the remote sandy beaches of Cape Cod and the outer islands. On her 21st birthday, she described her father's present as "I didn't know there was so much money in the world." When war came, Alice did a stint working for Grumman Aircraft Company (one of the largest providers of Naval aircraft) as a pilot and Link trainer operator.

Other women pilots I knew included Cecil "Teddy" Kenyon who used to fly for us at Skyways with her husband Ted. During World War II, she was one of three women who worked as a production test pilot at Grumman. We had other women at Skyways, such as Lorraine Defren, who joined our sales force in 1929. According to the aviation page of the *Boston Evening Transcript*, she was "the first girl connected with the sales department of any local flying service." The article

(above) Harriet Quimby, America's first licensed female pilot.

went on to say she was "talking up flying among her girl-friends, and may be responsible for the appearance of several new aviatrixes at the Boston Airport."

Miss Defren also organized a club for women pilots attached to Skyways. The ladies called themselves "Skymates," a name that would hardly be accepted today. Still in the *Transcript*, Lorraine explained that the Skymates planned to put on tea dances at the airport. "Being at the airport and seeing others fly, they (women) may catch the flying bug very early," she said. As originally formed, Skymates had 16 members. At the time, there was a freshly organized national club for aviatrixes called the Ninety-Nines (which had 99 members) and there were 126 women holding pilot's licenses in the United States.

Many other women in those days did not aspire to take the controls, but enjoyed flying, and comprised a significant portion of our clientele on sightseeing flights. When we were young and single, these ladies were our favorite passengers, and we were often the objects of their admiration. Some pilots used to take advantage of this admiration. During a 15-minute sightseeing hop, the motion of the plane might be enough to cause the passenger to grab hold of the pilot's arm. From there, it was but a small step for the pilot to take the frightened young woman's hand in his. After the flight, the passenger would be more than ready to accept an invitation to dinner.

(left) Teenaged Alice duPont getting into her Waco.

Among my lady passengers during the Skyways years, I flew a very nice, very matronly member of the Women's Christian Temperance Union. On November 3, 1933, she hired me to carry her to each of the six New England state capitals where she was carrying out a last ditch effort to defeat the campaign to repeal Prohibition. We got along fine during our 3 hours, 15 minutes flying time, but it was probably as obvious to my passenger as to everyone else that my heart wasn't in it.

The following day's paper carried a small piece with my photograph. "Snow Flies Dry but Votes Wet," read the headline.

Our trip was, alas for the lady, in vain. Prohibition, "the noble experiment," bit the dust just four days later when Utah became the 36th state to ratify repeal on November 7, 1933.

Aerial Photography

(right) Lorraine Defren, who worked in our sales force at Skyways, organized a club for women pilots in Boston. The ladies called themselves "Skymates."

CHAPTER 7

BIG BUSINESS

DATE	TYPE	AIR TIME	CO-PILOT	PILOT
1/29/30	Cessna	1 hour, 45 minutes	Crocker Snow	Freddy Ames

When we left Boston, the sky had been dimly overcast. As we neared New York City, the haze dissipated to reveal clear blue sky and a brilliant winter sun. We were on our way to meet Dick Hoyt, king of aviation mergers, to discuss marrying Freddy's East Coast, Skyways and Curtiss-Wright Flying Service. Freddy and I knew that this could be our insurance against Depression woes: we could become players in the declining field of commercial aviation. The familiar, distinctive contours of the New York City skyline loomed ahead, sunlight glinting off the towering skyscrapers. The world of big business and high finance awaited us in the shadows of those proud, jagged shapes.

At Skyways, we flew into the thirties with a sense of uncertainty. With little cash to spare, companies were disinclined to spend it on flying services. The general public was too worried about making a living to pay for sightseeing flights. Flight schools catered to military customers and those with Depression-proof incomes. The world of aviation was still filled with enthusiasm, but it was an excitement tempered by the reality of hard times, and an understanding that we had to band together if we were to survive.

Not long after the crash, Skyways director Lester Watson suggested that Freddy Ames and I meet his brother-in-law, Richard Hoyt, in New York. Freddy owned East Coast, one of our competitors at the airport. Like Skyways, East Coast was in an uncertain position, although Freddy's immense private fortune would probably ensure its indefinite survival. Dick Hoyt, famous New York financier and aviation tycoon, might help both our companies rise above the uncertain economic weather.

Dick was a colorful and influential figure. Senior partner of the New York investment banking firm Hayden Stone, he was also president of both the Curtiss Airplane and Wright Engine

(left) The Goodyear blimp flying over New York City in 1930. At the time, New York had the only skyscrapers in the country.

companies, operators of Curtiss-Wright Flying Service. He was later to become a director of TWA, North American, United, Aviation Corporation, Pan Am, and chairman of the board of National. A well-known deep sea sailor who competed in yacht races across the oceans, he summered on Buzzard's Bay, and commuted the 160 nautical miles to Wall Street in his 35-foot Baby Gar speedboat. This boat could really fly: it was powered by a 1,100 horsepower converted, liquid-cooled Allison aircraft engine, later to be used in World War II P-40 fighter planes.

Concerned about the near-term prospects for his businesses in the immediate post-crash era, Hoyt was merging the Curtiss and Wright companies to reduce overhead and improve efficiency. He suggested we might do the same by combining C-W Flying Service of Boston, East Coast, and Skyways.

On January 29, 1930, Freddy and I flew to New York for a meeting, both of us excited about our future prospects. The sky had been dimly overcast when we left, but as we neared the city, financial capital of the country, the haze dissipated to reveal clear blue sky and a brilliant winter sun. Ahead, we recognized the distinctive contours of the New York city skyline, where the sunlight glinted off towering skyscrapers.

The meeting went well. Dick was impressed with both our organizations and eager to go ahead with a merger. This would make our operation one of the largest at the airport, and a real competitor for Colonial Air Transport. Freddy, as sole owner of East Coast, agreed to merge immediately. I was responsible to 26 stockholders and a board of directors, and so had to ask for time.

It wasn't until March 4, 1932, that East Coast and Skyways agreed on the general plan of action that we submitted to Curtiss-Wright. As a first step, East Coast changed its name to Ames Aircraft. On March 14, we then formed a new company, Ames-Skyways Incorporated, naming Freddy president and me general manager. The merger looked like a good match. Not only were our hangars, shops and offices next to each other at East Boston, we also offered complementary services. Ames had the best engine and accessory repair shop in New England. It also had Wright engine, Hamilton Standard propeller, and Bendix accessory franchises, and was New England distributor for Beechcraft airplanes. Skyways had the New England distributorship for Bellanca, Stearman, DH Moth, Kittyhawk and Buhl Bull Pup planes, as well as a first class airplane repair shop. We took care of many service and storage customers, and did charter, student instruction, and aerial photography. In addition to our headquarters in Boston, we also had branches in Portland, Maine and on Cape Cod.

Ames-Skyway's crown jewel was Ames' engine shop foreman, Cockney "Arry" Ashworth, who was qualified to overhaul engines, magnetos and carburetors. He could straighten bent propellers, and handle almost anything that had to do with engines or their accessories. One of my first chores as general manager was to keep Harry happy by raising his salary from $0.80 to an unheard-of $1 per hour, which became $2 to our customers.

An essential part of the Ames-Skyways deal, and, later, of the Ames-Skyways Curtiss-Wright merger agreement, was that each of us would contribute our buildings, long-term operating rights and airport lease to the new company. This required

approval by the city of Boston. At a small celebratory gathering of the Ames and Skyways staffs, Bill Long, the jovial, rotund chairman of the Parks Department which administered the airport, congratulated us on the improved service and stability we were bringing to aviation in Massachusetts and wished us well. We thought we had nothing to fear from the government.

Our future dealings with City Hall were not nearly so pleasant. The progress of our merger slowed while the large Curtiss-Wright corporation struggled with the details of joining its Boston arm to us. By October, 1932 we were ready to go forward once again, and formally requested city assent to the necessary Curtiss-Wright lease assignments. But nothing went smoothly this time. The city claimed that our merger would give us a monopoly in storage and service of planes at the airport. During this time, Colonial Air Transport, now American Airways, had the same facilities as we would have

(above) Ames-Skyways' crown jewel was Harry Ashworth, our engine shop foreman, the most skilled mechanic at the airport. Here he straightens a bent propeller.

On the white board, partially visible text reads:

EAST COAST
AIRCRAFT SALES
MILLER FIELD
Revere - Mass.

Property of ...
to be Returned to

and was a much bigger operation. In addition, four other independent flying services operated out of East Boston, with plenty of room for new additional operations like ours, but hardly enough business to go around. By this time, both Ames-Skyways and Curtiss-Wright were losing money. The only way to make them profitable again seemed to be consolidating their activities.

Several months went by, filled with exchanges of correspondence between Ames-Skyways and City Hall, numerous meetings between lawyers, and much going back and forth about our hangar arrangements, but no assent from the city.

Frustrated by the delay, I asked my father for advice. As the first trustee of the Boston Elevated Railway when it went from private to public ownership, he knew Mayor James Michael Curley well and had earned his respect. In a meeting, the mayor had once related how the top man in Irish cities and towns was referred to as "The O'Reilly," or "The" whatever his surname was. Curley said that as far as he was concerned, Pa was "The Snow" in Boston and presented him with an Irish shillelagh. I still have it. It's a beauty.

Pa arranged for us to speak to the mayor. Curley's office at City Hall was oak-paneled, with a desk in the center of the room, and what looked like a telephone booth near the desk. It was. While I was in the middle of a recital of our problems, a man entered and whispered to Curley, who excused himself, entered the booth, closed the door, and conducted an inaudible but highly visible phone conversation.

(left) A sandblaster dressed for work at the airplane shop.

When we finished our interview, the mayor said we had made a good case and he would speak to the chairman of the Parks Department on our behalf. He added, however, that Bill Long was a stubborn fellow. Curley followed through by inviting Long and my father to meet him (without me) on January 23, 1933. Two days later I received a long, fulsome letter from Long beginning "My Dear Crocker," in which he, once again, refused to assent to our merger.

We then modified our plans to ensure that we could not be accused of holding any monopolies and applied again. Long's response to our new proposal was that it would be "carefully considered by the Board at its next meeting."

Very soon afterwards, Professor Hilding Carlson, who was in charge of Skyways' ground school, came to say he understood we were having troubles with the Parks Department. He said he had been asked to tell us that this was because we had the "wrong lawyer." (My father!)

Then he mentioned a name, and said he understood that if we hired this lawyer, everything would be taken care of at the next meeting of the Board of Park Commissioners. All we had to do was put the lawyer's fee of $20,000 in escrow at a specified bank, to be collected "only when you get your lease assignment approvals from the city."

Although the proposal sounded fishy, Freddy and I were almost ready to go along with it. When we informed Dick Hoyt of the situation, however, he told us not to play along. Curtiss-Wright would not participate in any bribing of public officials, period. Bill Long had now become even more intransigent. All our good faith negotiations had clearly been a costly waste of time, and, without greasing the right palms, it would be an equally costly waste to keep trying. We believed that it was the entry of New York money that changed the equation, making a few corrupt public officials greedy for easy profit. I often wondered what would have happened had we invested that $20,000 to stay in business and who would have gotten the bribe.

During the time that we were struggling with the merger, the connection between Skyways and Ames exposed me to various inventors looking for venture financing. Capital was hard to raise during the Depression, and Freddy Ames, known as an enthusiastic aviation booster and a very wealthy young man, attracted a number of creative individuals, eager to show off their wares.

Among these was Buckminster Fuller, who was later to become world famous for his free-standing geodesic construction, the best-known being the enormous geodesic globe at the entrance to Florida's Epcot Center. Bucky turned up one day at

(above) My father, Fred Snow, a partner in the venerable Boston law firm of Gaston, Snow and Saltonstall.

the airport with an automobile he designed. At the time he had a company called Dymaxion that, among other things, made hexagonal luxury houses created to be entirely self-sufficient and light enough to be moved from place to place with a dirigible. His Dymaxion automobile was a three-wheeled car powered by the new Model A Ford V-8 engine.

Freddy and I tried the machine out and enjoyed ourselves quite a bit. It was so lightweight and powerful it could accelerate like a Harley Davidson motorcycle. Many streets in those days had parallel pairs of flush trolley tracks down the middle. Bucky said he liked to demonstrate his car's maneuverability by going down one set of tracks at high speed, turning on a dime, and coming back on the other track. Freddy was sufficiently impressed to consider putting money into the venture, and almost did.

Shortly after this Boston visit, one of Bucky's colleagues was demonstrating the Dymaxion's maneuverability to another prospective investor. While doing a quick 180 degree turn, the car flipped over and seriously injured its occupants. Not much later, one of the prototypes was involved in a fatal accident, giving the car so much negative publicity that Bucky suspended production. The instability of the vehicle didn't surprise me when I remembered how easy it was to tip over while pedaling my childhood tricycle.

Another 1932 venture capital prospect was Alexander "Sasha" de Seversky, who docked at our East Boston seaplane ramp with a single-seat, high-powered, low-wing amphibious float monoplane. He had chosen to land on Boston Harbor because the all-way East Boston airport was too small. Seversky's plane looked like it was ready to win the Schneider Cup, the world's most prestigious international seaplane race. It was sleek, fast, and fun to fly. Seversky was looking for capital for his small company, hoping to build a whole line after his stylish prototype. He asked us to see if there was interest in his plane for sporting purposes.

I would have given my eye teeth to have one, but both Freddy and I felt that the market would be slim because of the plane's high purchase price and operating costs. In addition, its very high landing speed would limit its destinations to large airports or bodies of water. Seversky later contracted with the U.S. Army Air Corps, and his plane, on wheels and fitted with two synchronized machine guns, entered the service in July 1937 as the P-35.

Some time after Seversky flew away in his amphibian, two Englishmen named Crouch and Bolas showed up, hoping to interest us in an unusual airplane that they were building in Pawtucket, Rhode Island. The prototype of the Crouch-Bolas was a two-place, clipped-wing, twin-engine biplane, designed to operate out of short spaces and still have good cruising speed. The designers hoped to accomplish this with large diameter propellers that would not only provide thrust, but also generate induced lift by blowing air over most of the wing surfaces.

(right) Alexander "Sasha" de Seversky in his amphibious float monoplane at the East Boston seaplane ramp. Sasha wanted us to see if there was interest among sport fliers for this model of plane.

Shortly after the prototype was finished, one of the partners flew it to Boston. It was a strange-looking contraption, with its two engines midway between the fuselage and the wing tips so the slip-stream would cover the maximum amount of wing. It touched down at what seemed a high speed for short takeoffs and landings. When I quizzed the pilot, he explained that he hadn't flown much and hoped that I would test-fly the plane to see what it would do. He said that for maximum short-field performance, it should be pulled off the ground, full throttle, at less than the power-off stall speed. Likewise, to land short, the final approach should be nose up, full throttle, again below power-off stall speed.

My first take-off was conventional, but right away I noticed that even with the nose on the horizon the rate and angle of climb were exceptional. Leveling off at a cruising speed of about 130 miles per hour, I had to depress the nose to keep from climbing. So far so good. With power off, the stall came at about 55 mph, but as I gradually applied power while at the same time raising the nose, my airspeed dropped to 30 mph, and we were still flying.

Quite confident now, I came in to land, hanging on the props at nearly full throttle, and rolled only about two plane lengths after touching down. I was pretty sure we were onto something interesting, so I tried a short field take-off. With the stick back and throttles wide open, we were off the cinders in hardly more space than it took to land.

Among those watching my demonstration was Massachusetts Institute of Technology aeronautical professor, Otto Koppen, who would later design the Bollinger-Koppen single engine STOL ("Short Take-Off and Landing") Helio Courier. When I asked him what he thought of the Crouch-Bolas, he asked me how much time I had flying twins.

"None," I admitted.

Otto shook his head. "Do you realize what would have happened if one of those engines coughed while you were hanging on the props?" he asked. "You wouldn't be here now."

He then gave me a short lecture on sudden asymmetrical power loss during stalls, persuading me that the slightest loss of power on one side during my takeoff or landing would have rendered the plane totally uncontrollable. This ended my interest in Crouch-Bolas. It also taught me a lesson which I was to use often in accident investigation; that sudden loss of power on one side of a multi-engined airplane when under full power near stall speed can cause total loss of flight control.

Although the Depression was hard on small aviation concerns, commercial airmail and air passenger carriers were among the few businesses that actually grew during the early thirties. Air passenger transport became a significant part of the U.S. aviation industry in 1926 when 11 airlines carried a national total of 5,782 passengers. In 1933, 24 airlines carried 493,141 passengers from coast to coast, and 75,799 to Canada, Central and South America.

This growth was partly due to the Air Mail Act of 1930, which encouraged provisions for passengers while continuing generous airmail subsidies. Colonial, soon to become American Airways, reported a record 412 passengers between Boston and New York during the first week of March, 1931. In July, Pan American began service to St. Johns and Halifax in the Canadian Provinces. On August 1, 1931, Boston and Maine Airways, created by banker and financier Phillips Payson (Olcott's cousin), began scheduled service between Boston, Portland, Rockland, and Bangor, Maine, carrying 2,000 passengers in the first two months. B & M, which eventually became Northeast Airlines, New England's regional carrier, chose Skyways to service and fuel its planes in Boston. We also took care of Pan Am's planes.

Ames-Skyways almost had its own passenger route. Early in the thirties, the New York, New Haven and Hartford Railroad watched the rapid growth of air passenger service in its territory. The principals of the company concluded there was a potential market for frequent passenger air service between Boston and New York that was not being adequately met by American. Early in July 1931, the New Haven's assistant general manager asked me to look over their projections and preliminary studies with a view to a potential joint venture. According to the plan, the New Haven might put up the managerial experience, terminal facilities, and working capital. Ames-Skyways would maintain and operate the airplanes.

Intrigued, we set out to construct a realistic appraisal of the possibilities, first studying the cost-benefit ratios of two possible routes. One was between East Boston and North Beach (now LaGuardia), using speedboat connections to Boston's South

(right) Colonial, soon to become American Airways, did a good business carrying passengers between Boston and New York.

Station and buses to New York City's Grand Central Station. Another was between a new airport in Readville, a switching area southwest of Boston, and Holmes airport on Long Island, adjacent to the Long Island Railroad, permitting connecting rail service from the terminal airports to both city centers.

We considered three available airplanes: the 6-passenger Lockheed Orion; the 12-passenger Bellanca Airbus; and the 14-passenger Ford Trimotor. At a $15 fare each way, eight round trips a day, our computed break-even load factor for the Lockheed was 101%; for the Bellanca, 50%; and for the Ford, 64%. On paper, the single engine Bellanca came out ahead, but we felt that the perceived greater safety of the Trimotor, touted by Ford in all its advertising, should be considered.

However, events later in the year conspired to delay serious consideration of setting up any such venture. On November 6, 1932, while we were still in the middle of our protracted negotiations over the Ames-Skyways and Curtiss-Wright merger, I was playing golf at the Pocasset Golf club near Buzzard's Bay. During the match, the club pro came to inform me of an emergency call. It was George Barry, one of our Skyways linemen, who told me a plane had crashed in Randolph.

I felt a sinking in the pit of my stomach when I heard the

preliminary police report. It stated that two males, a female, and a small dog had died when a Cessna, flying low, suddenly dove in almost vertically with its engine running. The occupants died instantly.

Freddy Ames had inherited a stone mansion and several hundred acres of farmland in North Easton, headquarters of the Ames Shovel and Plow Company. Part of the property served as a turf landing strip for his four-place, Wright-powered Cessna. According to our lineman, Freddy had arrived at the airport that morning with his faithful dog, a Mexican Chihuahua, accompanied by Frances Burnett, a great friend and flying student of mine, and Frank Sproul, another friend and pilot member of the Harvard Flying Club. The three had loaded picnic hampers and set out for North Easton. Randolph was on their direct course.

Freddy's death was a terrible blow both for me personally and for Skyways. The Ames heirs lost interest in Ames-Skyways, which was soon dissolved.

In the same month, Franklin Delano Roosevelt won the Presidency. President Hoover, discredited, and without political clout, offered to collaborate with the president-elect on interim emergency measures to save a desperately sick economy. Roosevelt refused the offer. In the meanwhile, the

(above) Freddy Ames at the Boston airport.

country seemed more concerned with Prohibition than anything else. Bumper stickers reading "Repeal the 18th Amendment" and "Repeal the Volstead Act" were on about every other car on the road.

1933 and 1934 were the darkest years of the Depression. On November 22, 1933, we received a letter from the New Haven Railroad saying that they still were interested in developing an airline, but could not afford to invest in any capital equipment. The New Haven hoped that Skyways alone could finance the airplane operation out of its share of earnings. Skyways, however, was in no position to finance new ventures. In fact, any fortunes we may have hoped to make were beginning to resemble misfortunes.

On February 9, 1934, Roosevelt, contending that the previous administration had fraudulently handed out juicy airmail contracts to favored companies, canceled all airmail contracts and ordered the Army to fly the mail. Pilots who had been flying the mail previously were some of the best trained and most experienced in the country, with many hours of instrument time and an excellent feel for their routes. Army pilots, not nearly so well

Aerial Photography

prepared, had poor instrument training and little experience in bad weather flying. During the first month, 10 Army pilots were killed in unnecessary crashes. The country was outraged.

The subsequent Emergency Air Mail Act of 1934 put the mail back in civil hands. Nevertheless, Roosevelt insisted that the act bar from bidding any companies that had participated in what he called the "spoils conference" when the previous contracts were negotiated by Hoover's Postmaster General. Nothing really changed in the distribution of the contracts, however. American Airways simply became American Airlines; Eastern Air Transport became Eastern Airlines; Transcontinental Air Transport became Transcontinental and Western Airways. Most of the participants in Roosevelt's "spoils conference" ended up with essentially what they had had before. To comply with the terms of the law, however, they had to replace all their CEOs and major officers, so none of the companies could run as smoothly or efficiently as before.

After the death of Freddy Ames, the demise of the Curtiss-Wright merger and the failure of the New Haven Railroad-

---

(above) A plane flies over the Boston airport, welcoming our new President.

Skyways joint venture, Skyways went into a slow decline. Olcott Payson and I were now the primary stockholders, so we agreed that he would take over our Portland, Maine branch, near his home, and I would try to drum up new activity at Boston.

The changing national political slant of the New Deal contributed to the hard times we felt. One of the worst ideas of 1933 was the National Recovery Administration which gave the President broad authority to regulate every business in the country. By August 28, 1934, the NRA had developed a code of conduct for what it called the "Commercial Aviation Industry," involving everything but scheduled airlines and manufacturers. This code regulated all aspects of sales, service, charter, hours of operation, wages and prices. Employees were generally limited to eight hours a day, six days, and 40 hours in any seven-day period, and no one under 16 could be employed. It established minimum wages, and a vaguely defined "Code of Fair Competition."

The NRA sounded utopian on paper, but in reality, it dealt businesses a crippling blow. By 1935, when the U.S. Supreme Court declared the act unconstitutional, about the only reliable business Skyways had left was its hard core of loyal sportsman pilots and airplane owners.

(left) In early 1934, Roosevelt took airmail contracts out of civilian hands and ordered the Army to fly the mail. Generally unqualified for instrument flying, Army pilots had many unneccessary and fatal crashes.

CHAPTER 8

HIGH TIMES IN THE DEEP DEPRESSION

DATE	TYPE	LOCATION	PILOT
9/22/33	Stearman NC-2143	LIACC	Crocker Snow

After demonstrating a few short takeoffs, steep climbs and various stunts, I decided to try a dive followed by a vertical roll. As I was diving straight down, I was startled by a loud bang, and the Stearman suddenly shuddered from vertical to horizontal. Now, the plane was so tail-heavy, it was all I could do to maintain level flight. The stabilizer control had no effect, but at idle power and with lots of forward pressure on the stick, I was able to land. Afterwards, I discovered that the stabilizer-adjusting mechanism had failed, but that guides limiting up-and-down motion of the stabilizer still worked. It was a close call.

The Depression was hard on Skyways, but my own family lifestyle was hardly affected by it. We had a townhouse in Boston, and cottages in Newport and at my family's place at Buzzards Bay. We also belonged to clubs at Dedham and Hicksville, Long Island and continued our flying forays to private plantations on the offshore islands of South Carolina and Georgia.

My memories of flying during the Depression years are also inextricably linked to Stearman NC-2143, a special, one-of-a-kind airplane I had at the time. We first met at the 1932 Detroit Air Show where she was a numberless Boeing Stearman exhibit. She had no engine, propeller, or fabric covering. Though she was a mere skeleton of tubes, wires, ribs and spars, everything visible was chromed, varnished, and otherwise gussied-up to show what a fine job the company did with the part of her anatomy that was normally covered.

Earl Schaeffer, president of the Stearman division of Boeing, introduced us. Her name was Model 6-C, and she was the civil version of the Army's new trainer, the PT-9, powered by a 165 horsepower Wright R-540 engine. I was impressed

---

(right) My very special, one of a kind airplane, a much-modified Stearman Model 6-C, was a faithful companion on many flying adventures.

with everything I saw, but wondered out loud if she would have much pep with so little power. Earl laughed.

"She's built to military standards," he said. "And can handle any power you fit her with."

Stearman chief engineer Mac Short confirmed that, were I to buy the bare-bones plane, I should have no trouble getting her licensed with double the power she was designed for—he was keen to see how she would fly with a 300 horsepower Wright J-6. This convinced me.

It took a while to line up an engine and to haggle Earl down to a price I could afford. We finally agreed on $1,500 for the plane f.o.b. Boston, to be shipped May 19, 1933. Included in the price were "Engineering data for J-6 300 installation and for Department of Commerce approval. Also data on additional fuel tank and increased oil tank installations. Also for J-6 300 engine mount."

When we actually got to work, we decided to have Stearman build the engine mount since we could match neither their experience nor their price. Their quote, "on the basis of material plus labor at $1.50 per hour—total not to exceed $35.00." Today, with mechanics getting at least $40.00 per hour, the same job would cost at least $1,000.

Back in the Ames-Skyways shop we covered the fuselage, wings and control surfaces, overhauled and installed a 9-cylinder radial 330 horsepower Wright R-975 engine, along with its plumbing, electrical systems and instruments. Then we did things never done before or since to any other Stearman. We enclosed the engine in the latest, most aerodynamic aluminum cowling. We built a streamlined sliding hatch for the rear cockpit, and a removable cover for the front cockpit. We buried landing lights in the lower wings and faired the wing roots. Finally, we painted the plane jet black, with the lettering "NC-2143" in gold.

Two months after the Stearman's pieces were delivered to Boston, we completed our assembly job. On July 31, I test-hopped the result. She was a dream to fly, climbing to the clouds like a homesick angel. On August 4, Joe Boudwin, engineering inspector for the Aeronautics Branch, U.S. Department of Commerce, flew up from New York to inspect her for licensing. He had me do spins and stability tests, then spent an hour and a half in the air himself, after which he gave me a "License Authorization" pending permanent papers from Washington. Even he was impressed with my new plane's performance and handling. Beginning the next day, 2143 was a busy young lady.

During the early thirties, I divided my time between work at Skyways and my enjoyment of sport flying, much of it at the Long Island Aviation Country Club in Hicksville, New York. Even in the depths of the Depression, airplane manufacturers regularly developed new and improved models of their planes. Representatives from various airplane companies often turned up at the club to demonstrate their latest creations to members. One time when we were there, inventor Al Mooney arrived with a plane he called his "Mite." It was a single place monoplane with retractable landing gear—the first that I remember on such a small plane. While Mooney explained the instru-

(right) The Long Island Aviation Country Club had hangars next to the clubhouse. Here members lunch on the lawn.

Henry A. Liese Collection

ments and controls, several of us gathered around, eager to try out the machine

Luis deFlorez, president of the club, was first to fly. After a quick buzz, he made a smooth but noisy landing on the grass in front of the club house—with the gear up. When Mooney asked what had gone wrong, Luis sheepishly admitted that he had forgotten to lower the gear, but added in self-defense that he hadn't heard any gear-up warning horn, an almost universal safety device on retractable gear planes.

"Naturally you didn't," Mooney replied. "There isn't any."

Then he pointed to an inverted paddle, hinged at the bottom and topped by a black disk covering the face of the airspeed indicator. He explained, as he had before, that the paddle was designed to alternately cover and uncover the airspeed indicator if the wheels were up on approach. He felt that this was a better warning signal than a horn.

"Didn't it work?" he asked.

"I wondered what that damn thing was for," was Luis' abashed response. "It kept going back and forth across the airspeed indicator whenever I pulled back the throttle."

Peter Brooks, who had been my first flying student, kept his clipped-wing Monocoupe at Hicksville. This plane was

equipped for inverted flight, which he enjoyed practicing. He liked to make his landing approaches upside-down, rolling out at the very last moment. One day, while flying upside-down, he hooked his wing-tip on a telephone wire as he started his roll. He was unable to right the plane before it cartwheeled to the ground. Amazingly, Peter walked away from the crash with nothing more than bad bruises. His Monocoupe was not so lucky, and never flew again.

Most of what happened at the club was not nearly so dramatic, but there was a certain atmosphere about the place that would be hard to reproduce today. In addition to routine arrivals, departures, and student instruction, we had a number of interesting ways to use our airplanes. We had air meets, which usually included races, spot landings, and paper strafing competitions. The latter involved climbing to a given altitude and tossing out a roll of toilet paper, which unrolled on the way down. Then we would use our planes to cut the paper as often as possible before the pieces hit the ground. The one who cut the paper the most times was the winner—this required a highly maneuverable airplane and expert piloting.

Near the end of September 1933, I was flying NC-2143 at an air meet. I participated in paper strafing and bomb dropping

---

(above) Watching the air races in Florida. I am leaning on Alice duPont's car. Alair Crozer and Pierreport Johnson stand beside us.

contests, and won the prize for spot landing. Then I gave a show to demonstrate what my Stearman would do. After a few short takeoffs, steep climbs and various stunts, I decided to try a vertical dive from 5,000 feet, followed by a vertical roll. As I was diving straight down, I was surprised by a loud bang, and the plane suddenly shuddered from vertical to horizontal. Now the plane was so tail-heavy it was all I could do to maintain level flight. The stabilizer control had no effect, but at idle power and with lots of forward pressure on the stick, I was able to land. Afterwards, I discovered that the stabilizer adjusting mechanism had stripped its gears, but that guides limiting up-and-down motion of the stabilizer had worked and prevented a disaster. It was a close call.

I reported the event to Earl Schaeffer at Stearman. He responded that the stress analysis on the plane called for a 139% overload protection for the part that had failed. Furthermore, the Army's PT-9 handbook limited its maximum diving speed to the equivalent of its terminal velocity. Our 330 horsepower must have pulled us down faster than the 165 horsepower the plane was designed for. Earl's closing caution: "You just dived too fast. Do be careful and don't exceed the speed limit, for while it's a good airplane, it's not a pursuit ship and we don't want you to get in trouble with it."

But, despite my efforts, I did occasionally get in trouble with NC-2143. It was not, however, the kind of trouble my friend at Stearman warned me about.

During that same September, I accepted an invitation to a party in North Haven, Maine. North Haven was a popular resort for prominent Boston and New York families, such as the Lamonts, who made their name in banking. Their butler put on a yearly Labor Day barn party for the young people at the resort. My friend Harold Moon invited me to fly up and join the festivities. The party was rumored to be pretty wild, and so I agreed to go, mostly out of curiosity. When I asked where I could land, Harold replied, "on the golf course." He explained that his uncle Wheelwright, our host, was a member of the club and had said we would be welcome.

"The Wheelwrights will have two boats in the Pulpit Harbor race," he added. "You'll spot them immediately, since they're the only ones with colored sails."

Harold instructed me to buzz the colored sails when I arrived, and he would pick me up at the golf course as soon as he came ashore.

Accompanied by my friend Joe Burnett, I flew "down east." When we arrived at North Haven, we saw the waters of Pulpit Harbor dotted with sails. We soon spotted the two colored ones, and flew down near them to signal Harold of our arrival. Then we headed back to where the golf course waited, green and welcoming. We picked a vacant fairway, landed, taxied well into the rough, shut down the engine, and climbed out.

Soon two figures carrying golf clubs appeared. We knew they couldn't be Harold yet, and as they got closer, we saw that they didn't look friendly. In fact, their faces were dour, patrician and elderly. The first one looked us over appraisingly before introducing himself as the club's president.

"What are you doing here?" he asked gruffly.

I explained that we were guests of Mr. Wheelwright who had given us permission to land on the course. I added that Mr. Wheelwright's nephew would be picking us up soon.

This elicited what sounded like "hruuumph," followed by "Mr. Wheelwright had no authority to give you permission because we don't allow airplanes to land here. I guess as long as you have, you might as well stay, but don't do it again."

With that, the two gentlemen stalked off.

Not much later, Harold showed up. He appeared unconcerned about the trouble we had caused, perhaps because he was looking forward to the weekend's merrymaking. We soon forgot about our encounter.

The Lamont's butler's party was as wild as advertised. Since I was usually a fairly sober sort, I was pretty hung-over in the morning. While I was trying to recover, Harold came to ask if he could borrow my plane.

If I had been more in control of my senses, I would have had more judgment, but Harold was an excellent pilot and had already checked out in the Stearman. He said he just wanted to see the islands of North and Vinal Haven from the air. I assented, and he took off for his sightseeing adventure.

In the process of this trip, he buzzed Joe and me at the Wheelwrights, and then the local church during Sunday morning service. This was the final straw. I was ordered to get my airplane out of town forthwith. This was fine by me. A lady we had met invited us to land on her property further north, which we did. With the Stearman out of sight, I thought my problems with the country club elders were behind me.

A few days later I was back in my office in Boston when I got a call from Department of Commerce inspector Bob Hoyt, asking what I had been up to in Maine over Labor Day. When I pleaded innocence, he said if I had any influential friends I had better get in touch with them, pronto.

"I have orders direct from the White House to pick up your pilot's license, " he said. Then he added that it would take him "several days" to complete the necessary paperwork, giving me some time to maneuver.

This was obviously a crisis of the first order. After some brainstorming, I called my "solo in a day" student, Sandy Choate, whose family summered in North Haven. Sandy tracked down this information: the problem wasn't, as I had hoped, a case of mistaken identity. The complaint was not primarily related to Harold buzzing the church—although this little prank could not have helped matters. The grievance was from a race boat that was sailing near the Wheelwrights when we arrived at Pulpit Harbor. One of its crew was Mrs. Ellen Pratt, a pregnant young lady who was so frightened by our plane that her family feared she might miscarry. (She didn't.) According to her recollection of the event many years later, we "zoomed down several times over a dinghy near ours and did scare the wits out of many of us."

Sandy's father, Joseph H. Choate, was President Roosevelt's federal alcohol administrator. When he heard about the episode, he suggested to the President that something should be done about the reckless pilot in question. In fact, Joseph Choate and Mrs. Pratt's father, Penrose Hallowell, turned out to be the very two stern gentlemen who had first confronted us on the golf course. The orders to pull my license had, indeed, come direct from Roosevelt after he heard about my conduct from Mr. Choate.

Sandy took on the role of diplomat like an old pro. He argued my case with his father and with the bride's father, head of Lee Higginson, a Boston investment banking firm. Then he called me to report that Mr. Hallowell would be willing to see me at his Boston office.

"If you do a good job apologizing, it might help," Sandy suggested.

I duly went to State Street and was as contrite and polite as possible. I was not sure whether or not I had made any headway but a few days afterwards, Bob Hoyt called.

"Whatever you did, it worked," he said. "Washington rescinded its order to take away your license."

My membership in the Long Island Aviation Country Club gave me the opportunity to participate in such happenings as cross country air cruises. Most memorable were the 1933 and 1934 invitational winter cruises from Philadelphia, Long Island, and Boston, to Miami, Florida. These were sponsored by Colonel Henry Doherty (developer of Miami Beach) in con-

junction with the Florida Year Round Clubs, a loose federation of clubs offering sports such as golf, tennis and fishing. Presumably the colonel and Florida Clubs were hoping to attract customers from the northeast to southern Florida. The colonel, who was in charge of the itinerary, added a special twist to his cruise—finishing with a race from Orlando to Miami. His invitation intrigued me, both for the race and for the chance to see more of Florida.

I accepted Colonel Doherty's 1934 invitation. My guest and co-pilot was Dan Rochford, aviation editor of the *Boston Evening Transcript*. Dan reported on the cruise in *Sportsman Magazine*, of which he was also an editor. A grand total of 86 airplanes made the flight.

The trip to Miami was fairly uneventful. We took part in the final race and ended up eighth out of 60, earning a prize of $100. When we landed at Pan Am's field in Miami, the reddest of red carpets was rolled out. As Dan put it, "We had magic guest cards which were good for free rooms and meals at the Miami Biltmore, swimming at the Roney Plaza, fishing at Key Largo (with free autogiro service), aerocar service between hotels and the city and all the races, horse, dog and air."

(above) **The Miami Biltmore from between the Stearman's wings.**

On our way back north, we flew all day and all night to arrive at Boston through light snow at 3:40 a.m. It was, as Dan commented in his *Sportsman* article, a "long cold, tough ride." But it was also a good time.

The realities of my life in Boston were not so cheerful. When I returned from the cruise, I found that Lilias had left for Reno, Nevada. On April 7, 1934, she obtained an uncontested divorce, for reasons not entirely clear to either of us at the time or since. Perhaps it was the difference between the glamorous life at Newport that Lilias loved, and the sedate life in Boston and on Cape Cod that was more my style. At any rate, my log book records that I met my returning ex-wife at Roosevelt Field on Long Island on April 9, and flew her home to Newport. We were the best of friends then, and have always remained so. Lilias eventually married my good friend Pierrepont Johnson, pilot and Stearman owner. I had introduced them.

Soon after the divorce, I took part in more sport flying. The Dedham Polo and Hunt Club, about 20 miles southwest of Boston, regularly hosted the annual dinner of the Boston Bond Club. Lester Watson, Skyways director, ardent private pilot, and investment banker, used to invite me to these dinners, provided I would fly him out and back from East Boston. We landed on the 900-foot-long polo ground. One end was bounded by 50-foot high elm trees, the other by the club house and a raised, inclined driveway. This landing strip was certainly marginal, but good enough for my Stearman or Lester's DH Gipsy Moth.

After several years of landing on the polo field, I broached the idea of hosting an invitational air meet at the club, to which members of the Long Island and Philadelphia Aviation Country Club would be invited. Much to my surprise, the club officers were intrigued. My Bond Club flights, with their apparently routine arrivals and departures for home after dark, had given them open minds.

Asked what would be involved in hosting such a meet, I replied that we would have to remove a couple trees at the east end, put up a windsock, and grade ramps over a small part of the driveway entrance to permit taxiing to an open field at the other end for airplane parking.

The officers were amenable to everything but removing the trees, since they were not owned by the club, but by their neighbor, Roger Amory. Fortunately, Roger was head of Aviation Securities Corporation, which had financed Skyways' hangar complex at East Boston, and had no objections to our plans. We made the necessary alterations to the landscape, and were ready to go.

Luis DeFlorez was enthusiastic about the proposed meet, and asked the LIACC's president, James B. Taylor, Jr., to send me a list of members to invite. Jim's letter to me said "I understand the field there is rather small and I have marked with an 'X' the names that I am not sure of being able to get in and out of a small field. I may be wrong, and many of them would probably be insulted, but I am merely going by my knowledge of the amount of flying they do, and the kind of landings they make on our field."

(left) We were "Number 46" in the race from Orlando to Miami. The Stearman also sported my flying insignia, a pair of dice showing snake eyes.

I honored Jim's 'X's by not inviting them. One I remember well was Morehead Paterson, owner of a Wasp-powered Stearman Model 60.

A spring notice to Dedham club members said, "On Saturday, May 19, 1934, there will be an Air Meet at the Club. About 20 ladies and gentlemen who own their own planes have been invited to fly up from Philadelphia and Long Island."

We had worked out a program calling for a handicap race from Hicksville to Dedham, followed by bomb dropping, paper-strafing, a closed course race, and an aerobatics exhibition. The most dramatic event of the day occurred just before lunch. The cross-country racers arrived and landed without incident. We were all sitting on the club porch, when a big, light blue biplane hove into sight from the southwest. Someone remarked that it looked like Morehead Paterson's Stearman. We watched as the plane circled the field, lined up properly for a landing, came through the gap in the trees rather fast, and touched down about half-way along the polo field. I started running as the wheels tripped on the elevated part of the driveway, and the plane neatly flipped over onto its back, clear of both the driveway and the ramps connecting the parking area with the polo field.

It was indeed Paterson, flying solo. When I got to the plane, he was hanging upside-down by his safety belt. I asked if he was okay. He was quite cheery, replying, "Oh yes, I've done this before." Then he proceeding to unbuckle his belt and land on his head. After I helped him up, he asked if there was a phone handy so he could call his pilot to bring up his other plane.

Despite this rude interruption, all the afternoon's events were on schedule. The closed course race was the most fun. With a waiver of the federal air traffic regulations from inspector Bob Hoyt, we hedgehopped over the suburban country towns of Dedham, Westwood and Sherborne, legally buzzing the estates of many Dedham Club members. The day ended with a con-vivial dinner at the club. We held repeat performances of this meet in '35 and '36, with carefully selected guests.

In addition to organizing the first Dedham air meet, I also occupied myself with a new pastime which helped to keep me from feeling too down about my divorce from Lilias. I owed this diversion to my Buzzards Bay neighbor and friend, Wesley Dennis. Wesley was a gifted and successful artist who later became widely known for his illustrations of Marguerite Henry's *Misty of Chincoteague* and similar books about horses. Wesley's other love was polo. He and two other Cape Codders, Bill Danforth, Jr., and left-hander Leo Boyle, had been playing the game indoors over the winter in Boston's Commonwealth Armory. They wanted to put together a four-man team for the outdoor game, and asked me to join them.

I tried the sport and liked it. I soon bought two ponies and we formed a team, which we named the *Ramblers*. My first purchase, a black thoroughbred called Nutsy, cost me $350 and was

(left) The air meet at the Dedham Polo and Country Club was interrupted by the uninvited and unexpected arrival of Morehead Paterson who, unaccustomed to landing on such a short field, flipped his plane over on its back where it lies in the center of this photograph. Paterson was not seriously injured: his first request was for a phone so he could have his pilot fly up his other plane.

Aerial Photography

one of the best polo ponies I ever had.

Polo became one of my favorite sports, but it nearly ended my military flying career. We started playing on a hay field on Coonamesset Ranch in Falmouth after cutting the long grass with a horse-drawn sickle-bar mower. The field was conveniently located next to the small Coonamesset airport. Our usual competition was a team from Providence, Rhode Island, run by a livery stable owner named Rancourt. He had two young Italians, students at Brown, as the core of his team, with another Rhode Island native as a fourth.

In the summer of 1934, we fixed up a more sophisticated polo field, complete with sideboards and regulation goal posts, at the Skyways facility in Marstons Mills. On Sunday, August 12, we were playing our usual match against Rancourt's team. As we lined up for a throw-in, one of the Italians' ponies kicked me in the left knee and fractured it. It was compound fracture, opened up and bleeding.

One of the spectators was a doctor who used a stream of salt water to clean out the open wound before rushing me to the hospital in Hyannis. Then he flew me to Boston where my brother Bill met us. I asked Bill to call Dr. Thomas K. Richards, a knee specialist who took care of the Harvard football team and had treated me before. Unfortunately Tommy was rowing a shell down the Mississippi River with Harvard football great, Tack Hardwick. Bill's friend and orthopedic surgeon Bob Morris was available, however, and wanted to operate as soon as possible. This made sense to me, but turned out to be bad advice. The job was done the following morning at the Brooks Hospital on Corey Hill in Brookline.

A few days later, infection set in, and getting the incisions to

(above) Our polo team, the *Ramblers* (on the right) flew up to play against a team in Whitefield, New Hampshire just after the repeal of Prohibition. The other team got us quite drunk the night before the game. They won.

heal was a long and painful process. After three months in a plaster cast, the most knee motion I could get was 90 degrees, and that only after therapy by Dr. Richards, who told me that the operation should not have been done until the swelling had subsided. This would have greatly reduced the chance of infection and the resultant protracted immobility. While recuperating that summer, I often sat in the front yard of the family home with my leg propped up on cushions, practicing target shooting with my Colt Woodsman.

By November 26, 1934, I had recovered enough to satisfy the federal aeronautical inspector that my accident had not impaired my competence as a commercial pilot. Unfortunately Major Claude Cummings, chief flight surgeon of the First Corps area, had come to a different conclusion. He arbitrarily revoked my Army Air Corps pilot's medical certificate. If anything could have gotten me down more than my divorce, this was surely it. With my father's advice and counsel, I decided to fight the injustice all the way to the top.

Then, on March 5, 1935 Pa died suddenly of a stroke. I was stunned. I had now lost my guide, my protector, and my best friend.

Newspaper headlines appeared, letters and telegrams from

friends and business associates poured in, and leather-bound memorials arrived from the many companies Pa served as a director, trustee, or counsel. Until then, I had no conception of the esteem in which he was held by his many friends and associates.

Fortunately for my state of mind, there were soon out-of-the-ordinary matters brewing that I had to take care of. For example, the Town of Bourne, of which Buzzards Bay is a village, had appointed me to arrange an aerial display for the June 22, 1935 opening of the new Bourne highway bridge over the Cape Cod Canal.

There was no problem getting the National Guard and the Air Reserves to promise two three-plane formations each for a fly-over. With my knee, I could still fly, but I wouldn't be allowed to fly military aircraft, so I decided to effectively thumb my nose at Major Cummings who, though not a pilot, was sure to bum a ride on one of the military planes. As usual, inspector Bob Hoyt helped me out by waiving the minimum altitudes of flight for an additional three-plane formation of two Stearman C-3Bs and Stearman 2143.

Just at noon, 12 military observation planes flew over the canal from the Sagamore bridge in the east to the railroad bridge in the west. As they passed over the Bourne bridge, bands played

(above) While recuperating from knee surgery, I used to sit in the front yard of my family's home practicing target shooting.

and dignitaries cut the ribbon in its center. Moments after this, my three-plane formation, unseen because it had approached from the east below the banks of the canal, flew under the bridge wide open and wrapped the show up with an Immelman turn around it. The opening we flew under was just 54 feet high.

The pilots of the other two planes were Olcott Payson and Tom Ross. Years later, Tom came to thank me for my courage in including him in the show. I knew Tom as an excellent pilot, whom I could trust to do a safe and accurate job in such a display. He happened to be colored, which I don't remember thinking about one way or the other, but apparently it was unusual for a black pilot to be chosen for this kind of a celebration.

While this display didn't help get me back my military physical, it did make me feel better. In fact, I felt so good, I formally requested a Washington review of Major Cummings' action in revoking my military ticket. Six weeks later, I received a letter from the acting chief, medical division, office of the chief of the Army Air Corps, with instructions to see contract flight surgeon, Frederic E. Cruff for another examination. Private enterprise prevailed. Dr. Cruff gave me a waiver for "limited motion of the left knee," and I was back on military flying status.

Some months later, Stearman 2143 gained even more power. In the soggy spring of 1936, Frank Hawks, Texaco's speed-record-setting promotional pilot, hit a stone wall while taking off from a small grass field that served as the airport for Worcester, Massachusetts. He was flying the company's Travel Air Mystery S, which I had admired ever since watching it do a vertical slow roll on take-off at a Cleveland air show. At Worcester, the plane was washed out, and Frank's face was badly messed up. The Massachusetts General Hospital's top plastic surgeon got Frank's face repair job. Texaco gave Skyways the unhurried job of putting the plane together for permanent display in the Smithsonian Institution.

When we had sorted out the pieces, we saw that the Mystery S's custom built 420 horsepower Wright R-975C engine appeared to have only superficial damage. From the outside, it looked exactly the same as my 330 horsepower R-975. When the folks at Stearman confirmed that 2143 could handle the extra horsepower, and Wright said the engine's dimensions and weight were the same as mine, I made a deal with Texaco to swap. For safety's sake, we overhauled the R-975C before installing it in 2143. After an inspection and a flight test, I had a unique airplane powered by a unique engine. I often wonder if the Smithsonian knows that their Texaco Mystery S has my old engine in it.

During the time that we were fixing up the Mystery S for display, I frequently visited Frank in the Phillips House of Mass. General, bringing with me, at his request, a half pint of his favorite rye whiskey. He was fed through tubes because his lower and upper jaws were wired together. He wore a neck brace, and except for his eyes, his face was swathed in bandages. Nevertheless, he had figured out a way to have his swig. He would sit up, open his mouth by pulling down his lower jaw with

(left) Frank Hawks couldn't quite get Texaco's famous promotional plane, the Mystery S, off the grass air strip that served as Worcester's airport. Skyways got the job of repairing the plane, Massachusetts General Hospital of patching up Frank Hawks.

his right hand, insert the bottle with his left hand, and lean back.

In the summer of 1936, I went on the Long Island Aviation Country Club's invitational seaplane cruise. Had the regatta officials realized I didn't have a seaplane, I might have been dis-invited. The cruise was scheduled to depart Oyster Bay, Long Island, on June 4, with a first overnight at the Montauk Yacht Club on the eastern tip of the Island. Many arrangements for the seaplanes had to be made ahead of time, including the ship-ping and installation of seaplane moorings at the designated stops. My own plane was in the shop for her engine change, but my good friend John Lasell offered me his C-3R Stearman (on wheels) if he could go along as a passenger.

I made arrangements for overnight stops, entertainment and service for the cruise at Edgartown on Martha's Vineyard, and at Marion, Massachusetts. I was confident John and I could find a place to land close to the designated seaplane moorings and be able to join all the festivities. The heavily built-up envi-rons of Oyster Bay, where the cruise began, ruled out landing anywhere nearer than at a regular airport, so John and I joined the party at Montauk. We met the others at the Yacht Club, where we landed on a small patch of beach grass near the club house. From Montauk we flew to Edgartown, where we landed on a sand-spit next to the lighthouse.

One of the objectives of these cruises was to demonstrate how much fun could be had visiting places accessible only to seaplanes. The fact that John and I were usually waiting at the bar, clean and dry, while the rest of the flyers were still checking on their moorings was probably a bit annoying to the organizers. I was never invited on a seaplane cruise again.

By any measure, 1936 was a wonderful year for me. On March 11, I was invited to a small dinner party in Boston, where I met a most attractive expatriate young lady on a short visit to her mother from her home in England. Janice Vaughan Little had been brought up in Hamilton, Massachusetts, the equestrian center of Boston's North Shore, and home of the venerable Myopia Hunt Club. She was widely known as a daring and expert rider to hounds, steeplechase jockey, and show rider.

We got along famously. Two days later I started giving Jan dual instruction in 2143—a rare privilege, enjoyed by no one else. I hoped it would lead to a permanent relationship. I thought we were getting close when in June 1937, after 9 hours of dual, Jan soloed a Fleet trainer. Then she soloed 2143 after only a 10 minute check ride. It wasn't until May 21, 1938, that we were married at Olcott Payson's home in Falmouth Foreside, Maine.

From there, we let Stearman 2143 transport us to the Cloister at Georgia's St. Simon's Island, where we spent a dreamy week of swimming, bicycling, and relaxing before returning to our new home across Buttermilk Bay from the Snow family place. A few months later, we had a front row seat at one of the worst storms ever to hit that part of the world.

(left) Participants in a "fly-in" at Greenville, Maine. In the summer of 1936, I went on a similar trip, the Long Island Aviation Country Club invitational seaplane cruise, flying a Stearman on wheels.

CHAPTER 9

GREAT HURRICANE & AVIATION LAW

DATE	PLANE	FROM	TO	TIME	REMARKS
9/21/38	Stearman NC-2143	Buzzards Bay	Boston	0:25	Clear
9/21/38	Stearman NC-2143	Boston	Falmouth	0:55	Hurricane!

As I flew over Buttermilk Bay I was crabbing over 30 degrees, and I could see spume spitting from the angry whitecaps. On final approach to my northeast–southwest landing strip the wind was so strong from the southeast that I had to head south to keep the plane on a southwest track. For the first time I aborted a landing because of wind. Falmouth Airport, a dozen miles further south with two reasonably sturdy hangars, seemed like a better bet. When I got there and made a short left turn into the wind in the lee of the hangars, a 70 mile per hour indicated approach speed was getting me nowhere. I was just barely holding my own over the ground, so I increased power. Despite the turbulence, I was able to get very close to the hangar and land at almost no forward speed.

Buzzards Bay, 8:00 a.m., Wednesday, September 21, 1938. A typical Indian summer morning. A few cumulus clouds, a brisk wind from the southwest, and at least five miles visibility. Conditions were the same at East Boston and forecast to remain so. My regular commute from Buzzards Bay to my Skyways office at the airport would be routine. There was, as yet, no radar. We had no satellites, nor even weather flights. Early that morning, the Cunard liner *Corinthia* had reported a tropical storm off the Virginia coast, but the U.S. Weather Bureau predicted its track would be northeast over the ocean, passing far east of Cape Cod. Nothing really to worry about, I thought. Store it away for future reference. Little could I guess what was sneaking up on New England's shores.

(right) On September 21, 1938, the first hurricane to hit New England in 100 years moved up on its shores at an unheard-of speed of 70 miles per hour, taking the population completely by surprise.

Boston Globe

I took care of some paperwork in my office that morning. By lunch time, the wind had freshened and veered to the south-east—hardly what one would expect from a storm far out to sea. I was not overly concerned, but made an early start back just in case. Flight conditions were VFR (Visual Flight Rules) but the further south I went, the more I had to correct to port to stay on the well-remembered track home. Obviously the velocity of the easterly component of the wind was increasing.

Our home was perched on a headland on the north shore of Buttermilk Bay next to Gibbs Narrows which connects it with Little Buttermilk Bay. My 1,000-foot grass landing strip was on the south side of the bay on my family's summer place. As I approached, my thoughts turned to my pet Doberman Pinscher, Wiggy, who could distinguish the approaching sound of my engine and propeller from any other. As I flew over the house southbound, he would dash down the bank, swim the Narrows, run along the beach and through the woods to my landing strip, and, soaking wet, proudly ride home with me in my car.

When I passed over the house, I was crabbing over 30 degrees, and I could see spume spitting from angry whitecaps.

(above) When I took off for work in the morning, it had been a typical warm Indian summer day. Our house was perched on a headland on the shore of Buttermilk Bay. Gibbs Narrows (to the left) separated the house from my landing strip.

Not a good portent for landing. On shore, trees waved their leaves furiously. But there, running straight and self-confident was Wiggy, already halfway from the house to the Narrows, bounding over the stormy landscape. I couldn't let him down.

By 1938, I had regularly flown Stearman 2143 to and from unprepared landing spots smaller than Buzzards Bay in all kinds of wind and weather. I had come to believe that she would perform any task for me. So I decided to land. On final approach, however, the wind was so strong from the southeast that I had to head south to keep the plane on a southwest track to my northeast–southwest strip. This meant that the wheels on ground contact would be traveling nearly sideways instead of rolling straight ahead. Here, I thought, goes the landing gear or the right wing, or both. It wasn't worth the risk. For the first time, I aborted a landing because of wind.

Falmouth Airport, a dozen miles further south, seemed like a better bet. This was an all-way turf field, permitting a landing into the wind. It had two hangars with a clear grass space a few hundred feet long on their northwest sides. I decided to put down in the lee of the hangars.

(above) The hurricane permanently altered the New England shoreline, demolishing millions of dollars of property in the process, including over 2,600 boats.

Approaching the landing area after a left turn at 70 miles per hour indicated air speed, we were barely holding our own over the ground, so I increased power. Despite turbulence, which was less than I expected, I was able to land very close to the hangars at almost no forward speed. Fortunately there were enough people around to grab the wing tips and help secure the plane against the hangar wall.

I called Jan, who soon arrived by car. She had thoughtfully picked up Wiggy at Buzzards Bay where he was waiting for me. I still have a vivid memory of the ride home, watching the stunted Cape Cod oaks and pitch pine waving wildly in the wind. Neither Jan nor I realized what was in store, but back home we had a ringside seat.

With an incoming tide, the turgid waters of Buttermilk Bay were already well above their normal high water mark. A steady stream of flotsam sped by, en route from Buttermilk Bay through Gibbs Narrows into Little Buttermilk Bay. As the storm's intensity grew, we watched as my family's pier and boat house, located across the bay, tore loose and headed for us. Our own small boat house was half under water, but still holding fast, so I scrambled down the bank, ran a line in and out of a couple of windows and tied it to a tree. I might as well have tried to tether

(above) **The storm was doubly devastating wherever its landfall coincided with high tide, and all the more catastrophic for being wholly unexpected.**

120

a horse with a piece of thread.

When the winds finally died down that night and the waters receded with the falling tide, as far as we could see the beaches were littered with debris—much of it the wooden remains of houses, docks and piers. This had been the first hurricane to hit New England in 100 years, all the more catastrophic for being wholly unexpected. The awesome power of wind and wave had destroyed millions of dollars of property, wrecked lives and livelihoods, and instilled in all of us a healthy respect for the forces of nature.

The next day I took our chief of police, Bill Crump, on a survey flight. The destruction was absolutely devastating. Waterfront buildings were demolished, and large vessels had been deposited far inland. Promontories had disappeared, and many miles of shoreline had been rearranged. We learned later that the hurricane, with record low pressure at its core, had sucked up a huge mound of ocean, carrying it up the coast to dump it in harbors, bays and estuaries from Long Island to Maine. The weather observatory on 1,000-foot-high Blue Hill, southwest of Boston, recorded maximum wind speeds of 186 miles per hour, with sustained winds of 120 miles per hour.

But the greatest damage was done by high water wherever the storm's peak coincided with high tide. In front of our house, the water-level rose to almost 15 feet above normal flood tide. Although our house itself was spared, many large oaks and pines below the high water mark were uprooted. Fifty years later the Blue Hill Meteorological Observatory published *An Historical and Pictorial Summary of the 1938 Hurricane.* According to this report:

Twenty six thousand autos were smashed. Some 2.6 billion board feet of timber were thrown down, leaf pulp turned white houses brown. There were some 600 lives lost. 93,122 families suffered serious property losses. 2,605 boats were destroyed. Railroad service between New York and Boston was interrupted for two weeks. The total damage is reliably estimated to have been to have been at least $400,000,000; the greatest that ever occurred in a single storm anywhere in the world.

But the Great Hurricane of 1938 was not entirely an "ill winde that bloweth no good," since it gave a tremendous boost to commercial air traffic. With no useable roads (many major bridges were destroyed) or train tracks, the only practical way

---

(above) Although our house was spared, many large oaks and pines were uprooted by the combined forces of wind and wave.

to maintain economic and financial ties between Boston and New York was by air.

Before the Great Hurricane, the scheduled airlines, which had so well bucked the post-1929 depression, were losing money. This was chiefly an after-effect of Roosevelt's cancellation of the airmail contracts and the subsequent reorganization of the airlines. The Air Commerce Act of 1938, signed into law on June 23, was designed to help the airlines out of this financial muddle. It approved specific routes for scheduled common carriers, requiring them to obtain "certificates of convenience and necessity." Airmail contracts or other government subsidies protected airlines having such certificates from losing money on their passenger routes.

In 1938, American was the only scheduled airline authorized under the new law to provide service between Boston and New York. Using 23-passenger DC-3s, American transported an average of 100 passengers per day on a half dozen daily round trips. With only this capacity, they couldn't come close to meeting the new demand the hurricane created. The Civil Aeronautics Authority, created just three months before the storm, used its emergency powers to encourage other certified U.S. airlines to fly between the two cities on a temporary basis. Eastern, TWA, United, and National joined in the fray, transporting over a thousand passengers a day.

This surge continued even after the New Haven Railroad was back in business, introducing scores of thousands of frustrated ex-railroad passengers to travel by air. In fact, the Great Hurricane of 1938 marked the birth of air shuttle service, which eventually made the Boston–New York run the busiest in the world.

With the rise in commercial air traffic came an accompanying increase in the state and federal regulation of the airways, especially around larger cities. By 1938, I had become increasingly involved in the creation of these new aviation laws. This involvement stemmed, more or less directly, from the tragic death of my Ames-Skyways partner, Freddy Ames, in 1932. My partner's crash, one of many aviation accidents that I would investigate, brought me in contact with national authorities on aeronautics, and eventually led me to a career as the Director of Aeronautics in Massachusetts. Here is how it happened.

As soon as I heard of Freddy's crash on that October morning in 1932, I flew from Cape Cod to the Boston airport. There, I met Major Clarence Hodge from the Massachusetts Registry of Motor Vehicles, which was then responsible for investigating aircraft accidents. Major Hodge, just returned from the site of the crash, asked me if I had any information about Freddy or the plane that might help him in his investigation. I told him no. All I knew was what I had heard from our barker, George Barry, on the telephone: that the plane, flying low and level, suddenly dove straight down, killing its occupants on impact.

(left) In accordance with the Air Commerce Act of 1938, American Airlines was the only commercial carrier certified to cover the route between Boston and New York. After the hurricane, demand for commuter services was great.

Hodge nodded his head in agreement, commenting that there was an odor of liquor and some broken bottles in the wreckage.

There was nothing more for me to do at the airport, so I went to see Freddy's mother, Mrs. Cutler, who lived at the Ritz. There, I spoke to her husband, Roger, who was upset about a call from a news reporter shortly after the accident. The reporter said that the state investigator had mentioned the smell of alcohol at the accident site, inferring that drinking may have caused the crash.

Roger had refused to comment. He told me what he knew. That morning, Freddy had breakfasted with the Cutlers at the Ritz. He had been at a late party at his Harvard club, the Gas, but was stone sober. He had planned a day's sail on his boat, moored in Newport, and was meeting Frances Burnett and Frank Sproul at East Boston. Then they would pick up a lady friend at North Easton.

Roger was furious at the suggestion that the accident had been caused by a drunk pilot and asked me to do everything possible to find out what really happened. He also wanted Major Hodge fired, and wondered why the state's automobile department was running airplanes anyway.

I didn't know how I could help, but of course agreed to try. The opportunity came almost immediately.

Joseph Ely, Governor of Massachusetts and a close friend of Roger Cutler's, had recently received an invitation to send a delegate to the annual meeting of the newly formed National Association of State Aviation Officials (NASAO) in Nashville, Tennessee. At Roger's request, the Governor designated me his representative and I went.

This meeting really opened my eyes to the condition of aviation in the country, and I heard many fascinating discussions about national aviation affairs. I learned that the Commission on Uniform State Laws was working on a state statute to standardize aviation regulation and development throughout the country. I also discovered that Massachusetts was well behind the times in the way it handled the airways. The state's Registry of Motor Vehicles had an aviation division that was responsible for airport regulation, pilot licensing, and aircraft accident investigation. It had no development or promotional responsibility, and its methods were neither systematic nor consistent. Major Hodge, who was also a member of the Air National Guard, was the head of the aviation division.

When I returned from Nashville, my first task was to work up a report for the governor. I also began my own review of the available evidence on Freddy's accident, hoping to clear him of alcohol charges.

There had been no autopsies of the three people killed since the cause of death was obvious. The plane and engine maintenance records were clean. There was nothing to suggest engine or structural failure, although the condition of the wreckage was such that it could not be ruled out. I thought the odor of alcohol at the crash site was more likely to have come from liquor packed in the plane than from a drunken pilot, especially considering that our barker said he had helped load picnic hampers onto the plane not 10 minutes before the crash.

So where did we go from here? I wondered.

Frustrated, I shifted to a Sherlock Holmes approach—pick a plausible answer, and look for facts to support it. This differed from the classic, meticulous, investigation and reconstruction method in use at the time. What, I asked myself, would cause an airplane in level flight suddenly to go into a near-vertical dive? Short of shedding its wings (which hadn't happened), by far the most probable cause would be a strong forward force on the elevator control directly in front of the pilot.

The plane was flying low before it dove in. Was this a factor? In those days, there were no television towers, no FM antennae, and, except in New York City, no skyscrapers. Cross country flight at 1,000 feet above the terrain was common. Freddy's Cessna cruised at 120 miles per hour, or 176 feet per second, probably maintaining or exceeding that speed in its final dive. Assuming an altitude of 1,000 feet and 120 miles per hour air speed, this would leave only 5 seconds to impact once the dive had started. This seemed the only significance of the low flight.

Was a heart attack or a stroke the answer? Freddy Ames was under 30 years old, only slightly overweight, and there was nothing in his medical history to suggest it. Furthermore, I thought, heart attacks and strokes almost always gave some

warning, and with two other pilots aboard, it seemed likely that one of them would have had time to take over the controls.

There was one possibility that kept popping into my thoughts. Only about a month before the accident, Freddy asked me to drop by his Boston apartment on my way home from the airport. When I arrived, he took me to the pantry where a wooden keg lay on its side on the floor under the counter. It contained 50-year-old Kentucky Rye whiskey, left to Freddy by his grandfather. The keg had never been broached and this was to be the occasion. We inserted a spigot, wished each other happy landings, and drank.

A week or so later, while bending over to get himself a drink from the same keg, Freddy felt a sharp crack in his lower back. He couldn't straighten out or even get up from the floor, but crawled painfully from the pantry across the living room to the telephone. He couldn't quite reach it, and was only able to call for help by grabbing the cord and pulling the phone down to the floor. Some therapy and a few days bed-rest seemed to fix him up.

What if, I thought, Freddy had bent forward while flying the plane and his back had suddenly locked again, pushing him forward onto the elevator control? I knew that Freddy's tiny Chihuahua usually snuggled up on his lap as he flew. Suppose

Aerial Photography

(above) Major Clarence Hodge of the Massachusetts Registry of Motor Vehicles was in charge of investigating the Ames accident.

the pet had fallen or jumped to the floor of the cockpit? Any pilot's normal reaction would be to scoop him up before he got tangled in the rudder pedals.

This was the most reasonable explanation I could come up with. I tried it out on numerous pilots at East Boston and no one could suggest a better "most probable cause."

However rational my explanation, Major Hodge wouldn't buy it since there was no proof. However, my hypothesis convinced him to drop the liquor charge against Freddy. The official finding of the Registry of Motor Vehicles was that the plane went into a steep dive and crashed "for reasons unknown."

However, the Cutlers were not mollified. They wanted to see Major Hodge fired since he had insinuated that Freddy was flying under the influence. Roger Cutler also believed that it made no sense for the Registry of Motor Vehicles to be in charge of airplanes in the state. He wanted me to speak to the Governor about changing the situation. "I still am firmly of the belief, after studying the whole problem, that Major Clarence D. Hodge is not only a detriment to flying at the East Boston Airport but is also an entirely useless expense to the State of Massachusetts," he wrote to me in a February, 1933 letter.

I met Governor Ely and his secretary Mr. Bradford early in that same month. We agreed that the law putting the regulation of aircraft under the jurisdiction of the Registry of Motor Vehicles needed to be changed. The governor wanted to propose a bill to do this, to be filed in the 1934 session, and gave me the job of preparing it.

I got together with my friend John Lasell, now a member of the State Legislature, and we sat down to draft a proposal. At the suggestion of House counsel we entitled it "An Act Establishing a Uniform Aeronautical Code." John filed the bill during the 1934 legislative session. Meanwhile, I sent the proposal on to Fred Fagg, head of the National Association of State Aviation Officials, soliciting his comments. Fagg replied with a somewhat sarcastic letter, pointing out several weaknesses in our plan, including the fact that, although we entitled our proposed law a "uniform code," there was nothing uniform about it, since it corresponded to no other laws in existence. I recognized the merit of these criticisms immediately. We didn't push the bill, and were not surprised when it failed. The following year, James Michael Curley became governor, and I lost both my enthusiasm and my political connection.

Fortunately, NASAO thought I was still their Massachusetts contact, and continued to send me bulletins that kept me up-to-date on national issues regarding aviation. In 1938, I received a copy of the official Uniform State Aeronautics Act, from the NASAO headquarters. Shortly thereafter, Jan and I entertained her friend Bayard Tuckerman, a member of the Governor's Council. Our talk soon turned to various problems with the Commonwealth's handling of aviation.

(right) From my experience with the Freddy Ames accident, I developed a sort of a Sherlock Holmes approach to accident investigation. What might cause an airplane to dive to the ground? I would ask, then pick a plausible explanation and look for supporting facts.

126

(left) John Lasell, me, and Ted Holcombe. Lasell helped me write the bill that would establish the Massachusetts Aeronautics Commission.

Bayard was quite helpful. "If your problems can be solved by legislation," he said, "write up a bill and I'll see to it that it gets passed."

John Lasell, by then a member of the powerful Ways and Means Committee, was eager to help me again. Together, we carefully tailored NASAO's uniform act to fit Massachusetts' requirements.

As he promised, Bayard took me on a tour of the State House, where he introduced me to key committee chairmen, telling them that I had a good bill to reorganize aviation, and that he wanted them to support it. Boston's five daily papers had extensive, positive news coverage of the proposal, noting its almost universal backing in the legislature and citing the many highly respected aviation authorities who believed that Massachusetts needed to step into the air age and take advantage of available federal funds for doing such things as building airports.

Our bill called for a seven-member, bipartisan, unpaid commission directly responsible to the governor, with a full-time Director of Aeronautics. It passed easily, and was signed into law by Governor Leverett Saltonstall to become Chapter 39 of the Acts of 1939.

The very next day the Governor called me to his office. He said he understood that I was responsible for the bill he had just signed, and that he wanted me to run the new department. He also asked for my suggestions on whom to appoint to the commission.

This sudden involvement in aviation regulation came as a great surprise, but, since Skyways had now diminished to a small charter operation that took up very little of my time, I gladly accepted the appointment. Our top-notch commission was chaired by Chandler Hovey, senior partner at Kidder Peabody and board member of American Airlines. Gardiner Fiske, businessman and former World War I pilot was secretary. Jerome Hunsaker, Bob Love, and John Wells, together with ex officio members John Beal, Public Works Commissioner, and Eugene McSweeney, Public Safety Commissioner, made up the seven. At the first meeting on September 12, 1939, the commission chose me as its administrative officer, Director of Aeronautics. This was the beginning of my career in the creation, oversight and administration of aviation law.

Although my new job was absorbing and exciting, my thoughts were often occupied by foreign affairs. Events in Europe, which began unfolding during the middle thirties, had begun to follow each other more and more rapidly as the decade drew to a close. On the home front, we were preparing for our eventual entry into the war. I, like most American fliers, knew that it was only matter of time before I would be called upon to use my aviation experience and expertise for an entirely different purpose.

(right) In September, 1939, the Massachusetts Aeronautics Commission chose me as the first Director of Aeronautics.

CHAPTER 10

AIR POWER

DATE	PLANE	LOCATION	TIME	PURPOSE
3/15/38	BC-1A	Randolph	1:48	Check flight

With everything to lose, I willed myself to relax and go for broke. In quick succession I did a loop, which was easy; an Immelman turn, a roll on top of a loop (a fighter tactic to reverse direction), snaprolls in both directions, and then, thoroughly relaxed, a near perfect slow roll. The stick shook again and I turned around to see my check pilot grinning and holding his hand up to form a circle with thumb and second finger.

While Americans were worrying about the Great Depression at home, Europeans had an even more formidable enemy. The 1929 stock market crash helped trigger devastatingly hard times on the other side of the Atlantic. During the thirties, the mood of the people in some countries, particularly in Germany, took a desperate turn. Seeking sweeping change to better their condition, they turned for answers to the rising Nazi party and Adolf Hitler, its single-minded leader. In 1933, Hitler gained the Chancellorship and in 1935 withdrew Germany from the League of Nations and the Disarmament Conference in Geneva. Then he publicly announced his country's remilitarization, and in 1936, led the army in a show of force into the Rhineland, which had been taken from the country at the end of World War I.

In early 1938, German Nazis united with the Nazi party in Austria. Hitler's aims were clearly and explicitly expansionist: he advocated a "*Drang nach Osten,*" (literally: "the press toward the East"). After the union with Austria, Czechoslovakia was next on Hitler's list. His plan was to dominate Central Europe, and from there, take over as much of the East as he could. Although the Nazi movement was tremendously threatening, little had been done to stop it. Newspapers on both sides of the Atlantic reported Hitler's exploits with growing concern, but no military or diplomatic force had yet challenged Germany's

(left) B-17s flying in formation. World War II would clearly prove the efficacy of the airplane as a war machine.

charismatic leader. Europe's citizens and leaders seemed to be watching in mesmerized horror, certain that something would have to be done, but not sure when or how.

Given this tense atmosphere, it seemed inevitable to many Americans that we would eventually go to war on the side of the Allies. Soon after Germany and Austria united, Colonel Bob Walsh, who headed the Army Air Corps Reserve Office in Washington D.C., called to give me some advice. He told me that when we did enter the war, the Reserves would be called up, and currently qualified pilot-rated officers would get the best flying jobs. There was a pilot refresher course being offered in San Antonio, Texas. If I were to go, Bob suggested that I would be more likely to get a top flying job when the time came.

The prospect of flying new or different kinds of airplanes was enough incentive for me to sign up for this program post-haste. In addition to improving my chances of getting an exciting wartime assignment, it would also be an excellent excuse to do what I loved best: fly. San Antonio's Randolph field was the Air Corps' pilot training headquarters and I had heard that pilots there were experimenting with various new flying methods that

I was eager to see and experience. It was not long before my orders came, with instructions to depart for Randolph Field on February 15, 1938. I left by car and arrived two days later.

San Antonio was an attractive city, with its Spanish architecture, green parks, and brilliant flowering gardens along the lush banks of its river—scenery that made quite a contrast to the bleak wintery landscape back on Cape Cod. The people were friendly to anyone in uniform, perhaps remembering the Alamo or, more practically, because of the many benefits derived from the surrounding military installations. The outlying countryside was flat, arid, and ideally suited for flight training. Randolph itself was a small city encompassed on three sides by large, grass-covered landing fields.

There were several hundred cadets in advanced training. Fighter training, conducted in pursuit airplanes, went on at nearby Kelly Field. In 1938, America had little that could properly be called a bomber force. There were 20 of us in the three-month refresher course, divided into five flights of four students per instructor. Our instruction was to progress as rapidly as our individual capabilities permitted. Regardless of our reserve

(above) I arrived at Randolph Field, the Army Air Corps pilot training headquarters in February, 1938.

rank, we were all second lieutenants for this course. Our
immediate commanding officer
was a captain who made us well
aware of his silver bars.

In addition to my orders I had
a letter of introduction from
Colonel Walsh to Major K.P.
McNaughton, Director of Training at Randolph, who happened
to be a polo-playing friend of his.
Feeling a bit skittish as a second
lieutenant in the company of
colonels and majors, I had left the letter from Colonel Walsh in
Major McNaughton's office. On my second weekend in Texas,
he invited me to Miller Field, San Antonio's "skin" (dirt) polo
field where my host put me in a practice game. I had never
before, nor have I since, ridden ponies so perfectly trained. We
used nothing but rope hackamores and controlled our mounts
with our legs or by shifting our position on the saddle. Later, I
was lucky enough to play in a couple of matches.

Early in March, Major McNaughton, now a good friend
through our shared polo activities, told me about a blind
landing program going on at Randolph and asked me if I would
like to participate.

I jumped at the chance. Blind flight, more correctly called
instrument flight, means piloting an airplane without being

able to see out the window, a situation that normally occurs in
clouds or on very dark nights.
Instrument take-offs and flights
had become routine by the
middle thirties and were not too
difficult for experienced pilots.
However, then as now, actual
landings required some outside
visibility. Having followed
Jimmy Doolittle's career, I knew
that he had successfully made
the first blind landing at
Mitchell Field 10 years before. I was anxious to see what
progress had been made since then.

The Randolph program used BC-lAs, which were two-place
tail wheel monoplanes. For blind landings, the planes were
guided by two low-frequency radio homing beacons positioned
on the final approach path to the turf landing area. After lining
up with the two beacons and crossing the innermost beacon at a
prescribed altitude, the plane had to be kept level, both fore-and-
aft and laterally, while the pilot stayed straight on track with the
directional gyro. Then, with gaze constantly scanning the instruments, he would slowly let down, maintaining a pre-determined
speed and rate of descent by delicate moves of the throttle until
the main wheels hit the deck. At this point, he had to push the
control stick forward hard, and hold it there until the tail wheel

(above) While at Randolph Field, I got a chance to play polo as a substitute on Major Long's Dallas team.

came down. This last move prevented the plane from "porpoising."

Mastering the mechanics of blind landings was not as difficult as I expected, and it served to polish my instrument capabilities. I still remember the tension, the wait, seeing nothing outside the cockpit, trying to relax my grip on the stick, trying not to stare too long at the gyro, and anticipating the thud as the wheels finally hit the ground. The procedure was not very precise, and required a large, unobstructed area in which to land—not too practical for heavy airplanes with high landing speeds, nor for the long, narrow, paved runways coming into favor at the time. Even today, more than 50 years later, with the most sophisticated electronic control and surface guidance systems, blind landings are not in general use by either the airlines or the military. This means diverted or canceled airline flights or military missions when the destination airport is fogged in. Safe blind landings, necessary for all-weather operations, are still a prime objective of the government and the airline industry.

Several days after my blind landing session, my commanding officer called me in to dress me down. If I had time to spare, he said, on flying activities that were none of my damn business, he

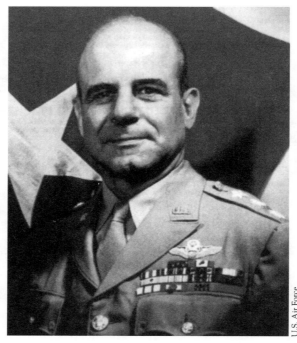

would give me something useful to do. He then handed me manuals on military doctrine, military law, and customs of the service to study. Fortunately, I had covered essentially the same material in Harvard ROTC, and was able to handle his subsequent substantial quiz.

By the Ides of March, I had completed all the requirements of the refresher flight training course way ahead of schedule. All, that is, except the hardest part, the final check ride. This was tougher than I expected. It was a clear, hot day, and things were going reasonably well until my check pilot asked me to show him a four point aileron, or slow roll. This, which had not been included in my course, is one of the more difficult precision aerobatic maneuvers to do well. It requires rotating the airplane horizontally 360 degrees about its axis, hesitating at 90, 180, and 270 degrees, while neither gaining nor losing altitude, and keeping the plane's nose at approximately the same point on the horizon. What makes a slow roll so special is that during the roll, the rudder and elevator controls progressively swap their functions. In normal flight the rudder moves the plane's nose right or left, and the elevator moves it up or down. At 90 and 270 degrees (with the plane on its side), the rudder moves the nose up

(above) Jimmy Doolittle was a pioneer in aircraft control at slow flight and the art and mechanics of blind landing.

or down on the horizon, and the elevator moves it right or left. At 180 degrees (upside-down), both the rudder and elevator controls have exactly the opposite effect as they do right-side-up.

I had never slow-rolled a BC-1A, and I was tense anyway, so my first attempt was sloppy. My second was worse. I overshot the 270 degree mark, and lost about 500 feet upside down. Instead of saying anything on the intercom, my check pilot, who was in the rear cockpit, shook his stick, the universal signal for "I'm taking over." Feeling this, I turned around to see him shaking his head and pointing to the ground with his thumb down. Great. I knew this meant we're landing. The ride is over. You're busted out.

I pleaded for one more chance. He agreed. With everything to lose, I willed myself to relax and go for broke. In quick succession, I did a loop, which was easy; an Immelman turn, a roll on top of a loop (a fighter tactic to reverse direction), snaprolls in both directions, and then, thoroughly relaxed, a near-perfect slow roll. The stick shook again and I turned around to see a grin and a hand held up to form a circle with thumb and second finger.

Twenty years later I met my check pilot at a Quiet Birdman meeting at the Miami Air Races. He confessed that our commanding officer had ordered him to give me a hard time. It seems the good captain had tried unsuccessfully to get in on the blind landing program, and was teed off that a reserve second lieutenant had beat him to it. I wasn't sure I blamed him.

At Randolph, apart from brushing up my flying skills, I also learned more than I had known before about the dispute within the military between those who believed in the efficacy of air power, and those who held that ground and naval forces were the ultimate military power. Although air power had been a major factor in World War I, the American military was reluctant to devote money or training to airplanes or pilots.

The acknowledged hero among military advocates for air power was Army Brigadier General Billy Mitchell. Billy Mitchell first attracted national attention when he organized and led the American Expeditionary Air Force in Europe during World War I. When he got to Europe, he discovered that the United States could not provide him a single combat-ready plane, so he had to borrow planes from France and England. He returned home, covered with medals, determined to build up American air power.

Over the heads of senior Army generals and Navy admirals, he complained bitterly about America's unpreparedness and tried to persuade the President and the Congress that the next world war would be won in the air. He believed that there should be an Air Force coequal with, and independent of, the Army and the Navy. At the time, top military officers steadfastly believed that airplanes were only good for scouting. On a challenge from Navy brass, which had asserted that battleships were invulnerable to aerial attack, Mitchell easily sank a cap-

(above) The Army Air Corps insignia.

135

tured German submarine, a destroyer, a light cruiser and the dreadnaught *Ostfriesland* with bombs dropped from Army planes, proving that air power could indeed be used in naval warfare.

Instead of taking Mitchell's lessons to heart, the Army grew defensive. In 1925, Billy Mitchell, arguably the best and the brightest high ranking officer in any of the military services, was court-martialled. At the trial, almost all the men who would become top Army Air Corps generals in World War II defended Mitchell at considerable risk to their careers, which were, indeed, compromised. The witnesses included Lieutenant General Touey Spaatz, who organized and commanded the Eighth Air Force, the first U.S. combat air unit in Europe in World War II, as well as his successor, Lieutenant General Ira Eaker. Major General Monk Hunter, Commanding General of the Eighth Fighter Command, and Lieutenant General George Kenney, Commanding General of the Allied Air Forces in the Southwest Pacific, added their favorable testimony. Major General Bob Olds, who organized the world-girdling Air Corps Ferrying Command, also testified, as did Lieutenant General Jimmy Doolittle.

Lieutenant Generals Ben and Barney Giles, who respectively became Deputy Commanding General of the Army Air Corps, and Commanding General of U.S. Army forces in the Middle East, added their voices to the chorus in favor of Mitchell. Brigadier General Rosie O'Donnell, who would be my immediate superior at the end of World War II, was also a vocal Mitchell supporter. My current neighbor General George Patton, Jr., tells me his father, the blood and guts Army General, admired Mitchell and thought his ideas were right on the money.

Despite all this testimony in his favor, Mitchell was convicted of "military heresy" and demoted to colonel. He then quit the Army and continued to carry out his campaign for air power until his early death in 1936. By this time, just about every military pilot considered Billy Mitchell a hero and a prophet. Those of us in the pilot refresher course at Randolph field hoped that we might one day get the chance to prove that Mitchell was right.

After my stint in Texas, I returned home to work and family at Buzzards Bay. Every morning I would get into Stearman NC-2143, kept at the landing strip at the Bay, and commute to my

(above) General Billy Mitchell with top WWI ace Eddie Rickenbacker. General Mitchell was the acknowledged hero of the military aviation fraternity. He believed the U.S. should have an Air Force independent of and coequal with the Army and the Navy.

office at East Boston. One late fall day, as I started the engine, the big Wright backfired with a loud bang. The cover glass blew out of the manifold pressure gauge, and flaming gas sprayed onto the cockpit fabric, which instantly caught fire.

There was a Pyrene fire extinguisher—standard military equipment—aboard, which I seized. I doused the flames and had almost put them out when I was overcome with choking fumes. I couldn't breathe. I had to get out of the cockpit, and before I got my breath back, the fire was out of control. My faithful, unique Stearman went up in smoke. The Stearman was special to me and had served me well, getting me in and out of countless difficult places. Losing her this way made me feel as if I had been unfaithful to an old friend.

But the Stearman did not die entirely in vain. In fact, my experience with the Pyrene fire extinguisher helped to get the dangerous substance removed from the cockpits of military planes all over the country. When I told Jerry Lederer, head of the Flight Safety Foundation, about the fumes that nearly suffocated me, he told me that when Pyrene gets hot it breaks down into highly toxic chlorine gas. He added that he had been trying to have Pyrene outlawed for use in aircraft. He later wrote to say that my experience had finally helped him make his point. Pyrene was replaced by a mono-ammonium phosphate, a safer dry chemical used to douse fires in power boat engines. Even in her final hours, my Stearman made an important contribution to aviation safety.

Sad as it was to do, I had to replace her. I chose a Luscombe Phantom, NC-1025. This was a sporty, two-place, high-wing monoplane which I turned over to the Civil Air Patrol in 1941 when I went to war. She was used for anti-sub patrol, and ended up in the Experimental Aircraft Association Museum in Oshkosh, Wisconsin where she still sits on display.

During the period before our entry into the war, a number of dates stand out in my memory, times when it seemed that our world was about to change dramatically. One I remember vividly was Sunday, September 1, 1939.

It had been an idyllic late summer's day at Buzzards Bay. Most tourists had left, and I was looking forward to some rest and relaxation now that the new Aeronautics Act was about to be signed by Governor Saltonstall. I would be able to enjoy tennis, swimming at high tide, and sailing in the freshening afternoon sou'westers. Soon the wildfowling season would open for black ducks and Canada geese on the Barnstable marshes. Trouble in Asia or Europe seemed remote. I spent the day enjoying the perfect weather at the beach.

That evening, Jan and I had guests for dinner. We were having coffee and liqueurs on the terrace overlooking Buttermilk Bay, and, as we watched the evening fog creep towards us from the head of Buzzards Bay, our guest, Richmond "Tote" Fearing, likened the creeping fog to Nazism. We talked of how lucky we were to be in our particular circumstances.

I had a shortwave radio, used mostly for aircraft communications and time signals, so we decided to try to tune in some foreign news. There was no television then, and few daily radio news broadcasts. After fiddling with the appropriate knobs for a while, we happened upon an emotional, staccato tirade in

German, punctuated by frequent and thunderous "*Sieg Heils.*" Tote, who was fluent in German, gave us a running translation and commentary. We soon realized that we were listening to Hitler announcing the invasion of Poland.

This, I thought, is it. It would be a different world tomorrow.

How wrong I was. For the rest of 1939, it seemed that all Germany wanted was Poland and the Polish Corridor. The situation of Poland's allies on the Western Front was aptly called the Phoney War. It became almost hard to take this small man with the toothbrush mustache seriously. It was easy then to forget the Reich's long range goal of a *Drang nach Osten.*

Hitler surprised most everyone yet again with the Werhmacht's lightning drive through Scandinavia and the Low Countries in March. In May 1940, the British turned in desperation to Winston Churchill, the country's leading opponent of the policy of appeasement, and one who had never taken Hitler lightly.

Churchill promptly pleaded with the United States for military planes. He felt this crucial to the survival of France and to repel the expected invasion of the British Isles. Even though President Roosevelt was an ardent Anglophile, he was nearly powerless to help. Our under-equipped Army and Navy had very few modern aircraft, certainly none to spare. FDR was also bound by the 1935 United States Neutrality Act which prevented us from giving or selling any of them to a combatant. Furthermore, there was anything but consensus among Americans that we should throw our lot with England and

France. The *America First* committee, with a huge following, felt we should stick with the advice of our founding fathers and keep out of foreign entanglements. I, for one, was impressed by the words of Charles Lindbergh, then a colonel in the Army Air Corps Reserve. Returning from a visit to Germany in late 1939, he was convinced that the Luftwaffe was irresistible and urged that we stay out of the war. The quick fall of Denmark, Norway, Belgium and Holland in the spring of 1940 seemed to prove his point.

Dunkirk, the fall of France in June 1940, and especially the August Battle of Britain changed many minds, and persuaded Congress to pass the Lend-Lease Act, allowing us to lease or lend aircraft and supplies to the Allies without compromising our stated neutrality. So far as the United Kingdom and China were concerned, this effectively bypassed the Neutrality Act. FDR signed Lend-Lease on March 11, 1941, and immediately appointed his alter ego, Harry Hopkins, as administrator. The U.S. then sent troops to Greenland and Iceland to protect the sea and air lanes between America and Great Britain. These were manned mostly by National Guardsmen and Reservists.

Meanwhile, we were preparing for war at home. In 1939, believing that air power would play a vital part in the war's outcome, the President and the War Department instituted the Defense Landing Area Act (DLA). Assuming that coastal military airports in the northeast and southeast would be strategically useful during the war and valuable commercial assets afterwards, DLA directed the United States Corps of Engineers to build an

---

(right) After the Stearman burned, I bought Luscombe Phantom NC-1025. Here Jan and I fly over Cape Cod.

airport at any location agreed upon by the Army Air Corps and the Civil Aeronautics Authority if a local public agency provided the necessary land.

Because of the extensive aviation and business experience represented on the new Massachusetts Aeronautics Commission (MAC), plus engineering and public safety help from its two ex-officio members, we were able to hit the ground running. Our staff was small but eager: Mary Urann, an excellent secretary; Joe Wallis, an airport engineer on loan from the Works Progress Administration, and Frank Sweeney, a state police pilot, also on loan. Finally, we inherited Major Hodge from the Registry of Motor Vehicles. He proved himself quite a diplomat on Beacon Hill, and turned out to be a valuable asset.

One of the first obligations of the MAC was to "prepare and revise from time to time a plan for the development of airports and air navigation facilities in the Commonwealth." When we first got down to business in the fall of 1939, Massachusetts had no state airport plan. Our first task, then, was obvious. Cooperating with the Public Works Department, we inventoried our existing facilities, and related them to the department's highway plan, which included a circumferential highway (assigned the number 128) surrounding Boston and extending to the Atlantic on

(left) When England entered the war, many Americans believed it would only be a matter of time before we would be fighting on the side of the Allies.

both ends. Working with maps and visual reconnaissance, first from the air and then from the ground, we picked four airport locations, approximately equally spaced along the path of what would be Route 128. The locations were in South Weymouth, Norwood, Bedford, and Beverly. We also strongly recommended a second major airport to relieve congestion at Boston.

By November 30, 1940, the end of the MAC's full fiscal year, we had developed a preliminary state airport plan. Designed to create "airports adequate to the present needs of military, commercial and private flying as part of a continuing program designed to take care of such future needs as can be reasonably foreseen," the plan was approved by the Civil Aeronautics Administration and the War Department for DLA participation in December, 1940. We also recommended that the Commonwealth should terminate the city of Boston's lease on the East Boston airport and return it to state control.

My next task was to persuade the communities where our proposed airports were to be situated to provide the required land. In most cases, this was surprisingly easy. I had expected that Bedford, potentially the most interesting as the second major airport for Boston, would be easy to sell, since at that time, the site was a pig farm. We thought that Bedford and its surrounding communities would be happy to swap this farm for a valuable post war airport. How wrong we were!

I did not realize that, not far from the piggery, the prominent Boston attorney, Sam Hoar, kept a private wildfowl preserve along the banks of the Concord River. Sam warned me that he was going to do everything he could to protect his birds from being disturbed by airplanes. I spent endless hours at town meetings and with planning boards and selectmen in Bedford and the contiguous towns of Lincoln, Lexington, and Concord. People were polite, but firmly against the airport.

One of the staunchest supporters of the Bedford airport was a popular statehouse reporter for the *Worcester Telegram* named Larry Hanscom. He said that if I could get Governor Saltonstall to propose that the state pick up the Bedford project, he could help with members of the legislature to make it a state airport. Saltonstall requested an appropriation of $64,000, the appraised value of the pig farm, for a DLA state airport at Bedford. The vote in the House of Representatives ended in a tie, which was broken May 14, 1941 by the rare, favorable vote of the Speaker, Chris Herter, former editor of *Sportsman Magazine* and future Secretary of State.

The state took the land on June 19, 1941, and construction began immediately. When Larry later died in a Civil Air Patrol accident, the new airport was named Hanscom Field. Larry's confidence, and mine, in the importance of the Bedford site proved well-founded. After the war, Bedford helped spawn the beginnings of Route 128's Technology Row, with nearby research facilities for Massachusetts Institute of Technology's Radiation Labs, the U.S. Air Force Lincoln Labs, and Raytheon.

Soon after work started at Bedford, Governor Saltonstall called me in to meet Navy Lieutenant Commander Rosendahl, who said the Navy wanted the site for a lighter-than-air base. He explained that he needed to operate semi-rigid blimps in anti-submarine patrol along the New England coast.

I pointed out that Bedford was separated from the ocean by the busy Washington–New York–Boston airway, which the blimps would have to cross, and suggested South Weymouth instead, which was closer to the ocean. Rosendahl agreed, and the resultant airport became the South Weymouth Naval Air Station.

In the immediate pre-war years, I also served on Governor Saltonstall's three man War Preparedness Committee. Together with Powell Cabot, head of the state Office of Economic Development, and Roy Williams, President of Associated Industries of Massachusetts, my mission was to evaluate, encourage and promote participation by Massachusetts industry in the rapidly expanding war effort.

With this practical experience in public business, it was easy for me to become involved in part time military projects. By the middle of 1941, I was dividing my time about equally between Air Reserve activities in Washington and Maine and my state job. Although my work in Massachusetts was important for the war effort, my thoughts were frequently in Europe, and I hoped to be able to play a more active role in the defense of the country, using the skills I had sharpened in the pilot refresher course at Randolph Field. It was not long before I would have that chance.

Aerial Photos International

(above) Lawrence Hanscom, a reporter for the *Worcester Telegram,* was one of the staunchest supporters of the proposed airport in Bedford.

(left) The Bedford Airport, potentially the most interesting of our DLA airports to serve as an overflow for Logan after the war.

CHAPTER 11

SETTING UP THE FERRY ROUTE

DATE	PLANE	FROM	TO	TIME	PILOT
02/26/42	Lockheed Hudson	Goose Bay	BW-1	4:53	Crocker Snow

We still had plenty of fuel, so we headed back to the coast, dropped below the overcast, found what we were sure was Simiatuk, and started VFR up what we thought was Tunugliarfik. There are three fjords close together; Brede to the north, Igalike to the south, and the one we sought in the middle. We had picked the wrong one, which soon came to a dead end. Fortunately, there was room for a 180 degree turn. As we reached Simiatuk again, we saw another fjord just to our right. This had to be the one. It was. After flying for about 20 minutes at 300 hundred feet, between sheer cliffs rising into the clouds, we spotted the steel mat runway angling off to our right from the water's edge. We must have been some surprise, approaching unannounced out of the mist at one of the world's most remote places.

In April 1941, Harry Hopkins called on Army Air Corps Colonel Bob Olds to put together an overseas air ferry network to get American supplies and aircraft to the Allies. Bob Olds, whom I had first met through Colonel Bob Walsh, asked me if I was interested in going on active duty and joining his team. He predicted that when (not if) we got into the war, I would be called up regardless, probably for assignment as a flight instructor at some miserably hot southern training station. By

joining him now, he promised I would be "close to the throne."

At the time, I was designated by Governor Saltonstall of Massachusetts as a person who would not be called upon for active duty unless it were absolutely necessary: My work with the Defense Landing Area Act and on the War Preparedness Committee was considered important enough to warrant my staying at home and continuing on. However, in July, 1941, I received orders to report to Selma, Alabama, where the Army

---

(left) Tunugliarfik Fjord. We flew down this long corridor of sheer cliffs to find Bluie West -1, one of the stops along the new North Atlantic Ferry Route to the U.K.

had a flight school. This was clearly one of those miserably hot southern training stations Bob Olds had warned me about, and I was not happy. I still needed to be released from the governor's war pool to be able to follow these orders, but it seemed that, unless I did something about it, my war-time activities would involve breathing dust and teaching the rudiments of flight control to eager young pilots.

Bob Olds came to my rescue. He sent me a letter in July, saying, "It is necessary that you be immediately available for assignment to the transfer point development project." I soon obtained a letter of release from Governor Saltonstall, and on September 10, 1941, reported to Air Corps Ferrying Command headquarters in Washington for briefing and assignment.

Washington was bulging with Army and Navy officers in mufti. We were ordered to refrain from wearing uniforms in public—apparently the Commander-in-Chief wasn't ready for the public to realize that we were preparing for war. Colonel Olds' staff was small and dedicated. I particularly remember Major Will Tunner, who went on to command the Hump operation, and later the Berlin airlift, as well as my reservist friends Felix duPont and Bob Love.

There were few regular officers to spare for the Ferry Command, so Olds had blanket authority to sign up reserves and offer direct commissions to qualified civilians. There was an equal shortage of military aircraft for us to use. Consequently we were authorized to contract with the airlines for flying services.

Our first theater of operations was to be the North Atlantic, the shortest route to the hard-pressed United Kingdom. We would need terminals in the U.S. and in England, with suitable stops in between. Our immediate task was to establish the western terminus of our first ferry route. It had to be as far northeast as practical; accessible by highway and rail; and close to a center of population large enough to support a myriad of civil services. Canada's Royal Air Force Ferry Command was operating out of Dorval airport in Montreal. They wanted us to join them, making such improvements as we needed. However, Colonel Olds chose Presque Isle, Maine, because it was closer to England, and American money spent there could benefit the U.S. after the war. Our Corps of Engineers was already building an airport there under the DLA Act.

We were to use Gander, Newfoundland and Prestwick, Scotland (both already operational) for long-range flights. For short range aircraft, we would have Goose Bay, Labrador, (under construction as a joint Canadian–U.S. venture); Bluie West-1 (being built in southern Greenland by U.S. military engineers); and Reykjavik, Iceland, marginal in size and soon to be replaced by much larger Keflavik on the western tip of the island. A quick paper study showed that none of the legs of the route for short-range aircraft was more than 800 nautical miles long. A surprise to me was that, of all the airports, Presque Isle had the coldest winters and the most snow.

My first assignment was to represent the Ferry Command in the construction and outfitting of air bases at Presque Isle and Houlton, Maine. Presque Isle was the center of Aroostock County's potato growing country in the far north. This was no small distinction; it was said that, in boom years, sales of Rolls

Royces in Aroostock County exceeded those in Boston. Houlton was bisected by the Canadian–American boundary. It was designed this way intentionally to circumvent the Neutrality Act. Airplanes would land on the American side and get pushed across the border so that Canadian pilots could fly them away. After the passage of the Lend-Lease act, this subterfuge was no longer necessary.

My first assigned transportation was a Howard DGA, a very nice single engine, high-wing monoplane that was renamed a C-70 when it was drafted into the military. Soon a C-39 (in civilian garb a Douglas DC-2 twin-engine passenger plane) complete with copilot and mechanic, was added to the stable for carrying emergency supplies and personnel between Moncton and Goose Bay for the MacNamara Construction Company that was building the airport.

The 3,000 foot landing strips at both ends of my run—Moncton and Goose Bay—were rolled and hard-packed snow with spruce boughs marking their boundaries. Because of the intense winter cold, on overnight layovers we either had to drain the airplanes' engine oil and keep it warm, or, before trying to start, operate the oil dilution system. This meant squirting gasoline into the engine crankcase to thin

---

(right) We established the North Atlantic Ferry Route as a safe way to get planes, munitions and supplies from the U.S. to hard-pressed England.

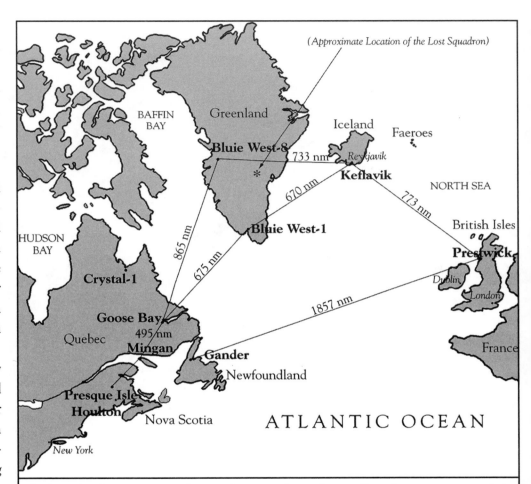

Air bases for short range aircraft were close enough together to allow planes to return to their starting point without running out of fuel if the destination airport was below minimums for landing. Planes with the range to make the direct flight from Gander to Prestwick usually followed a "pressure pattern flight" which enabled them to fly with a tailwind most of the way over the ocean. The route was longer than 1,857 nautical miles on the direct course, but much faster and more economical.

the oil. When the engine started, the gasoline was supposed to evaporate. Why this process didn't start a fire I'll never know. The C-39 was equipped with steam heaters for the cockpit and cabin. On very cold days or on stopovers these would usually freeze up. In winter, passengers and crew dressed in fur-lined or electrically-heated suits, helmets and flying boots, just in case.

Canadian National Airlines served Moncton from the west. If the weather was particularly bad, the approach path was lighted with red flares shortly before scheduled arrival time. If there was icing on the ground, which was frequent, we protected the wings and tail with cloth covers as soon as the props stopped. Because of these primitive precautions, commercial airline cancellations for weather were rare. Even my single DC-2 operation maintained a fairly reliable schedule between Moncton and Goose Bay.

Still, the operation wasn't entirely routine. I recall, for instance, one frightening mid-winter flight when, while crossing the 60-mile-wide straits of Belle Isle, just over halfway from

Gander, Newfoundland to Goose Bay, Labrador, we lost the oil pressure on both engines. With a mountain range behind us, icy water below, and no place to land short of our destination, there was nothing to do but proceed with our hearts in our mouths and our fingers crossed. Fortunately we made it without incident. Our post-flight inspection revealed that the oil in the lines between the engines and the gauges had congealed: the engine oil pressure was fine, but the gauges in the cockpit couldn't tell us so.

On December 7, 1941, I was flying a C-39 from Montreal to Moncton. Early in the afternoon, I made a fuel stop at Presque Isle. The only teletype on the base with access to flight plans and weather was in Northeast Airlines' small operations shack and passenger shelter. I was waiting there while the C-39 was being refueled. Suddenly the teletype machine let out a succession of peremptory *ting, ting, tings*. This was an attention signal, often followed by a severe weather warning, or word that a general officer was on the way in. Instead, it spelled out the words, "The Japs have bombed Pearl Harbor."

(above) Stops along the North Atlantic route were frigid in winter and required some special precautions to keep the planes operating.

(right) Some parts of our route took us over vast expanses of snow and ice.

At first those of us in the shack thought this was someone's poor joke, but as more information came over the wires we knew the information was for real. We were now at war, playing for keeps. There was even a sense of relief among our small staff that all the waiting was over. Our efforts would now have a clear objective—winning the war.

The following day the President spoke to the nation by radio. Together with many townspeople and our small military contingent, I heard his broadcast in Presque Isle's movie theater. I had never voted for FDR, but on this day, I thought his shocked, short and stirring "Day of Infamy" speech, ending with a call on Congress to declare war on Japan, was just right for the occasion.

My job was now to prepare the facilities at Presque Isle and Houlton to handle the expected flow of aircraft across the North Atlantic. Then, on January 23, 1942, I was called to Washington and presented with War Department Special Orders Number 3, designating me (a first lieutenant!) to be commanding officer of the North Atlantic Sector of the Air Corps Ferrying Command, extending from Presque Isle to Prestwick, Scotland.

My first reaction was that the career military personnel barrel must be nearly empty, which I guess it was. But Bob Olds and his A-3 (operations staff officer) Major Tom Mosley, gave me and four other newly-appointed sector commanders a pep talk that filled me with confidence and made me proud to be a part of Olds' team. I was certainly close to the throne, and vowed to do my best.

My assigned mission was to maintain and operate facilities for the movement of military aircraft and crews between the U.S. and the European theater via the North Atlantic. We were also to provide air transport for military passengers and cargo, using commercial airlines under contract as much as practical. There was considerable doubt at the time that the British Isles would be able to weather the expected German invasion. To prepare for this, an alternative way to get military aircraft within range of Europe was in the mill. Code-named the Crimson Route it went from the West Coast of the U.S. via The Pas, Manitoba; Southampton Island at the top of Hudson's Bay; Crystal-3 in Baffin Land; Bluie West-8 in northern Greenland to the Faero Islands, 400 miles off the coast of Norway. We were directed to survey the Crimson project. There was also a standby plan for evacuating the British government over our route, using flying boats, which were to land on the Thames.

All this to do, and no staff to do it with. Fortunately, I was able to get instant commissions for a number of Harvard and Massachusetts Institute of Technology friends. My brother-in-law, Norman Vaughan, an experienced explorer, who handled Byrd's sled dogs on the Admiral's 1928 expedition to the South Pole, was one of my first recruits. His job was to command Crystal-1, a key far northern base under construction at Fort

(right) Crystal-1, the base at Fort Chimo, Labrador, was part of the Crimson Route, an alternative, polar path to Europe to be used in the event that Germany occupied the British Isles and their navy patroled the North Sea.

Chimo, Labrador. He also became our search and rescue expert, a profession that he continued after the war with the International Civil Aviation Organization.

Other recruits included Charlie Hubbard, an All-American football guard at Harvard, deep sea sailor, tennis, squash and wild fowling companion, who had explored much of Labrador by air. He was in charge of our weather net. Waddy Walker, head of a Boston investment banking firm, turned out to be a topnotch adjutant. John Yerxa, of a Boston mercantile family, did a superior job handling our supply problems. He later became a vice president and Boston station manager for Pan American Airlines. John Thayer, a bon vivant, was a natural to set up our officers club and run our motor pool. Washington helped by sending up Lieutenant Harry Jones, a rated military pilot, who became our operations officer, and Lieutenant Raymond Ickes, our "expediter." While no such title existed in our table of organization, it did make sense since Ickes had an independent pipeline to the throne itself. His father, known as the Great Curmudgeon, was President Roosevelt's Secretary of the Interior.

Our hierarchy was not as clear-cut as one would expect in a military organization. Some of our recruits were commissioned as lieutenants, and two, for no discernible reason, as captains.

Thus, they outranked me, their commanding officer. The Presque Isle base commander was regular Army Colonel Rafael Baez, who sported a waxed mustache and carried a swagger stick. His job was to provide the facilities and services required by the rated tactical commander. Me. All of this made for interesting relationships.

On January 31, 1942, the War Department contracted with 17 domestic airlines on a cost-plus fixed fee basis. Northeast Airlines was immediately assigned to the Air Corps Ferry Command, and was soon installing navigation equipment—four-course radio ranges and homing beacons—along the North Atlantic route. To save critical time, radio equipment at low activity domestic airports was moved to ferry route stops. The first four-course radio range was transplanted from Montpelier, Vermont to Prestwick, Scotland.

Since I was settled in Presque Isle, I moved my family up from Boston. The caravan consisted of Jan, three children, one Swedish cook, and a mother Doberman Pinscher with five puppies. We had rented an attractive log cabin just off the airport. It had a rather primitive heating system—a wood furnace in the cellar. We also had a large fireplace, but on winter nights we needed our Hudson's Bay blankets (bought in Moncton) to stay warm.

(above) My brother-in-law, Norman Vaughan, a life-long sled dog expert, commanded Crystal-1.

By this time, we were beginning to move B-17 Flying Fortresses and B-24 Liberators from Gander non-stop to Scotland. However, our light bombers such as the DB-7 Douglas Boston, the B-25 Mitchell, the Martin B-26 Marauder, and our fighters didn't have the necessary range to be ferried to Scotland without using intermediate fueling stops, which were not yet ready. In the meanwhile, these planes were being sent by cargo ship, many of which were lost to German submarines.

With Goose Bay and Reykjavik now on the line, BW-1 in southern Greenland was the missing link. It was great news, therefore, when on February 19, 1942, the Navy's low frequency net delivered me a radiogram. Addressed to "Commanding General North Atlantic Sector, Air Corps Ferrying Command" and signed "Giles, Commanding Officer Greenland Base Command," it said that BW-1 was operational and ready for inspection. It took me a few days to find an available airplane with enough range to get from Goose Bay to Greenland and return nonstop if necessary. There was as yet no instrument approach at BW-1, and no way for Goose to get current BW-1 weather.

The Royal Canadian Air Force was kind enough to provide a co-pilot and a Lockheed Hudson, in which I checked out in a sightseeing flight to Hamilton Falls. We flew 175 miles west of Goose over trackless spruce forests and snow-covered muskeg with no signs of life or civilization. The weather was clear, with bright sunshine. The falls were a dramatic sight—countless

(above) P-38s and B-17s flying in ferry formation from Presque Isle.

tons of tumbling water, first passing through a narrow gorge and then leaping into a small lake at the bottom of a bowl with sheer walls of ice and snow. We flew low, took lots of photographs and occasionally thought we heard the thunder of the water when we throttled back. My Canadian check pilot doubted if many people other than nomadic Indian trappers had seen this magnificent spectacle. Now called Churchill Falls, the waterfall is the site of a huge hydroelectric complex, supporting an airport and the Town of Churchill, home to several thousand people.

On February 26, the Canadian weather forecaster at Goose predicted clear skies over Goose, Lake Melville, and the Davis Straits all day. He expected some low clouds along the west coast of Greenland, but thought they would be broken 50 miles inland at the base of the ice cap, where BW-1 was located. Our chart showed it to be at the head of Tunugliarfik Fjord. The mouth of the fjord was distinguished by Simiatuk Island. Simiatuk in Eskimo means "cork," as in a bottle.

The flight over the Atlantic by dead reckoning was uneventful until we neared Greenland, where we saw lots of "growlers" (small icebergs). The low clouds were there as predicted, with a 500 foot ceiling below them, which we stayed under, dodging icebergs, until we made landfall. Seeing nothing ahead that resembled Simiatuk and the mouth of the fjord, we turned south along the coast, still at 300 to 400 feet. Because the wind had been southerly coming over, we guessed we had most probably drifted north.

Soon we thought we knew where we were. With the information that Tunugliarfik fjord had solid rock walls as high as 5,000 feet, we decided to gamble on the forecast of broken clouds inland, climbed on top westbound, and headed back to the northeast at 7,000 feet. The undercast, about 2,000 feet below us, was solid as far as we could see, lapping the slope of the icecap, obviously beyond where BW-1 had to be. We still had plenty of fuel, so we headed back to the coast, dropped below the clouds again, found what we were sure was Simiatuk, and started VFR up what we thought was Tunugliarfik.

There were three fjords close together: Brede to the north, Igalike to the south, and the one we sought in the middle. We knew we had picked the wrong one, because it soon came to a dead end. Fortunately, there was room for a 180 degree turn. As we reached Simiatuk again, we saw another fjord just to our right. This had to be the one. It was. After flying for about 20 minutes at 300 feet between sheer cliffs rising into the clouds, we spotted the steel mat runway angling off to our right. We must have been some surprise, approaching unannounced out of the mist at one of the world's most remote places.

After a rattly landing on steel matting, we were met by the commanding officer, Colonel Ben Giles, his supply, weather, and communications officers, and a few enlisted men. This, except for engineers and construction workers, was his entire staff. After returning the colonel's snappy salute, I shed my Arctic parka. Only then did Giles realized that the "Commanding General" he had turned out the garrison for was

(left) **Hamilton Falls, now Churchill Falls, was a magnificent spectacle, which, in 1942, was familiar only to nomadic Indian trappers.**

nothing but a lieutenant. He took it in stride however, and we later became good friends.

Following a quick lunch at the base, I inspected the airport, which had one 5,000-foot east-west runway sloping up two degrees from west to east—a plus, since the approach from the west was good, while that from the east was blocked by the lower reaches of the nearby 7,000-foot high icecap. Thus, landings had to be made from the west where the up-slope acted as an extra brake on the landing run, and takeoffs to the west where the downslope reduced the length of the ground run on takeoff.

After I made the inspection, Ben Giles and I discussed approach procedures for ferry flights and readily agreed on two points. The scud-running technique we had employed to find the runway would not be safe. Until the programmed Simiatuk radio range and BW-1 radio beacon were in operation, BW-1 would be useful only in clear weather, which was not a common condition on the North Atlantic. We agreed that getting navigation aids in place was our top priority. Early the next morning, my copilot and I returned to Presque Isle. I then reported to Washington and went to work.

Our most important job in the late winter and spring

(left) We knew we were flying up the wrong fjord because it soon came to a dead end. Fortunately, there was enough room to turn around.

was to get all our airports and radio navigation facilities in shape. In April, after I had been promoted to captain, I flew a C-47 to Iceland, via Labrador and Greenland, for on-site inspections. We landed at Reykjavik Airport on Sunday, April 26. Shedding my furs in the operations shack, I was greeted with a stentorian hail, "Snow, what the hell are you doing here?"

It was Jimmy Mills, husband of my old flying student Alice duPont, who had been sent to Iceland with a Mitchell Field Reserve detachment in early 1941. Jimmy invited me to Sunday dinner at the Borg, Reykjavik's leading hotel. Apparently, Sunday dinners were special occasions in Iceland, for which all the blue bloods dressed for dinner. Fortunately, I had brought my tunic. On the way to the hotel we passed a large, landscaped lake. Since those in Maine, Labrador, and Greenland were still frozen, I was surprised to see no ice. Jimmy said that, as far as he knew, the lake had never been frozen. Iceland's weather was neither hot nor cold, but generally raw, damp and unpleasant.

The people eating at the Borg were well dressed and attractive, especially the ruddy-cheeked blond young ladies. It didn't seem the worst place to spend the war, but Jimmy confided that his main job was flying laundry between Reykjavik and Acureyri, a summer resort on the north shore where most of the senior military officers were quartered.

When I returned to Presque Isle, I found that Northeast had substantially completed its first task of installing radio beacons. American and Transcontinental and Western Airways were to furnish additional service in the North Atlantic Sector. The president of American, C. R. Smith, had been given a direct commission as colonel and was now deputy to Olds. TWA's new job was to fly non-stop between Gander and Prestwick; Northeast's was the route segment between Greenland and Prestwick; and American was supposed to feed Northeast from the Presque Isle terminal.

It soon became apparent that many southwest bound American flights originating in Goose Bay were overflying

(above) After we landed at BW-1, Colonel Ben Giles and his staff greeted us on the runway. It was only after I shed my arctic parka that Giles realized that the "Commanding General" he was expecting was only a lieutenant.

Presque Isle for New York, giving weather or mechanical problems as their excuse. Since the observed weather on a number of overflights was well above minimums, I suspected that the pilots knew there was little west-bound cargo destined for Presque Isle, and that more of the crews had families or girlfriends in New York than in northern Maine. They probably felt that no harm would be done in skipping their assigned stop, since they would still pick up the important loads at Presque Isle on their way back northeast.

The hitch, from my standpoint, was that American was submitting vouchers for the unproductive 1,000 mile round trips. When I sent headquarters a list of New York flights for which American should not be paid, our headquarters fiscal officer called to say that the airline was raising hell about my action. I had the temerity to wonder out loud if American thought it had a friend in court, since its president was Bob Olds' deputy. Shortly afterwards, I received a curt note from Colonel Smith himself, saying that when he worked for American he did everything he could to help them, but that now his loyalty was to the U.S. government.

Many years after the war, I ran into Ernie Gann, noted author of great aviation novels like *The High and The Mighty* and *Fate is the Hunter*. Ernie had been an American Airlines captain stationed at Presque Isle during the war. He said at first that he couldn't believe that my suspicions about some pilots overflying Presque Isle could have been true, but wrote me back after talking to another American Airlines captain to say that a few of American's pilots (not well regarded by their peers) had been doing exactly what I claimed.

During May, elements of the Eighth Air Force started drifting in to stage for their trip to the United Kingdom. Early in June, the commanding general of the Eighth, Major General Touey Spaatz, a very impressive officer, dropped in on his way to England. The general's plan was to have his P-38s escorted by B-17s, with each flight made up of four fighters under the wings of the more completely equipped bomber. He suggested that for the following ferry flights (many of which would be flown by pilots fresh out of school) we should have especially competent pilot/control officers at each stop. We agreed, but finding the bodies was a problem.

The general had only one serious concern about our operations. This was that all air-ground weather reports were being encoded in what was called ALACO, and that the code was changed daily. General Spaatz was against using code for weather reports. He felt that any possible help to the Germans from sending weather in the clear would be outweighed by the reduced probability for mistakes on our part. As it turned out, he was right.

(left) On one flight over the North Atlantic, I took a side trip to see this newly-erupted volcanic island south of Iceland.

CHAPTER 12

ARCTIC FLIGHTS

DATE	PLANE	FROM	TO	TIME	PILOT
7/18/42	C-53	Keflavik	BW-8	5 hours	Crocker Snow

We were gassed, fed, and ready to go, but the weather had deteriorated, with heavy rain, a 100 foot ceiling, and 1/4 mile visibility. This was way below official minimums of 300 feet and one mile, so, anxious to get back because of the men down on the icecap, I exercised my recently-acquired privilege as a rated senior pilot to clear myself. I was soon to regret it. After takeoff we had trouble climbing or getting up air speed, although all power indications were normal. Ordinarily we would have turned back, but the ceiling and visibility were too low for landing. Nothing for it but to keep going and hope for the best. We soon discovered that the left landing gear was down and would not retract. We picked up quite a lot of ice crossing the Denmark Strait. This, and the drag of the now iced-up gear, made it a tossup: either we would reach BW-8 or join the party on the icecap.

On June 20, 1942, by War Department General Order Number 8, the Ferrying Command was transformed into the Air Transport Command and the North Atlantic Sector was reborn as the North Atlantic Wing. Colonel Ben Giles, promoted to general, became its commanding officer and asked me to stay on as his deputy. Back in Washington, it was politics as usual. Bob Olds was kicked upstairs to become the Commanding General of the Second (training) Air Force, a dead end for those hoping for a combat command. The story was that the White House had learned that Olds had supported Wendell Willkie in his run against Roosevelt in 1940, and had been slated to become Secretary of War if Willkie won.

While we were processing the Eighth Air Force for movement to England, we had several prominent visitors. The then Senator from Missouri, Harry S Truman, was one. He was being flown on an inspection of military bases by a member of the

(right) Navigator Elias Bacha at the nose of the Big Stoop, one of two B-17s to go down on the Greenland Icecap, along with six P-38s.

initial 1939 Massachusetts Aeronautics Commission, my friend John Wells. Harry Hopkins came to see his handiwork in action. He brought along General George Marshall, an imposing officer with great ability, noted for his description of completed staff work—no paper longer than one page, and so structured that if he agreed with it, his initials would make it the basis of a formal order for action. Chandler Hovey, first chairman of the MAC, was another welcome visitor. He came with Bill Bump of American Airlines, who had been the first president of the revived Harvard Flying Club in 1926.

Over the summer we began processing aircraft in earnest. On June 26, the first flight of Eighth Air Force B-17s left Presque Isle for England, followed the next day by more B-17s, P-38s, and C-47s. My logbook shows July as a busy month, with over 100 hours of pilot time. Especially memorable was my first crack at a really high performance, current airplane, the two-place DB-7B. This came with the Eighth Fighter Command, which had used it for staff transportation. Stripped of armor and weapons it was a thrill to fly—I remember watching the airspeed hit 200 before reaching the end of the runway.

Also memorable in many ways was a C-53 (a DC-3 reconfigured for military transport) flight to Prestwick and back. The Army, faced with a shortage of experienced pilot officers, had drafted a number of airline pilots, commissioned them captains, and put them through a short course in military flying. We got three of them to be to be stationed at our airports to act as operations officers. Our plan was for all of them to see the route eastbound, taking turns flying copilot. We would leave one at Prestwick and drop one off at Keflavik and one at BW-8 on the way back.

We departed Presque Isle on July 14. The trip was a great education for me, both because my copilots knew more than I did about flying DC-3s, and because it was my first summertime flight east of Canada. Southern Greenland was no longer the grim, forbidding winterscape of my previous visits. West of the frozen icecap, it was dotted with crystal clear, blue-green lakes between rolling hills covered with brilliant green foliage. Whatever forgotten Norseman named the world's largest island must have first seen it in summer.

We spent the first night at BW-1, which was crowded with B-17s and P-38s waiting for good weather to Iceland. We took off for Reykjavik early the next morning. At about the same time, two flights of B-17-escorted P-38s left BW-8 in northern Greenland, bound for Iceland.

Our flight was routine, with only the usual wet cloud cover—not enough to cause trouble. We gassed at Reykjavik, and went on to spend the next night at Stornaway, an island off the coast of Scotland. For breakfast we gorged on eggs, ham and milk, all of which were rationed in England.

We dropped off a pilot at Prestwick and started home on July 17, landing at newly activated Patterson Field in Keflavik, about 20 miles west of the capital city. There we heard that eight planes, two B-17s and six P-38s, enroute from BW-8 to Iceland, had gone down somewhere on the Greenland icecap. No one knew what caused the mishap, but the crews were in radio contact with BW-8, and reported that, aside from being

extremely cold, they were all in good shape.

On July 18, we were gassed, fed, and ready to go, but the weather had deteriorated, with heavy rain, a 100 foot ceiling, and only about 1/4 mile visibility. This was way below official minimums of 300 feet and one mile, but, anxious to get back because of the men down on the icecap, I exercised my recently acquired privilege as a rated senior pilot to clear myself.

I was soon to regret it. After takeoff we had trouble climb-ing or getting up air speed although all power indications were normal. Ordinarily we would have turned back, but the ceiling and visibility were too low for landing—nothing for it but to keep going and hope for the best. We soon discovered that the left landing gear was down and would not retract. We picked up quite a lot of ice crossing the Denmark Strait. This, and the drag of the now iced-up gear, made it a tossup: either we would reach BW-8 or join the party on the icecap.

(above) Lieutenants J. Bradley McManus and Robert H. Wilson in front of Bradley's P-38. Bradley had attempted a wheels-down landing on the frozen icecap.

We made it, though with little fuel to spare. Our C-53 had a safety feature, pins that could be inserted in the landing gear when on the ground to keep the gear from collapsing or being inadvertently retracted. After landing at BW-8, sure enough, we found a pin still in the left gear.

More important, we received the happy news that a Navy Catalina flying boat out of BW-l had spotted the airplanes lost on the icecap. The Navy plane had dropped emergency supplies, including bedrolls, blankets, canned foods, magazines and whiskey. The Navy pilot, Lieutenant Atterberry, reported all the crews safe. They had sawed off the propellers of one of their B-17s so that they could keep the motor running and stay in radio contact with BW-8 without wearing out their batteries. Over the next few days, Lieutenant Atterberry flew over them several times, dropping more supplies and lending moral support.

Back at BW-8, we learned some curious details about the ill-fated flight. At convoy departure time, 03:45, Greenwich Mean Time July 15, BW-8 was clear and remained so all day. The enroute forecast called for nothing worse than scattered to broken layers of clouds. Reykjavik had been forecast to remain above its minimum approach ceiling of 4,000 feet for the duration of the flight. Five and a half hours after departure time, BW-8 received a radio request from the lead B-17 for its weather, and replied, as required by regulations, in ALACO code for the day. Shortly afterwards there was another call, this

(left) Fighter pilots by the wreckage of Lieutenant McManus' P-38. Once the lost squadron had been spotted on the icecap, they were kept well-supplied with necessities.

time for BW-1 weather, which was transmitted, also in code. Just before noon BW-8 heard faint distress calls in the clear saying that six P-38s were down on the icecap with their pilots apparently okay, and that the transmitting plane, a B-17, was about to join them.

The next day, I was ready to leave BW-8, dropping off my last co-pilot there. Given the recent circumstances, I was a bit reluctant to make the flight back to Presque Isle solo. Fortunately, I found a weather officer who had done a little private flying, and had just received orders transferring him to Washington. He was delighted to occupy my right seat on what would be a routine flight.

We arrived at Presque Isle to find that the last of the Eighth Air Force, eight P-38s and two B-17s, had left the day before with Monk Hunter and his staff. This departure not only gave us smaller units to handle, it also removed what had become somewhat of a personnel problem, and a personal problem for my family. Apparently General Hunter had taken quite a shine to my attractive, 32-year-old wife, and become very persistent in his attentions—so much so that his aide, our old friend Cocie Rathborne had moved into our log cabin while I was away, explaining that I had asked him as company for my wife.

On July 20 came my second promotion in three months, this time to major. I hoped my rise in status would continue like the story of the Western Union messenger who entered the Pentagon to deliver a telegram and came out a general.

Now that I had returned to my post, my immediate job was to

(right) Lieutenant McManus, making the best of the situation.

165

investigate the icecap situation. Seven days after the planes went down, a rescue party, consisting of a dog sled and three expert skiers (Naval Lieutenants Fred Crockett and Don Shaw, and Army Corporal Harry Kent) had reached the marooned men and escorted them back to the coast where they were picked up by boat, transferred to a PBY flying boat, and transported back to BW-1. I collected statements from the pilots in an attempt to unravel the mystery. Why would two B-17s and six P-38s, all apparently in good flying shape, with ample fuel to reach their good-weather destination have crash-landed, lost, on the Greenland ice cap? Statements from three of the pilots, all consistent, painted a clear picture of what had happened.

The convoy had departed BW-8 for Reykjavik, 733 miles, or about five hours to the east. The P-38s had over eight hours of fuel aboard; the B-17s a couple of hours more. At briefing before takeoff, the B-17 radio operators were supposed to have been furnished with ALACO weather codes for the day. Since these were changed daily, having the right ALACO code on hand was essential to decipher weather information. BW-8 weather was clear, and remained so all day. BW-1 weather was marginal most of the day.

While flying over the ice cap, the formation ran into a low layer of stratus clouds, forcing them to gain altitude, going up into ever more frigid conditions. Encountering cumulus clouds shortly thereafter, the planes climbed even higher, where the air

---

(left) While stranded on the icecap, the crews set up a shelter under the stabilizer of one of the B-17s. Here they make hot chocolate on a makeshift stove.

temperature hit −25° C. Uncomfortable even in their arctic flying suits, the men tried to drop below the overcast to warm up, but when they did so, they hit snow squalls. Now the planes were icing up and growing sluggish, so the group was forced back into the higher air.

At this point, they had been flying for over three hours, and should have been within 200 miles of Reykjavik. The lead ship attempted to get a weather report for the destination, but was temporarily out of radio contact both with the destination and with the weather ship flying about an hour ahead. Unsure whether they would be able to land at Reykjavik, their planes also now suffering from the cold, with frozen airspeed indicators, the pilots decided to turn around and head back for BW-8.

Although when they left the airport it was in the clear, the report they got from BW-8 now was that it was closed in with a ceiling of 1,000 feet and visibility of 1/8 mile—well below minimums. A second radio transmission confirmed the first report of bad weather at BW-8, but gave the encouraging news that BW-1, 400 miles away, was clear and unlimited. Now, the convoy changed course and tried for BW-1. But they never made it. At 11:45 GMT, eight-and-a-half hours out, flying over a trackless expanse of ice and snow, the planes drifted off

---

(right) Lieutenant Rudder, Captain Webb and Private Cook have fun with the parachutes used to drop them food from rescue planes.

course. Lost, the P-38s started running out of gas. Followed by the B-17s, they landed on the icecap just west of BE-2 on Greenland's east coast, 200 miles north and east of BW-1.

When I began to investigate the situation, several people put forth the proposition that a surreptitious German radio station on the east coast of Greenland or on a German submarine had led the flight astray with fictitious weather information. But there was nothing to support this hypothesis. I couldn't help recalling General Spaatz's concern about the hazards of encoding our ground-to-air weather communications. Suppose something had slipped in the encoding process? I decided to try this theory out for size.

When we decoded the July 15 ALACO weather for BW-8 and BW-1 using the airborne code for July 14, we had exactly the misinformation the Greenland flight had received. This satisfied me that the previous day's ALACO code had by mistake been issued to the lead B-17s, which might have happened because the pre-flight briefing, at 02:00 GMT July 15, occurred at 10:00 p.m. local time, July 14.

There was no smoking gun to prove my point beyond any doubt. With one irrelevant exception, the crews had, after landing, properly destroyed all classified material, including their weather codes. However, we were satisfied that such a mixup in codes was a much more credible cause for the confusion than misleading information from some unspecified enemy source, and this was our official finding.

(above) The "Lost Squadron" prepares to leave for the coast with rescuing skiers and their sled dogs.

After the downed crews had been rescued by Navy Lieutenant Fred Crockett, we sent my brother-in-law Norman Vaughan in alone by dog team to remove a secret Norden bombsight which had inadvertently not been destroyed. His biggest problem was removing the device from its B-17, but he succeeded. The eight planes, arranged in a perfect semi-circle on the ice, stayed where they had landed.

As a postscript to this story, some 40 years later, Norman became intimately involved in the daunting mission of attempting to recover the planes themselves. He became a partner in the Greenland Expedition Society (G.E.S.), which conducted several summer season trips to the icecap before locating a B-17, buried under 250 feet of hard-packed snow and ice. In 1990, the following summer, the Air National Guard flew heavy equipment to the site as a training exercise and excavated a hole large enough to send down a man in a sling, who reported that the aluminum skin of the plane had been squashed flat. Despite this discouraging news, the society went on looking for a P-38, reasoning that the smaller, more compact plane had a better chance of holding up under the weight of snow and ice. Two years later, the G.E.S. tunneled down to a P-38, 260 feet below the surface. Over the next month, they

(right) Members of the Lost Squadron, safely back at base. Front row: Captains D. W. Webb & R. B. Wilson; Second row: Lieutenants J. B. McManus, J. C. White, B. B. Bayless, R. H. Wilson; Third row: Lieutenants M. L. Mitchell, C. F. Rudder, E. Bacha, J. D. Hanna, H. L. Smith; Fourth row: Corporal Daniels, Sargeants Parizek, Poirrier, Speilman, Okley; Fifth row: Private Cook, Sargeant Hahn; Privates DeWitt, Gilbet, Henry and Guoan.

laboriously dismantled the perfectly preserved plane and hauled it, piece by piece, up a 12' by 4' shaft cut into the blue green ice. The plane, Harry Smith's P-38, made its way back to Middlesboro, Kentucky, where, renamed "Glacier Girl" it was reassembled. The remaining planes will sink deeper into the ice as they move inexorably westward and down until the icecap spits them out at its western extremity.

Soon after the North Atlantic Sector was established, we had put in a requisition for a Navy flying boat, the amphibious PBY-5A. Since most of our route was covered with water, we felt we needed an amphibian for air-sea rescue and to service remote weather and radio stations with no nearby airports. We didn't get our PBY at first. Instead, an OA-14, a small, twin engine four passenger amphibian, known in civil life as a Grumman Widgeon, showed up at our base. This was a fine airplane, but it didn't have the range, capacity, or seaworthiness that we were after. However, it did come in handy.

One of my father's law partners, Merrill Griswold, owned B Pond, a lake in the logging country in northern Maine, accessible only by seaplane or tracked vehicle. In the late summer, Merrill called to say he was heading for his camp, and wondered if I would like to fly over and do a little fishing. I asked if I could bring a friend, and invited my new commanding officer Ben Giles. On leave, we fired up the Widgeon early in the morning of August 28 and headed west. That part of Maine was densely forested, sparsely populated, and filled with rivers, lakes and streams.

We had some trouble locating B Pond, but finally spotted it with its camp, float, canoes, and a float plane on the beach. Merrill had a friend with him who turned out to be an expert dry fly fisherman who joined me in fishing several streams around the lake, while Merrill and Ben fished the lake from canoes. Between us, we caught quite a mess of brook trout, togue, and small mouth bass, many more than enough for a very pleasant—and instructive—dinner.

Ben had recently been through Army War College, where geopolitics and economics were part of the curriculum. Merrill, besides being a noted corporate lawyer, was a practicing financier. Among other ventures, Merrill organized the first U.S. mutual fund, Massachusetts Investor's Trust. The after-dinner conversation turned to the cost of the war and how it was going to be paid for. I remember Ben saying, "War is waste, but when you get into one you have to win it, no matter what the cost." As the war progressed, I saw plenty of evidence of the truth of this statement. But I am getting ahead of my story.

Soon after we returned from our pleasant fishing interlude, we had a chance to use the Widgeon for more appropriate business. A tactical B-25, enroute to Europe, went down somewhere between the St. Lawrence River and Goose Bay. Captain Messer, one of our ex-airline pilots, returning from Goose Bay to Presque Isle, spotted the plane on course and apparently intact, close to an uncharted but identifiable river in the wilds of Labrador. He reported the crew apparently in good shape.

(right) My good friend and commanding officer, the remarkable Ben Giles in my office at Presque Isle.

On October 25, I flew the Widgeon to Goose Bay; gassed up; retraced Captain Messer's course and soon located the B-25. I had to land some distance down-river where there was a long enough straight stretch of water for a loaded takeoff. Though winding, the river was wide and clear enough that I could taxi back and forth from my landing spot to where the crew had set up camp.

All airplanes using our North Atlantic route were equipped with survival gear including water, K-rations, mosquito netting, fishing gear, matches, an over-and-under 22 caliber rifle and a 410 gauge shotgun. The downed crew had made good use of their equipment. When I arrived they were roasting venison over a campfire. That, plus fresh-caught brook trout, was a tasty supplement to their K-rations. Everyone was in good shape, and seemed almost reluctant to leave their sportsmen's paradise for the war zone. The pilot explained that he had lost most of the power on both engines, but had been able to land under control in a thicket of small spruce trees. He did a good job, since no one was hurt.

The airplane was not too badly damaged either, though we had to abandon it due to the near impossibility of recovery. Many years after the war, Reverend Bobby Bryan, skilled bush pilot, great sportsman, and head of the Quebec-Labrador Foundation, gave me a photo he had taken of the remains of a B-25 he stumbled across in interior Labrador. We thought it was the same one.

We also used the Widgeon to land engineers for ground surveys of a site for an emergency landing field between Presque Isle and Goose Bay. I had first cased the territory in the DB-7, and found what appeared to be just the ticket. It was a large, flat plain just inland of the small fishing village of Mingan, Quebec, on the north shore of the St. Lawrence River across from Anticoste Island. We did ground surveys, which were favorable, and went ahead with the project.

On October 8, a Navy PBY-5A, the plane we had requested months before, landed at Presque Isle and taxied up to Operations. The pilot, a civilian, said his orders were to deliver the airplane to us and to return to the West Coast with his crew immediately. He said he couldn't stay long enough to check us out.

(above) The PBY-5A flying boat was the Navy's workhorse amphibian. On wheels, it handled much like any other plane, but to take off or land in the water required special skills.

"Anyway," he said, "on wheels it flies like any other airplane. I couldn't help you on the water, because I've never flown a seaplane." He did add that we would need a qualified crew chief or flight engineer, since all the fuel management was located in the center-section, out of reach of the pilots.

An immediate canvas of stationed and transient personnel disclosed no PBY pilots, but did uncover a crew chief with Navy PBY time. Together, we studied the PBY's operations manuals, and I decided to give the biggest airplane I had so far flown a try.

The Navy apparently did more for creature comfort than the Army. The PBY had a well-equipped galley, hot and cold running water, and a couple of bunks. It was also festooned with radio antennae of various shapes and sizes, most of which were designed to use exotic electronics, not included in our package, nor, I suspected, designed for our weather. This suspicion was later confirmed in a flight that encountered moderate icing. I lost a lot of antennae one-by-one, but my essential radios still worked.

On wheels, the PBY did handle much like any other airplane, except that it creaked and groaned like a wooden sailboat in a storm. After a few successful touch-and-go landings at Presque Isle, we headed for Squapan Lake, about 10 miles southwest. With a little practice I was able to grease the big boat in with hardly a ripple when we touched down in the water. Two days later I flew it to Mingan and back. I felt I was getting the hang of it, and that the PBY would be very useful to us.

On October 18, a Navy officer showed up with orders to proceed to BW-l. He had been a PBY squadron commander at Pensacola, and was happy to lay over for a few days to give us the benefit of his experience. Accordingly, we climbed into the plane and I proceeded to show him what I could do with it. He asked me to demonstrate a few takeoffs and landings on wheels, which I did. Then we headed south to Squapan for some water landings. Taking extra pains to show my skill, I came into a light breeze, and made one of my best and smoothest water landings ever. Turning to savor the expected approbation, I found my co-pilot ostentatiously wiping his brow, and saying, "For Christ sake, don't ever land a PBY amphib like that again!"

He then explained that the standard PBY flying boat hull had been modified with a bow compartment for the retractable nose wheel. Any slightly nose-down or level landing like mine, with any kind of a chop, would cave in the weakened bow and the main hull would rapidly fill up with water. With a sharp V bottom, the hull was designed to take large vertical loads, but very little on the nose.

We went up again, this time with him at the controls. His demonstration of the right way to land scared me about as much as my landing had scared him. He stalled at about 25 feet above the water, held the yoke way back, and we dropped almost vertically to land with a tremendous splash. This, he said, was not just the safest way to land in light air, but the only way to land in a heavy sea. He also advised against trying to take off in even a moderate sea. Good advice, as it turned out.

I then checked out our most experienced pilot, Jack Zimmerman, who had been chief pilot for TWA. He was a wonderful person, and had taught me a great deal about flying the

L.H. ELEVATOR   R.H. FIN   POINT OF IMPACT   R.H. RUDDER

OIL COOLER SCOOP   LEFT WING   LEFT FIN   TAIL OF FUSELAGE WITH R & L STABILIZER

2" OF RIGHT INNER FLAP   UPPER ½ L.H. RUDDER—PILOTS HATCH

R.H. AILERON LESS TIP

DC-3. We placed Jack in charge of ferrying people and supplies to Mingan in the PBY. Based on my limited experience and my check ride, I advised Jack not to take off from Mingan if the wind was parallel to, or onshore of, the north bank of the St. Lawrence, especially if the tide was coming and the wind was westerly, which created a vicious chop. After several weeks of routine operations Jack did just that. Viewed from the shore, the plane traveled from left to right, slowly picking up speed with spray flying above its high wing, seemingly struggling to get off, then stopping dead on the water and slowly sinking until the wing was awash.

Before a rescue boat could reach the plane, Jack and half the occupants had drowned, trapped in the cabin. The survivors reported that soon after the takeoff run had started, water poured in through a hole in the bow. Jack felt the safest course was to try to get off, and cushions and clothes were stuffed into the hole, but too much water had already come aboard.

My last memory of Presque Isle was, tragically, another fatal accident. Commanded by a young and eager officer, a B-25 squadron had arrived for processing enroute to the U.K. On October 21, after several days of bad weather along the ferry route, Goose Bay opened wide as did the segment from St. Lawrence on. At Presque Isle we still had a low overcast with a ceiling of 500 feet, but it was reported clear on top. The squadron commander assured me that all his pilots were Instrument Flight Rules qualified, and should have no trouble climbing on instruments through an overcast, especially if the rest of the trip would be in the clear. To be on the safe side, I hopped into a C-70, topped the clouds at 5,000 feet, and had unlimited visibility as far north and northeast as I could see. Back on the ground, I reported this to the squadron commander, and his flight was soon on the way, one by one.

It seemed like only a few minutes after their takeoff when the phone started ringing. Caribou and Ft. Fairfield police just north of Presque Isle were calling to report two fatal crashes. The rest of the squadron arrived at Goose Bay without trouble. The only plausible reason for these accidents was that the pilots were not qualified for blind flying, and lost control while trying to climb through 4,500 feet of overcast. This tragic and unnecessary accident taught me a valuable lesson that was to stand me in good stead later on. Don't trust an instrument rating issued at an Army flying school.

(left) A diagram of one of the accidents that was to be my last memory of Presque Isle. The only plausible reason for this accident was a poorly trained pilot, who was unable to climb through 4,500 feet of overcast on instruments.

CHAPTER 13

SECURITY SECRET

DATE	PLANE	FROM	TO	TIME	REMARKS
01/15/43	C-53	Middletown	Nowhere	0:00	Canceled

When we learned that Stalin wanted only our planes and not our pilots, the mission was scrubbed. The two C-53s, specially modified for cold weather flight through Siberia and some of the iciest places in the world, would be quite useful on the North Atlantic Ferry Route. I suggested they be sent there. Instead, they were dispatched to sweltering North Africa.

The six months following Pearl Harbor were a bitter time for America. The Japanese, having sunk most of our Pacific Navy and destroyed the greater part of our Army and Navy aircraft, were almost unopposed in implementing their "East Asia co-prosperity sphere policy." This consisted of conquering and subduing every country they could find, and appropriating whatever they could for their own purposes. Even before the December 7, 1941, debacle they had taken control of much of China, leaving the country's nominal leader, Chiang Kai-Sheck, stranded in remote Chungking.

The Japanese then turned their attention to the Philippines, a U.S. Commonwealth, where General Douglas MacArthur served as field marshal. The Japanese air force hit Manila's Clark Field unexpectedly, just hours after Pearl Harbor, destroying 475 Army and Navy planes on the ground. These planes had been flown there to defend the city, but not one of them so much as taxied down the runway before the bombs hit. With his air force annihilated, MacArthur had no choice but to declare Manila an open city and abandon his post. He retreated first to embattled Bataan, and two days after Christmas, withdrew to the supposedly impregnable rock, Corregidor.

(left) Tom Watson, Bill Hicks, and General Follett Bradley pose in front of the plane that would take them to Moscow for secret meetings with Stalin. Bradley's plan was to convince Stalin to let America set up air bases in Siberia.

Washington promised to send help to the Philippines, but help never came. After three months of bloody fighting, it became apparent that Japan would prevail. President Roosevelt therefore ordered MacArthur to withdraw while he could, and proceed immediately to Australia. From there, he was to take command of all military activities in the southwest Pacific. Although the general objected to abandoning his men, he escaped on March 11, 1942, leaving General Wainwright and over 47,000 U.S. troops to surrender to the Japanese.

Two days after Pearl Harbor, Guam, a U.S. possession in the Mariana chain of islands east of the Philippines, fell without a fight. Two weeks later, after a gutsy defense by a small contingent of U.S. Marines, nearby Wake Island became a Japanese base.

On April 10, 1942, Japanese war planes sank two British cruisers in the Bay of Bengal, the key to the Indian Ocean. On June 22, a Japanese submarine shelled Canada's Vancouver Island. Meanwhile, Japanese troops attacked the U.S.-owned Kiska Island in the Aleutians, garrisoned it, and began an occupation.

In all the gloom, there were two bright spots. Between December 18, 1941 and July 4, 1942, Brigadier General Claire Chennault's American Volunteer Group, flying out of Kunming at the Eastern end of the Burma Road, conducted a successful mini-war against the Japanese air force. Chennault's "Flying Tigers" were equipped with 55 new P-40 Tomahawks, crated for shipment to England, but turned down there as obsolete. Their noses were painted with multi-toothed sharks, whose wide open mouths seemed ready to take a bite out of the enemy. They were manned by 70 trained Army, Navy, and Marine Corps pilots. The Flying Tigers were credited with destroying over 500 Japanese planes and their crews. On their way to this accomplishment, they lost only 12 pilots and planes in action, and 9 others in training and ferrying.

The second bright spot was created by Major Jimmy Doolittle. On April 18, 1942, Major Doolittle planned and carried out a courageous and well executed bombing raid on Tokyo with 16 B-25 light bombers. These planes were launched from the Navy carrier *Hornet*. Even though the raid did little physical damage to the city, it made for great PR. Landing at Kunming at the end of his historic flight, Doolittle was greeted by his friend Chennault. Chennault immediately removed one of his own stars and pinned it on Doolittle—now General Doolittle—who was unaware until that moment of his promotion en route.

While most of this was happening, I was occupied in the North Atlantic, but news of the Pacific appeared regularly in the press. At the time, most of my friends believed that the *New York Times* and *Time Magazine* were better purveyors of classified and timely military information than were conventional military channels.

It bothered me that MacArthur had been placed in charge of all operations against Japan. I couldn't forget that he had been a member of the court-martial that pilloried General Billy Mitchell, who was a vastly better war prophet than any members of the court or 95% of the regular Army generals and Navy admirals. I was afraid that in MacArthur's mind, our potential air

power would play second fiddle to the Army and the Navy.

I need not have worried. General MacArthur, who had a front row seat from which to observe how effectively Japan used its air power, had changed his mind. Now, he agreed that Billy Mitchell's followers were right all along. He therefore proposed an island-hopping campaign from the Solomon Islands to the Mariana chain. The Marianas were roughly 1,250 nautical miles from Tokyo. General MacArthur hoped to make them into strategic United States footholds from which to attack Japan.

There were only two small hitches to this plan. The first was that the Marianas were firmly under Japanese control. The second was that the only plane capable of carrying bombs and ammunition on a 2,500 mile round trip mission was the B-29. This plane, the "Superfortress," was being developed by Boeing, but wouldn't be available in quantity until late 1944. MacArthur knew that even if his Marianas plan worked, it would be enormously expensive in casualties, money and time. Military minds looked for solutions elsewhere, thinking that there must be a better way. I was to be closely involved in a possible alternative.

In late December, 1942, I was unexpectedly relieved of my

(above) Brigadier General Claire Chennault's "Flying Tigers" used P-40 Tomahawks to conduct a successful mini-war against the Japanese.

duties at Presque Isle, and ordered to Air Transport Command Headquarters in Washington. I wondered why. There, on January 8, 1943, I received War Department Special Order Number 7. This put me on temporary duty for approximately 60 days, "to carry out the instructions of the Secretary of War."

Soon after I received these orders, a memorandum arrived from my commanding general, Hal George, another Billy Mitchell disciple. This memorandum instructed me that I was to "survey a proposed foreign route for the delivery of aircraft, personnel, matériel and mail by air." It didn't tell me where this foreign route would be, nor why I was chosen for the special duty. In fact, it turned out that not even General George knew the answers to these questions. When I found out, I was forbidden to tell him, or anyone else.

I reported to the Directorate of Personnel, where I was told to go to a designated room in the Pentagon at 7 a.m. the following morning. I was also given a parking sticker for my car on the River Terrace lot. This was the smallest and most convenient parking area of all, normally reserved for service secretaries and general officers. If none of the other circumstances surrounding my new orders revealed to me how important they were, this parking assignment did.

Needless to say, I was intrigued. The next morning, I went to the appointed room. The first thing I saw was a guard posted at the door. He let me pass. Inside the room, maps and charts of east Asia and the northwest Pacific lined the walls. About a dozen field grade officers, from weather experts to weapons and supply specialists, had arrived for the meeting. There were also two briefing officers from Chief of Staff General George Marshall's office, who soon let us know why we had been called to Washington.

We learned that our mission, headed by General Follett Bradley, was classified Security Secret, the highest classification, even above Top Secret. We were not to discuss it with anyone outside our group. If we had any research to do, we were not to visit any library, military or civil, nor consult any agencies or individuals, government or private, personally or by phone. To protect the secrecy of our mission, an officer would be assigned to each of us to do all outside research and consultation.

After this interesting preamble, we were told what the Bradley Mission was all about. We were to work out a plan to get planes, personnel, supplies and matériel from the United States to the Vladivostok region of Siberia, from where we would be able to wage war against Japan. My job was to survey and recommend a military air route or routes from Alaska to Vladivostok. Working with individual weather, communications and supply experts called into the program, I was to lay out the route and find suitable locations for air bases along the way. Each one had to be capable of handling, fueling, and resupplying B-17s and other, smaller aircraft. The terminal airport most accessible to the industrial centers of Japan must have, or be capable of providing, hard stands, abutments, bomb and other munitions storage for 100 B-17s, plus living quarters for their crews and other necessary personnel.

(left) Jimmy Doolittle led a bombing raid on Tokyo in April, 1942, using B-25 light bombers launched from the Naval carrier *Hornet*.

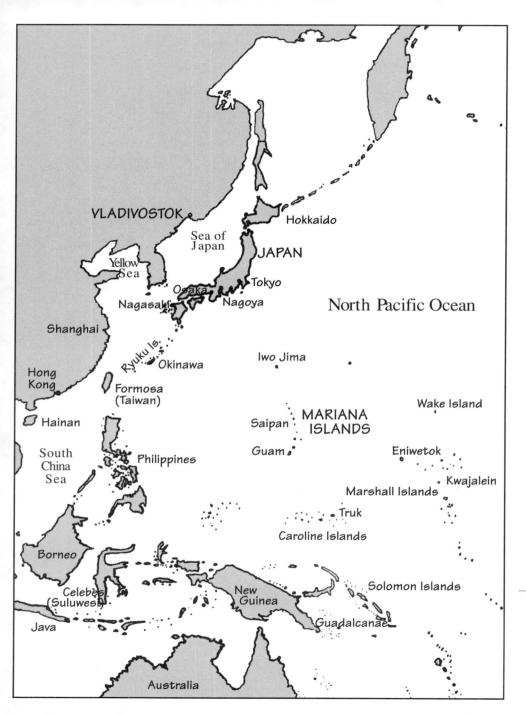

VLADIVOSTOK

Hokkaido

Sea of
Japan

JAPAN

Yellow
Sea

Osaka Tokyo

Nagasaki Nagoya

North Pacific Ocean

Shanghai

Ryuku Is.

Okinawa

Iwo Jima

Hong
Kong

Formosa
(Taiwan)

Wake Island

Hainan

Saipan

MARIANA
ISLANDS

South
China
Sea

Guam

Eniwetok

Philippines

Kwajalein

Marshall Islands

Truk

Caroline Islands

Borneo

Celebes
(Suluwesi)

New
Guinea

Solomon Islands

Java

Guadalcanae

Australia

Copies of pertinent communications between President Roosevelt and Stalin, both past and present, would be available for our comment or information. Two C-53s were assigned to the mission. They were already at the Middletown air depot, being modified for the inhospitable Siberian weather. I was to pilot one. General Bradley's pilot, Captain Watson, already at the depot supervising the modifications, was to pilot the other.

We were asked if there were any questions. I asked two. One was, "How about General MacArthur's island hopping plan?"

The answer was: "If this works, it won't be necessary."

My next question was: "Is it all right for me to check up on my plane while it's being modified?"

The answer was: "I'd think you would. According to your 201 file, you have had some arctic experience on the North Atlantic Ferry Route."

Early the following morning, I flew to Middletown. There I found a captain and the two C-53s. When I introduced myself, I noticed a label on the young man's leather A-2 jacket reading, "Captain T. M. Watson, Jr."

"Are you, by any chance related to the president of IBM?" I asked.

He nodded briefly. "My father," he replied.

(left) As this map shows, the Vladivostok region was much closer and more accessible to mainland Japan than were the Mariana islands.

Then he said he was glad to see me, since he knew I had set up the North Atlantic Air Ferry Route and was accustomed to very cold weather flying. He told me what had been done so far and asked my advice. I made a few suggestions—or that is how I remember the encounter. After the war, our families became great friends, and years later, Tom informed me that I had told him that much of what had been done was useless, and practically insisted that they start all their preparations over again. Despite my none-too-diplomatic behavior, Tom and I got along well from the beginning.

I soon learned more about the history of my mission. Chief of Staff General Marshall and the Army Air Corps head, General Hap Arnold, were planning to bomb Japan with B-17s, which had been highly effective in the European theatre, and were expected to be equally devastating in Japan. Since Vladivostok was only 565 nautical miles from Tokyo, it would obviously be a much less expensive place from which to carry out an attack than from the Mariana islands. Not only would this plan save valuable fuel which would be wasted in 1,250 mile flights to Japan, it would also save precious time. Vladivostok was within the B-17's range, so we would be able to begin our bombing raids right away, rather than wait for the manufacture and delivery of the B-29.

The generals had sold Secretary Stimson on the idea, who in turn sold the President. The diplomatic wheels began turning. The problem was persuading the Russians to let us set up American bases in Siberia. At the time, the Russians were most concerned with beating back the Germans, who were pushing them hard from the west. The U.S. was already supplying Russia with money, munitions and airplanes. As our allies, it seemed reasonable to assume that they would not object to us using land in their territory to fight off our enemies, especially since Japanese aggression was almost guaranteed to focus on Russia if we did not crush it.

On June 17, 1942, Roosevelt sent a message to Stalin saying that events in Alaska and the North Pacific suggested that the Japanese were preparing to attack Russia's maritime provinces. He promised to provide U.S. bombers for defense, if Russia would make suitable airports in Siberia available for the planes. On July 1, Stalin proposed a Moscow meeting to discuss this plan, and on July 18, he accepted Major General Follett Bradley as Roosevelt's emissary. Four weeks later, Bradley, his aide and pilot (Tom Watson) departed Mitchell Field on Long Island in a B-24. Threading the needle of war zones in Africa and the Middle East, they arrived in Moscow on August 5, but it was a month before Bradley had Stalin's approval to make a survey flight from Alaska to Vladivostok. On October 10, the Bradley party started for home through the frozen Siberian tundra, but didn't reach Fairbanks, Alaska until November 30. In a December 18 message to Stalin, Roosevelt aimed at clearing up any uncertainties in the proposal. He said:

> In the event that Japan should attack Russia in the Far East, I am prepared to assist you in that theatre with an American Air Force of approximately 100 four-engine bombardment airplanes as early as practicable. . . . Although we have no positive information that Japan will attack Russia, it does

appear to be an eventual probability. Therefore, in order that we may be prepared for this contingency, I propose that the survey of air force facilities in the Far East, authorized by you to General Bradley on October 6, be made now. He [Bradley] will also determine the extent of advance preparations practicable and necessary to ensure effective participation of our units promptly on initiation of hostilities.

With the diplomatic go-ahead, the Bradley Mission began in earnest.

My first task was fairly simple—a paper study. I had to establish criteria for an air ferry route from Nome, Alaska to Vladivostok. The air bases had to be accessible for resupply by sea or large river, located at a community big enough to accommodate the civil needs of crews in transit and military station personnel, and located not more than 800 nautical miles apart.

I analyzed 10 locations, including Verkoyansk, where winter temperatures reached -80 degrees Fahrenheit. We had no problem eliminating that one. The most logical, direct, and easiest to supply of the remaining nine were Anadyr, Magadar, and Komsomolsk. All were close either to the Bering Sea or to the Sea of Okhotsk. My only problem was sticking to the 800 mile separation. Two were slightly closer together, and two were further apart, but well within the round-trip range of a B-17. The total route distance between the termini of Nome and Vladivostok was 3381 miles.

I sent my five page report and recommendations to General Bradley, hoping that he would accept them and we would get under way as soon as the modifications of the aircraft were completed.

My next and most interesting task would be to conduct the actual survey of the route, checking out the proposed bases in person. I had arranged for Air Force Reserve Major Andy Ivanoff, my old partner in Skyways, to come along. Andy was a naturalized Russian, fluent in his native tongue, which I figured might be useful in Siberia, even if all he did was tip me off on what he overheard of conversations between Russians. It did not take us long to make the necessary preparations for our trip.

But then, on Wednesday, January 13, Stalin sent a message to Roosevelt, saying, in essence, that he, Stalin, had been misunderstood; that Russian experts were quite capable of making the survey of the air route themselves; that Russia was at war with Germany, not Japan; and that he would be happy to have Russian crews take over the promised 100 B-17s and their weapons in Alaska.

This was not at all what we had in mind. We scrubbed the deal.

I recommended that the two C-53s, modified for Siberian weather, be assigned to the North Atlantic Wing of the Air Transport Command. They were instead sent to sweltering North Africa. Typical.

(left) An American-built Douglas Transport at Teheran, flown by a Russian pilot. The Russians relied heavily on American planes in their battle against Germany.

CHAPTER 14

BOMB COMMANDER

DATE	PLANE	FROM	TO	TIME	PILOT
08/23/43	Hurricane	Heston	Bovington	0:20	Crocker Snow

From the air, the English landscape was confusing. Every field was almost identical to every other one. There were no radio aids to navigation. A large number of grey, sausage-shaped barrage balloons hung in the air to protect important cities from aerial attack. These balloons were tethered to the ground by steel cables, which would wreak havoc on any plane that encountered them. With all these difficulties, compounded by my unfamiliarity with the area, it took me 20 minutes to cover the 16 miles from Heston to Bovington.

After the demise of the Bradley Mission, I was temporarily without an assignment. Drawing on my North Atlantic experience, I persuaded General George to let me look into ferrying unescorted fighters across the Atlantic. He made arrangements for me to test-fly the Army's four operational fighters, the P-38D, the P-40E, the P-47C, and the P-51E, which I did on instruments and at night. Between flights, I ran into an old friend, Colonel Ben Kelsey, an engineering test pilot at Wright-Patterson Field. He had been experimenting with the possibility of ferrying the twin engine P-38 across the South Atlantic. He found that this fighter had greater range with one engine feathered than with both of them operating. I concluded that all of our single-engine fighters, properly equipped for radio navigation and communications (and flown by competent instrument pilots) could handle the North Atlantic route.

The P-40 was easiest to fly, but its performance was out of date for combat. Otherwise known as the Tomahawk, the P-40 was the one of the most extensively built American fighters of

(left) Members of the Snow Provisional Group in front of a B-17. We had an outstanding group. After our proficiency checks, I received a commendation from the commanding general of the Second (training) Air Force, saying that our crews' efficiency was "considerably higher than that of other comparable units." Unfortunately, this letter arrived too late to be passed on to the crews that had earned it.

World War II, but its performance at higher altitudes was undistinguished. The P-47 Republic Thunderbolt was one of the great fighters of the war. Designed around a powerful radial engine, it had a cruising speed of 300 miles per hour and a range on internal fuel of 800 miles. Equipped with ferry tanks, it could go quite a bit further, but it was heavy on the controls, and not as stable as the others. The P-51 Mustang, often cited as the greatest single seat fighter built in World War II, was my pet. It had superior performance, maneuverability and a maximum range of over 2,000 miles. With its smooth, elegant lines and responsive handling, I could easily understand why it was so universally admired.

My conclusions and recommendations about ferrying the fighters were transmitted to the Director of Military Require-ments. Six days later he issued a memorandum saying, "It is mandatory that all ferry routes be prepared to successfully permit ferrying of fighters." He went on to discuss details of additional air and ground radio navigation and communications needed, pilot qualifications, and special briefings for fighter pilots. So that was a success.

My next assignment, dated February 10, 1943, came from headquarters of the Air Transport Command (ATC) in Washington, signed by Colonel Larry Fritz, formerly of TWA's top management and now assistant chief of staff of the general staff corps. It ordered me to headquarters, where I was to be "responsible for handling and coordinating all matters pertaining to the movement of tactical units, including coordination and liaison."

(above) The P-51 Mustang, often cited as the greatest single-seat fighter to come out of World War II, was my pet.

My job sounded important (and was) but it wasn't exactly my cup of tea. A memo from my very efficient secretary tells the story better than I can. This was the start of a typical day:

1. Please call:
General Evans	4269
General Harper	6110
Colonel McCoy	6536
Lieutenant Smith	73993
Lieutenant Wooten	71328

2. Colonel McCoy wants a report of the Blitz for General Arnold at 9:00 tomorrow morning. He did not say which one. I assume you know which he means.

And so on. There was a lot to do, but none of it was terribly exciting. Even teaching cadets to fly would have been better. At least then I would have been in a plane.

After a few weeks of this, I broke down and asked Ben Giles for help in getting a combat assignment. He introduced me to a friend of his, General Eugene Eubank, who was in charge of assigning commanding officers to combat groups. When I told General Eubank about my recent experience with fighters, he said I was clearly qualified to command a fighter group, and he would not hesitate to give me one. But he added that I would probably be replaced as soon as I got to the theater of operations.

When I asked why, he said I was too old.

I was 38.

My experience in medium bombers—the DB-7, A-20, B-25 and B-26, was, he said, equally irrelevant, because they were all being phased out.

"So what do you know about heavy bombers?" he asked.

I explained that I once had a short ride in a B-24 at Presque Isle, and had been responsible for getting a lot of B-17s across the North Atlantic, but had never even sat in the cockpit of one of them.

"Good," he said, "We're badly in need of heavy bomber group commanders."

The general added that he had a provisional B-17 group just starting training at Dyersburg, Tennessee, and would name me to command it.

I thought he had misunderstood me. The B-17 was the only one of all the airplanes we discussed that I had never flown. But no, he said, not to worry.

"All your pilots will have excellent primary and advanced pilot training. Your job will be running the show."

I persuaded the general to let me spend eight days at the Army's B-17 instructors' standardization school at Spokane, Washington, but I was to go directly from there to Dyersburg.

In a week of concentrated flying and ground school, including blind takeoffs and actual instrument approaches, I learned a lot about the B-17. Boeing's Flying Fortress, powered by four 1,200 horsepower Wright Cyclone radial piston engines, was designed to accommodate a 10-man crew. Equipped with 10 machine guns and the capacity to carry over 17,000 pounds of

(left) Working at a desk job wasn't my cup of tea. Fortunately, with the help of Ben Giles, I was able to get an assignment as head of a provisional B-17 group training in Dyersburg, Tennessee.

bombs, it was one of the most famous of all World War II aircraft. Despite the fact that it was the largest (and the first four engine airplane) that I had been in charge of, I found it easy and pleasant to fly.

I reported at Dyersburg on May 29, 1943. There were no suitable quarters available for me on base, so, with a promise of rooms in the Bachelor Officer's Quarters as soon as they could be arranged, I checked into the motel in town. It wasn't to be a restful night.

About midnight I was wakened with the news that one of my crews had crashed taking off on a night training flight. The airplane was demolished, but there were no serious injuries. The base commander, Lieutenant Colonel John Moorman, told me that a similar accident had occurred a few days earlier. Then, four crew members had died. In both cases, the pilots spoke of an overpowering force that pushed the control yoke forward just after takeoff. Colonel Moorman said the prevailing opinion was sabotage of the autopilot, and that the FBI had been called in.

The next day I did some investigating of my own, and learned that Second Air Force training standards called for simulated combat conditions whenever possible. For night operations, this meant hooded runway edge lights and no landing lights on takeoff. The nights of the accidents, takeoffs were to the west, towards the Mississippi River, over marshy land with no lights for reference. To me, this meant blind, or instrument takeoffs, with some resemblance to the B-25 accidents that were my last vivid memory of Presque Isle.

I immediately assembled my pilots, and found that they all had Second Air Force instrument cards issued at Blythe, California. When I asked what were the most important things to remember on an instrument takeoff, they all agreed they were to maintain a positive rate of climb and to stay well above stall speed.

This answer gave me my clue. The rate of climb indicator is barometric. When a plane is in an established climb or descent, it is quite accurate. However, during a changing rate, such as in a takeoff, it lags considerably behind the actual rate of climb. In fact, I have often seen mine temporarily indicating a climb when I was descending, and vice versa. The only safe takeoff procedure is to maintain the correct airplane attitude, either from outside visual clues or by reference to the gyroscopic artificial horizon, which shows changes of attitude instantaneously. The cause of these accidents was most likely not sabotage, but pilots trying to climb too steeply. The "overpowering force" was a stall.

I immediately canceled all night training. Within a couple days, I had photoelectric cell-operated lights installed on 10-foot poles in the flatland 1,000 feet west of the far end of the east-west runway. Then I checked out each of my flight commanders under the hood, and found most of them unqualified for instrument takeoffs.

The next few days were devoted to concentrated instrument instruction of my six flight commanders. I then authorized them to instruct and check out their individual pilots. After 10 days of this, I authorized the resumption of night training, but with landing lights on during all night takeoffs.

This was the end of our training accidents. Esprit de corps, essential to an effective fighting team, improved dramatically, and I got in many hours in the B-17. It was a forgiving airplane, so easy to fly, we called it our four engine primary trainer.

Heavy bombers were thought to be unique in their capability to defend themselves against enemy fighter planes. The B-17 had five pairs of 50 caliber machine guns. Two of these, the top and chin turrets, were aimed by a Sperry computer sight, with which the gunner merely kept cross hairs on the target—the sight computed the lead. The others were eyeballed by the gunner. For gunnery practice we were furnished with unlimited quantities of shotguns and clay pigeons, and encouraged to use them. This was to have some unforeseen negative consequences.

For more real life practice, our gunners shot at cloth sleeve targets towed behind Martin B-26s. Many of these B-26s, piloted by Army Air Corps pilots, crashed because the airplane was like a skittish horse, sensitive and difficult to manage. We gave up the training and grounded the B-26. But before long a number of WASPs, young and attractive lady pilots, reported for duty to fly our tow-target missions. The women, with much lighter hands than their male predecessors, had little trouble with the B-26, and our gunners soon became proficient in leading moving targets. In combat we found that we had overlooked an important factor—neither the clay pigeons nor the tow targets were shooting back.

There was only one cloud on the horizon, and it was a distinctly man-made one. Early in August, we moved to Grand Island, Nebraska, our staging station, where we would be checked for proficiency and outfitted for our trip overseas. I hoped that none of the Snow Provisional Group would miss the added experience of flying their own B-17s to England.

The outfitting was a bit more than I had expected. Each crew member was issued 61 items of equipment, over 200 pounds worth, including folding canvas cots, tents, mosquito netting and mess kits. Much of this seemed unnecessary for a civilized, temperate climate like the British Isles, but I was told that only the combat theater could change the list of equipment. No wonder we had a such a hard time getting our men overseas, overloaded as they were. I was beginning to see for myself the truth of Ben Giles' remark about war being waste.

Our travel orders instructed 29 of our crews and me to proceed by train to Presque Isle and then by transport aircraft to England. The remaining eight crews were to go by train to the port of embarkation and across the Atlantic by boat. When I learned that 40 B-17s, destined for the Eighth Air Force in England, were waiting at Grand Island for ferry pilots, I pointed out that my crews were competent to fly them. The experience would be good for them, and both airplanes and crews would arrive where they were needed a hell of a lot sooner. Although everyone apparently agreed with me, we couldn't unsnarl the red tape.

On August 10, 1943, 46 highly trained 10-man B-17 crews, lugging 50 tons of unnecessary baggage, boarded a troop train, leaving idle, combat-ready B-17s languishing behind. The B-17s were eventually flown overseas by ferry crews that then had to be returned to the States. With dumb mistakes like this, I often wonder how we won the war. It must be only because our enemies made more or dumber mistakes.

(above) B-17s taking off on a training flight. Once my crews had had sufficient training on instruments, we had no more accidents.

I had a short, sentimental visit at Presque Isle. Many of my old comrades were still there. Ben Giles was still in command, now of a vastly expanded North Atlantic division of the Air Transport Command. He estimated that it would take seven C-54s just to transport our equipment.

As I showed Ben, my orders were to accompany my provisional group "to its overseas destination on TD [temporary duty]. Upon completion of this temporary duty the Commanding General, Theater of Destination, will release this officer and return him to the 21st Bombardment Wing by the first available air transportation." While in England, I was also to get the latest dope on operational problems and innovations on the front, both to bring training procedures in line with the latest combat experience, and to further my own education.

Ben saw another angle to my orders. He amended them to read:

SPECIAL ORDERS
Part 1, SO #212 this hq., dtd 17 Aug 1943 as concerns Major CROCKER SNOW 0230124 AO is amended to read "Auth. is granted to make such variations in this itinerary and to proceed to such additional places as may be necessary to fulfill instructions issued by CG, NAW, ATC."
By command of Brigadier General GILES

This, he explained, would enable me to go to Africa, the Middle East, South America, or anywhere else the Air Transport Command operated by military aircraft. He urged me to take advantage of the opportunity, saying it would improve my usefulness to the service. Then he set me up on the next passenger flight to the United Kingdom.

We landed at Prestwick on August 22, where I hopped a shuttle to Hendon outside of London. There, I ran into Captain Frank Crowley of Boston, an ex-member of the First Pursuit Squadron at Selfridge, whose airplane and flight jacket insignia had always been "lucky" 13. Frank gave me the current "gen," British for scoop. He said there was no shortage of luxuries on the island (except for women's silk stockings) but that all necessities were tightly rationed. He also said he had a half dozen airplanes available for qualified U.S. officers who needed to get around England. One of these was a Hawker Hurricane, the English fighter plane next in popularity to the Spitfire. I vowed to find a good use for it.

The next day I reported at Pinetree, the Eighth Bomber Command headquarters at High Wycombe, a converted girl's school, the Abbey. There, I ran into Duke Sedgewick of Boston in the A-2 (combat intelligence) section. He told me about their Operational Research Unit, made up of civilian P.h.D.s

(above) Our gunnery crews practice shooting clay pigeons from a moving Jeep.

and scientists who were doing a remarkable job of analyzing and improving combat tactics.

Learning that none of my squadrons had arrived at Bovingdon, the transfer point for all replacement crews, I decided to get right to work. First came the problem of unnecessary combat crew baggage. General Anderson, commanding general of the Eighth Bomber Command, agreed that most of it was not needed. He instructed his chief of staff to take care of the matter immediately. He then offered me a car and driver, an officer from his operational training section. This enabled me to obtain a great deal of information which might otherwise have been difficult to get.

The good general also authorized my use of the Hurricane. This turned out to be great fun, useful in adding a new trophy to my log book, but not a very efficient form of local transportation. Because of my unfamiliarity with the English landscape, the lack of radio aids to navigation, and the large numbers of grey, sausage shaped barrage balloons surrounding important cities, it took me 20 minutes to cover the 16 miles from Heston to Bovingdon.

While in the U.K., my itinerary included Brampton, headquarters of the First Air Division, where an old friend from the Massachusetts Air National Guard, Bart Beaman, gave me a broad overview of the air war. I also went to Bushy Hill, headquarters of the Eighth Fighter Command. Later, I visited Molesworth, home of the 303rd Group, which was to be the future home of most of the Snow Provisional Group crews. Here I really hit pay dirt. The group commanding officer, Lieutenant Colonel Stevens, put me in touch with some of his most competent flight crews. He also sent me (as an observer) on a fairly easy bombing raid to the Watten submarine pens on the coast of France.

Here are the highlights of my report of what I learned about bombing operations in England:

Tactics: For defensive reasons, daylight bombing was carried out in very large formations, usually a combat wing of three groups, at altitudes above 25,000 feet. The position of a group in an attacking force had a material effect on its bombing accuracy: after the second group the bombs might as well have been left at home. A substantial part of our striking Air Force was thus engaged in providing defense for the lead groups who did the work.

Fighter Cover: Royal Air Force cover by Spitfires was excellent. They flew at bomber level, and if any aircraft were forced out of formation, flew tight cover for them. On the other hand, our P-47s, because of their poor rate of climb, had to fly at altitudes substantially higher than the bomber formation, and were required, once they had lost altitude in a fight, to hit the deck and come home. This led to an unfortunate situation: the bomber crews thought our fighter pilots were yellow.

Gunnery: When discussing tactics with experienced B-17 crews, many of them observed that they would just as soon be accompanied by a squadron of B-24s on a raid as have fighter

---

(left) When I arrived in Prestwick, Frank Crowley, on the left, told me that all necessities were tightly rationed, but that luxuries were in ample supply—except for women's silk stockings, the gift of which would be more precious than a bottle of Chanel #5.

cover. Their reason: the German fighters would concentrate on the B-24s, and leave the B-17s pretty much alone; why, they weren't sure.

This last observation was so intriguing that I decided to see if the scientists at Pinetree had any ideas. It turned out that their Dr. Edwin Hewitt had just completed a study which was very much to the point. In training, bomber crews received extensive practice in hitting moving targets. They learned, of course, that this required leading the target—shooting ahead of it. B-24s had nothing but manually sighted 50 caliber machine guns.

Hewitt realized that except for the risky bow or tail approach, an enemy fighter with its fixed, forward firing guns, could only hit a moving bomber by constantly aiming in front of it. This resulted in what he called a "curve of pursuit" in which a threatening fighter moves, relative to a bomber, towards the bomber's tail. This is easy to understand if you move your left hand (representing the bomber) forward, while your right hand (the fighter) comes in from the right, pointing constantly a decreasing distance in front of your left hand. Hewitt concluded that a B-24's guns, aimed in front of a threatening fighter, would never hit it. A B-17 Sperry sight was not confused by the fighter's apparent direction, but led the fighter's *relative* motion which was backwards, and aimed behind its tail.

Presumably the Luftwaffe had learned the hard way that B-17s were apt to down their fighters, while B-24s seldom did. The study's conclusions were called "almost beyond belief." I was thoroughly briefed in all of its details, and urged to spread the word the moment I returned to the States. This information was obviously of vital importance, and I realized that the sooner I could get it home to the training fields, the better for our troops. It looked like I would not be able to take advantage of Ben Giles' thoughtful arrangement for a tour of the world's battlegrounds.

Meanwhile, I had plenty of time to observe other logistical mistakes that we were making, all of them a waste of time, money, and, probably, lives. For instance, when the Watten mission, on which I was an observer, took off from Molesworth, there were five fully armed B-17s left behind because there were no combat crews to fly them. At the same time, most of my 37 trained crews had been cooling their heels at Presque Isle for nearly a month. Meanwhile ferry pilots were still pouring B-17s into England.

After a hectic and frustrating week of this kind of observation, I decided it was time for R&R. London was pretty grim. Barrage balloons were everywhere, polka-dotting the horizon. Walking about the parts of the city that I remembered best from between World Wars—Picadilly Circus, Trafalgar Square, Green Park, the Ritz, Jermyn Street—I found bomb-demolished buildings and uncleared rubble all over the place. Nevertheless, there was lots of traffic, and people seemed to be going about their business much as usual.

I had dinner with my friend, fighter pilot Cocie Rathborne, which turned out to be a night of pub crawling to Glenn Miller's music with a pair of attractive young Women's Auxiliary

(left) B-17s flying in combat box formation on a mission to bomb European targets.

196

Ferrying Squadron members. We traveled about blacked out London in a military staff car without lights and at such breakneck speed that I was sure our driver was a frustrated P-47 pilot. The whole affair must have been relaxing, because I foolishly bet Cocie $1,000 (two months pay on my major's salary) that the war in Europe would be over by May 15, 1944. I was only a year off! I still have Cocie's signed receipt, which I obtained after paying him at a champagne dinner in New York after the war.

All too early the following morning, the duty officer at Etousa Headquarters in Grosvenor Square tracked me down. The Air Transport Command was carrying a V.I.P. to Washington, leaving Prestwick in the afternoon, and it was hoped I might escort her. She was Lady Peggy Dill, whose husband, Sir John Dill, British War Minister, was in Washington.

I arrived in Prestwick at the appointed hour, where I met Lady Dill, a well-dressed, youngish and pleasant companion for a trip across the Atlantic. Also on deck were Lieutenant Colonel Beirne Lay, post war author of *12 O'Clock High*, the story of a B-17 group in England; Bob Hope, and Hope's companion, Frances Langford. Our plane was a C-54, flown by Bob Buck, chief pilot for TWA.

(left) Although London had its share of bomb-demolished buildings and other reminders of the war, some sections were untouched and the streets were still busy.

Our first stop was Meeks Field in Keflavik. When word got around that Hope and Langford were aboard, strange things began to happen. The weather forecast for the rest of the flight to Presque Isle turned sour, and the ground refueling system developed problems. There was nothing to do but R.O.N. (Remain over Night). The Hope-Langford team was persuaded to entertain a standing-room only audience in the mess hall, the largest habitable building on the base. This was the first and only time I saw Bob Hope perform live, with his inimitable, tongue-in-cheek one-liners. He was great, and it was easy to see why he was in such demand for building U.S. troop morale.

We took off the next day (our "mechanical difficulties" from the night before had miraculously cleared up). Arriving at Presque Isle on September 4, I found 14 of my B-17 combat crews still there, with 10 more at Houlton. There were also 7 B-17s, waiting for civilian ferry pilots to deliver them to the U.K. Ben Giles said he had tried unsuccessfully to get permission for the waiting crews to fly the planes over, but meanwhile was letting them fly locally to keep their hands in and their spirits up.

While in Presque Isle, I also ran into Nancy Love, who was ferrying a B-17 to the U.K., with another friend, Betty Gillies, as co-pilot. I was delighted to see them, and admired their skill, but was concerned about the adverse effect of this operation on the already-waning morale of my side-tracked crews.

When I arrived back at headquarters, 21st Bomb Wing in Topeka, Kansas a few days later, I submitted my report about the state of operations in England, and the important flaw in our gunnery tactics. I was then immediately ordered to headquarters, Second Air Force in Colorado Springs, on temporary duty, to discuss my findings. The Second was the training command responsible for all Army Air Corps flight and ground training. The staff quickly grasped the importance of the gunnery problem, and things happened fast.

If the logistics of ferrying the planes and crews across the Atlantic was painful, the dialectic of changing gunnery tactics was not. On September 15, 1943, I reported to the 46th Bomb Operational Training Wing at Dalhart, Texas, with broad author-

(above) Bob Hope was on my flight back to Presque Isle. When we landed in Keflavik, Iceland, word soon got around that Hope was in town. Our plane instantly developed mysterious "mechanical problems" and we had to spend the night. Hope, of course, had nothing else to do, so he put on a show.

"All the News That's Fit to Print."

The New York Times.

LATE CITY EDITION
Cloudy and warmer today; fresh winds.
Temperatures Yesterday—Max. 30; Min. 9
Sunrise, 5:13 A. M.; Sunset, 5:34 P. M.

Copyright, 1943, by The New York Times Company.

Entered as Second-Class Matter,
Postoffice, New York, N. Y.

VOL. XCIII..No. 31,381.

NEW YORK, SATURDAY, DECEMBER 25, 1943.

THREE CENTS NEW YORK CITY

EISENHOWER NAMED COMMANDER FOR INVASION; 3,000 PLANES SMASH FRENCH COAST; BERLIN HIT; ROOSEVELT PROMISES NATION A DURABLE PEACE

STRIKE CALLED OFF BY 230,000 IN TRAIN AND ENGINE UNIONS

But Non-Operating Men Meet Carriers and Reject Offer Made for Overtime Pay

GIVE BYRNES NO ANSWER

He Says Agreement Must Meet Requirements Set Forth in the Stabilization Program

By LOUIS STARK
Special to The New York Times.

WASHINGTON, Dec. 24—The Brotherhood of Locomotive Engineers and the Brotherhood of Railroad Trainmen today canceled notices for a strike of their 230,000 members on Dec. 30 in view of President Roosevelt's offer and their acceptance of arbitration by the Chief Executive.

The conductors, firemen and switchmen's unions, also members of the "Big Five" operating and transportation brotherhoods, representing more than 120,000 employes, have rejected arbitration by the President and have not called off the strike of their members set for Dec. 30.

The other major development today in the railroad wage situation was a three-hour conference in the office of James F. Byrnes, chief of the Office of War Mobilization, participated in by committees of the railroads and of spokesmen for the fifteen non-operating unions, whose 1,100,000 members are scheduled to strike on Dec. 30.

At this meeting it was reported that the non-operating unions asked for a wage increase of 6 cents an hour as compensation for overtime after forty hours. These employes receive overtime after forty-eight hours of service. The

17 Perish as Fire Sweeps 42d Street Lodging House

Scores Hurt in 'Bowery-Type' Building Disaster, Worst of Its Kind Here in Years—Many Trapped Asleep

Sixteen bodies had been removed last night from a five-story brick structure at 437-439 West Forty-second Street, between Ninth and Tenth Avenues, the four upper floors of which were occupied by a "Bowery-type" lodging house, after one of the city's worst fires in years virtually had consumed the entire interior.

A seventeenth victim died at 7:15 P. M. in Roosevelt Hospital, to which most of the score of injured were removed.

The actual loss of life probably never will be known. With most of the victims burned beyond recognition and in many cases nothing remaining but bones, the task of counting the dead and identifying them was proving almost impossible. Authorities, after checking for hours, could not even determine

how many persons were in the building at the time of the fire. They were faced with the fact that the lodging house had beds in three-foot by six cubicles, separated by flimsy plywood partitions, and in hall-like dormitories "accommodating" 248 persons. It was said the beds were well filled with restaurant and other night workers.

The fire, believed to have smoldered for three hours, started at 2 P. M. as if set by a hundred torches. Trapped in their sleep many were burned to death in their "cells," rooms so tiny that a lodger had literally to crawl into bed through a special door on a central vertical hinge that folded to permit entry.

The victims groped through corridors

Continued on Page Twenty-six

WLB PEACE OFFER WIRED STEEL UNION

Davis Tells Murray Retroactivity Can Be Reconsidered Within Wage Formula

Special to The New York Times.

WASHINGTON, Dec. 24—William H. Davis, chairman of the War Labor Board, telegraphed today to Philip Murray, president of the CIO United Steel Workers, that if labor members of the board desired to reconsider their vote on the retroactive pay issue "the public members will favor such reconsideration."

But, while he indicated that a retroactive basis might be ap-

CITY AN OPEN HOUSE FOR WARTIME YULE

Heart-Warming Parties for Service Men and Women Are Chief Among Festivities

New York was far from a big, cold, gray city as it ushered in its third wartime Christmas last night with heart-warming church services, gay parties, gifts for the ill and unfortunate, and messages of good-will that brought cheer to its teeming millions and to the men and women visitors in the services.

It will not be a white Christmas, according to the weather man, but it will be cold.

RECORD AIR BLOW

'Forts,' Liberators and Medium Bombers Rock 'Special' Targets

ALL CRAFT RETURN

RAF Pounds the German Capital With 1,120 Tons Before Dawn

By DAVID ANDERSON
By Cable to The New York Times.

LONDON, Dec. 24—The greatest number of American heavy bombers ever to take off from Britain attacked "special military installations" of the Germans along the coast of northern France today as part of record operations of probably 3,000 Allied warplanes across the Channel.

Before dawn hundreds of the most powerful bombers of the Royal Air Force struck Berlin again with more than 1,120 tons of high explosives and fire missiles.

Several features of this two-fisted battering by the Allied air forces on the eve of Christmas made the day a memorable one for the enemy, even taking into account the Anglo-American achievements of recent weeks.

Headquarters of the United States Eighth Air Force announced that 1,300 planes handled by American crews took part in the daylight missions.

An even greater number of RAF, Dominion and Allied planes were out. Every one of the bombers and fighters of the joint forces returned to its base, according to a communiqué issued by headquarters of the United States Army here and the British Air Ministry.

Included in the American force were the largest formations of Flying Fortresses and Liberators ever sent into the air. Since an estimated 750 United States "heavies"

TO KEEP IT BY ARMS

President Says 4 Nations Agree on This for as Long as Necessary

'COST MAY BE HIGH'

German Might Must End, He Says on Air, Warning 'Japs' of Bad News

The text of the President's address appears on Page 8.

By JOHN H. CRIDER
Special to The New York Times.

HYDE PARK, N. Y., Dec. 24—President Roosevelt promised the country and the world this Christmas Eve that they could look for insured peace with "certainty," even though "the cost may be high and the time long," and said that the United States, Great Britain, Soviet Russia and China were agreed to use force to maintain that peace "for as long as it may be necessary."

Speaking from the study in the Franklin D. Roosevelt Library, one of his favorite rendezvous, with his family gathered informally around him, the President gave his first comprehensive report on his recent conferences in the Middle East over the most extensive broadcast facilities ever set up in this country.

For the first time the President tempered his "unconditional surrender" ultimatum of Casablanca by stating that the United Nations did not want to enslave the German people but wanted them to have "a normal chance to develop in peace as useful and respectable members of the European family."

There appeared to be one of the great achievements of the conference at Teheran—a united view by

Gen. Dwight D. Eisenhower
The New York Times, 1943

Pope Prays for Just Peace Kept by Wise Use of Force

By The Associated Press.

LONDON, Dec. 24—Praying that this may be the last war Christmas and that a truly Christian peace may be celebrated in the coming year, Pope Pius XII today called for the world's responsible leaders to check the instincts of hate and vengeance and give rise to "the resplendent dawn of a new spirit of world union."

Raising his voice to a vibrant, ring in outlining "the principles

The text of the Pope's address appears on Page 10.

GENERAL IS SHIFTED

Choice of 'Big 3' Parley, He Has Montgomery as British Field Leader

WILSON IS SUCCESSOR

Mid-East Head Honored —Spaatz to Direct U. S. Air Strategy

Special to The New York Times.

HYDE PARK, N. Y., Dec. 24—President Roosevelt announced today the appointment of Gen. Dwight D. Eisenhower to lead the invasion of Europe from the north and west, and from London came word that Gen. Sir Bernard L. Montgomery of North African fame would head the British troops under General Eisenhower to form a proved and hard-hitting team to lead the assault on Adolf Hitler's "Fortress Europe."

The President's announcement of General Eisenhower's selection at the recent Teheran conference to lead the main attack against Germany also was set to rest the old rumors regarding the probable appointment of Gen. George C. Marshall, Army Chief of Staff, to that post.

The President, in his radio report today on the recent conferences at Teheran and Cairo, also named Lieut. Gen. Carl A. Spaatz as commander of "the entire American strategic bombing force operating against Germany."

This was taken to mean that while General Eisenhower will confine his command to the mass attack on Europe from the north and west, General Spaatz' command over all American strategic bombardment of Germany extends to operations against all neighboring bases.

Quashes Marshall Rumors

ity to develop appropriate new gunnery training procedures. The same day I was designated deputy to the commander of the 333rd Combat Crew Training Group, Colonel E.T. Kennedy, a fine officer to work with and for.

Our first step was to stop all skeet and trap shooting practice. The next was to convince all concerned that to hit a threatening enemy fighter coming in from anything but 6 or 12 o'clock, a bomber's guns had to be aimed behind the fighter instead of ahead of it. Despite hours of brainstorming none of us were able to come up with a practical and non-lethal way to permit gunners to practice this. We were, however, able to demonstrate the virtues of the Sperry computing sight by hooking one up to a shotgun, and showing how easy it was to clobber clay pigeons just by keeping the cross hairs centered on the target. Our most important task was to prepare a training manual. The big job now became one of unlearning the gunners of their previous training. This was soon implemented at all our training bases.

A month after my arrival at Dalhart, orders came transferring me to the 46th Wing, as Director of Training. This was probably a promotion, but it was a blow nevertheless since I had expected a combat B-17 group command. Making the best of it, however, I devoted my energies to setting up and running a serious all weather flying course, including blind takeoffs.

On Christmas day, 1943, headlines proclaimed that General Eisenhower had been chosen to lead the invasion of France and Germany, and that General Touey Spaatz, whom I admired greatly, would command all U.S. invasion air forces. I was afraid the war in Europe might be over before I got a piece of the action. My fears were well-founded. As it turned out, my war was to be on the other side of the world.

(left) With General Eisenhower designated to lead the invasion of France and Germany, we hoped it would only be a matter of time before we would win the war in Europe.

CHAPTER 15

SUPERFORTS AGAINST JAPAN

DATE	TYPE	MISSION	HOURS	TARGET	RESULTS	A/P CM
7/7/44	B-29	Training	13:50	Cayo Travieso	Excellent	Crocker Snow

All of the holes in the radar storm picture we were approaching suddenly disappeared. In moments we were surrounded by the most beautiful display of St. Elmo's Fire I have ever seen. Halos of shimmering green luminescence enveloped the four whirling propellers and myriads of green sparks played about the metal filigree that framed the plexiglass greenhouse in front of us.

O n January 10, 1944, I received orders to report to headquarters of the 20th Bomber Command in Salina, Kansas, where I was assigned to the 73rd Bomb Wing, soon to be commanded by General Emmett ("Rosie") O'Donnell. About two dozen field grade officers and I gathered to hear our marching orders. Much to my surprise, I learned that instead of the B-17s for which I had been trained, we would be equipped with the new Boeing B-29 Superfortress, the largest and most sophisticated bomber in combat operation.

The B-29 was a four-engine plane designed for a crew of 11, with a fuselage divided in four parts: the bomb bay, and three pressurized sections. First came the nose, which housed the six-man flight crew and the bombardier; then came the waist, accommodating two gunners and a fire control officer; and finally came the tail, which had barely enough room for a single gunner. The fire control officer, located in a plexiglass bubble in the roof, could fire any of the plane's pairs of 50-caliber, Sperry computer-aimed machine guns. Only 87 B-29s had been produced so far, and these, as the 58th Wing, were going to India to carry out propaganda raids against Japanese-occupied territory in Asia.

Our target was to be the Japanese heartland. The 73rd Wing would be first on line. Our chain of command was direct

---

**(left)Boeing's B-29 bomber, with an unprecedented bomb load, range, and firepower, was introduced in 1944.
At last we had an airplane that could reach Japan from the Mariana Islands.**

from the Joint Chiefs of Staff through the 20th Air Force and the 21st Bomber Command. We would not be under the control of the theater commander. The 73rd Wing was made up of four bomb groups with three squadrons, each with ten B-29s. Flight and ground personnel were arriving daily at air bases in the southwest.

After this exciting introduction, we were provided with specifications and capabilities of the B-29, notebooks and E6B calculators. With the information that the average length of our missions would be about 2,500 nautical miles round trip, we were each to calculate and propose appropriate flight profiles, tactics, and fuel and bomb loads.

This exercise took several days. My conclusion was that the B-29's range, load-carrying capacity, and state-of-the-art APQ-13 radar bombing and navigation system would enable the plane to be a self-sufficient fighting machine. This would let us strike at night and in bad weather, using darkness and clouds as our primary defense, as distinguished from the clear weather, high altitude, mutual-protection daylight formations used by American B-17 and B-24 forces in Europe.

A couple of days after our theses were submitted, four of us, three Majors including myself, and a Lieutenant Colonel, were told that because of superior papers and personnel records (201 files), we had been selected to organize bomb groups. Mine was the 498th in Clovis, New Mexico. I was thrilled. It looked as if I might be about to play a small part in proving that strategic air power could indeed win wars, as General Billy Mitchell prophesied.

Eager to get started on my new mission, I made my way to Clovis. An agricultural distribution and railroad center, Clovis is located in the state's arid eastern plains close to the Texas border. Its Army air field was noted for causing "Clovis throat," a raw cough and soreness caused by clouds of alkali dust generously distributed by the almost constant dry winds. Not quite sure that my exciting assignment was for real, my first act was to issue an order to make it all official. With the invaluable help of Lieutenant John Zechman, I issued General Orders Number 1. Dated January 20, 1944, it read, "Pursuant to Para. 1, Special Order Number 11, Headquarters 73rd Bombardment Wing (VH), SHAAF, Salina, Kansas dated 17 January 1944, and under the provisions of AR 600 70 the undersigned officer hereby assumes command of the 498th Bombardment Group (VH)," signed C.S. Eight copies went to the commanding general, Second Air Force, and two to the 73rd Bomb Wing. There were no repercussions, so I was finally satisfied that I was really in charge.

My first job was to review reams of 201 files from which to select the best candidates for staff positions. I was pleased to see that none of the pilots were fresh out of school. A few were recently commissioned airline pilots. Most of the rest were bomber or fighter pilots with combat experience in Europe or Africa. I tended to favor those with college educations, especially ROTC graduates, a selection method that worked well in

(right) Our B-29 group had to wait for its airplanes. While we waited, our crews trained in different planes such as a version of this B-25, a five-seat attack bomber with cannon mounted on the nose.

the Ferry Command. When the key spots were filled, the rest of the organization took care of itself, and I could get to work on what we were all there for, flying.

The only airplanes available were UC-78s—four-place, twin-engine wood and fabric Cessnas, derisively known as "bamboo bombers." They were, however, well-equipped with instruments and radios, and the theory and practice of instrument flying is the same whatever the type or size of plane. We kept our bamboo bombers busy with four pilots aboard, taking turns flying under the hood and later in all kinds of weather. This made the pilots happy and had the ground crews well-occupied, but did nothing for the bombardiers, navigators, radio operators, flight engineers, or gunners. We therefore set up ground school training for them.

Many of our combat crews came from a decommissioned Caribbean anti-submarine group that operated the B-25G, a five-seat attack bomber with a 75mm cannon mounted in the nose. No one else seemed interested in these mongrel light bombers, so we were able to get some for advanced flight training of all essential crew members. There were still no B-29s in sight, but in early March we located some B-17Fs and were able, at last, to start training entire air and ground combat crews as a unit.

My days in charge of the 498th Group were numbered. West Point graduate Colonel Wiley Ganey, slated to take over command of the group, arrived at Clovis on March 14, piloting a two-place A-25. I met his airplane at the ramp and was kept waiting on the hot asphalt, exposed to Clovis' famous dry winds, for at least 15 minutes while he diddled in the cockpit.

Uh-oh, I thought, this is the champ, putting the challenger in his place by making him cool his heels waiting in the ring.

I couldn't have been more wrong. After inspecting our set-up and operations, he was generous in praise of what we accomplished with so little material. Taking official command, Colonel Ganey designated me his deputy, with additional duties as Operations and Training Officer (Group S-3).

Colonel Ganey told us that in early April, we would be moving to Great Bend, Kansas, where our maintenance and supply echelons were being established. He also had the news we were all waiting for—that we should begin getting our B-29s when we arrived there. He told me privately that we would eventually be operating out of the Mariana Islands, still, at the time, in Japanese hands.

Colonel Ganey recommended that I read a recently published book called *Japan's Islands of Mystery*, by Willard Price. It was fascinating. It explained why it would have been "suicidal" for Russia to give us bases in Siberia (the abortive Bradley Mission), and predicted that Russia would delay action until Japan had been "beaten to her knees." The Micronesian islands were both Japan's strongest defense and our greatest opportunity, the book said, to get within bomber range of Tokyo. Island hopping—i.e. taking the key islands in the 2000-mile chain from Australia to Japan, and letting the rest die on the vine—was the way to do it. This is the strategy that we followed, for which General Douglas MacArthur got credit. If Price's book had been a War Department document it would have been classified Top Secret.

On April 13, 1944, the 498th Group Headquarters and all of our Clovis personnel moved to Great Bend Army Air Field. I had been lucky enough to find a nice house there to accommodate Jan, our three children and our faithful Swedish cook. We did a fair amount of entertaining, and were introduced to the Army custom, at cocktails, of all the ladies sitting together on one side of the room, and the officers on the other—a derivative, perhaps, of yesteryear's custom of separating ladies from gentlemen after dinner. Another custom, a morale builder, allowed command and staff pilots to take family members on local flights. I took Jan and the children up regularly.

On April 20, 1944, our first B-29 was ready for delivery at the Boeing plant in nearby Wichita, Kansas. Since we had no pilots qualified to fly it, I went there with 498th Group staff members Major Walter Todd as co-pilot, and Lieutenant Dick Gast as flight engineer, to be checked out and to bring her home. Boeing's factory manager turned out to be Earl Schaeffer, my old friend from Stearman days, so the red carpet was rolled out.

After absorbing all I could about the design, construction, armament and electronic equipment of this great airplane, I found it quite easy to fly, especially since the flight engineer did most of the work. He was responsible for everything to do with the four Wright 3350 horsepower radial air-cooled engines, except opening and closing the throttles. He also had to be able to calculate the plane's weight and fuel remaining at any moment—useful information, since on approach to landing, the correct air speed in miles per hour was the same as the plane's current weight in thousands of pounds.

After landing back at Great Bend and answering a multitude of questions about the plane, I had two priority tasks. The first was to qualify the pilots and squadron commanders on the B-29. The second was to incorporate the B-29 in our existing flight and tactical training manual, using personal experience. This dictated that I get plenty of time in the airplane, which was fine by me.

Right away we ran into a minor problem based on the manufacturer's aircraft operating standards. I had no qualms about

(above) General MacArthur got the credit for developing the tactic of island hopping, in which U.S. forces would take key islands in the Pacific from which to wage war against Japan. This strategy was outlined earlier in *Japan's Islands of Mystery*, a book by Willard Price.

any of our pilots handling the B-29 in the air because of their considerable experience in other, smaller airplanes— the principles of flying were the same. But I wanted them to get enough landings and takeoffs to make these operations almost automatic. Electric motors raised and lowered the heavy, six-wheeled undercarriage, and the airplane manual recommended that at least 20 minutes elapse between gear ups and downs to prevent overheating the motor. We soon found that if we raised the gear on take-off (which was normal procedure) and obeyed all the other rules, one practice landing and takeoff used up 40 minutes of flying time. This much wasted time and fuel was unacceptable, so we just left the gear down and made touch-and-go landings as though the plane were a fixed-gear primary trainer. Some eyebrows were raised, especially by a technical representative from Wright-Patterson Field, but we went right on ahead.

The tactical issue proved more problematic. General O'Donnell had accepted my idea of using individual rather than formation operations. We therefore selected a small, unoccupied coral islet, Cayo Traviesa, off the southwest coast of Cuba and marked it with a bulls-eye and rings. This island was about the same distance from Great Bend as Tokyo was from the Marianas. We then ran radar bombing missions, using practice smoke bombs. Radar screen and visual spotting cameras recorded the results.

We flew these training missions day and night in June, July, and August, the months when the south-central U.S. could be counted on to provide spectacular thunderstorms. Our radar could be tilted down for ground mapping, or up for weather penetration. We felt that this, and our pressurized altitude capability, would enable us to avoid the worst part of these storms. Usually we did.

One time when I was aboard, all the holes in the radar storm picture we were approaching suddenly disappeared. In moments we were presented with the most beautiful display of St. Elmo's Fire I had ever seen. Halos of shimmering green luminescence surrounded the four whirling propellers, and myriads of green sparks played about the metal filigree framing the plexiglass in front of us. It got a bit rough, but, in severe thunderstorm turbulence, I had learned never to try to maintain a given altitude,

(above) **The view from inside the nose of the B-29.**

208

but instead to keep the airplane level. It worked. We sat back and enjoyed the show.

I didn't realize it at the time, but the most significant event of the whole tour at Great Bend was a visit by Major General Curtis LeMay. General Arnold had asked LeMay, just returned from a successful and productive tour of duty in the European theater, to see what he thought of the combat-readiness of the 73rd Wing. Because the 498th had written the training manual for the Wing, Headquarters sent him to us. Since I was Group Operations and Training officer, he was passed on to me.

By then I had well over 100 hours of B-29 pilot time, much of it teaching others. Teaching any subject, I have found, is the best way to test and perfect my own knowledge of it, so I felt well-qualified to discuss B-29s with anybody. In answer to LeMay's terse questions, I described our conclusions about the most desirable B-29 tactics, and how we had built our training program around them. The general had little to say, chewing instead on the unlit stump of his cigar. At one point, he asked how much high altitude formation we had practiced.

(right) We carried out numerous practice missions to Cayo Traviesa, Cuba, a small, unoccupied coral islet. Here, we dropped 10 bombs: the one that hit the target was counted both for its hit and for falling within the target radius.

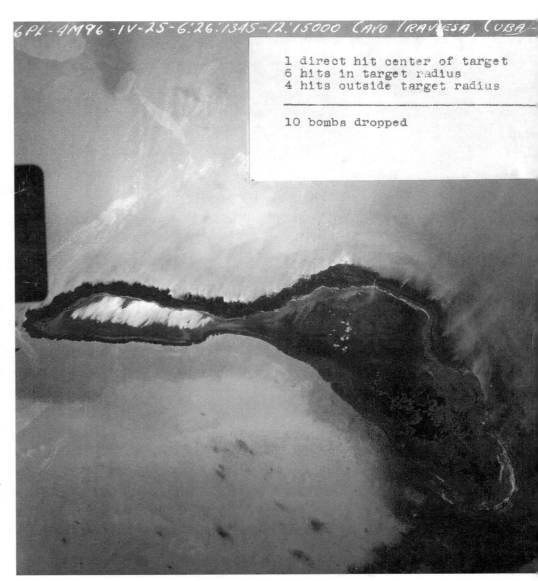

6PL-4M96-IV-25-6.26:1345-12.15000 CAYO TRAVIESA, CUBA-

```
1 direct hit center of target
6 hits in target radius
4 hits outside target radius

10 bombs dropped
```

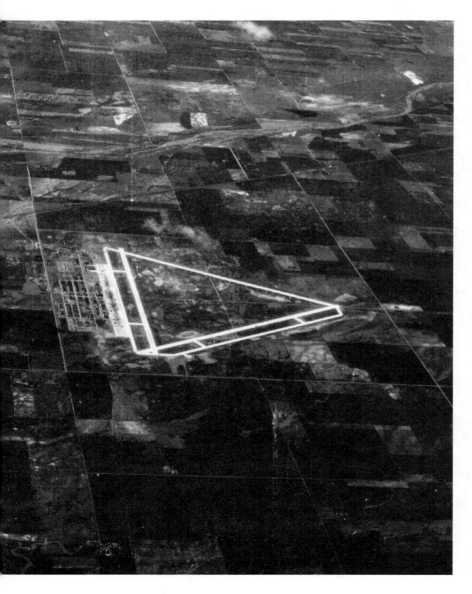

None, I replied, because it would be a waste of time and it would be dangerous. I explained that the pressurized plexiglass nose often fogged up suddenly, especially at altitude—enough so that we had rigged our B-29s with numerous small rubber-bladed off-the-shelf electric fans in order to be able to see out. Cover of darkness and clouds would provide better protection for individual B-29s than would high altitude formations, which required clear weather and daylight.

LeMay thanked me.

In July, we learned that Saipan, the northernmost of the Mariana islands large enough to accommodate our needs, had been secured by the Army, Navy, and Marines, and we would be moving overseas shortly. The planning and coordination necessary to have organized our four B-29 groups to base in Saipan was breathtaking. When the groups first formed in January, our planes were not yet built, and Saipan, together with its surrounding islands, was still firmly in Japanese control. Engineers, supplies, and heavy equipment must have been started on their way long before the island was taken.

On September 1, 1944, our wing, the first to complete its training, moved to Kearney, Nebraska, our overseas staging base. We were proud of the fact that from the group's inception on January 20, we had neither injured a flight crew member nor, with one exception, damaged a plane. The exception occurred when one of our airplane commanders, returning from a training mission, told the tower that the landing gear wouldn't go down.

(left) A typical American B-29 base. Since B-29 bases looked similar from the air, pilots often set down at the wrong one.

The tower called me. I said to land the plane as close to the Boeing factory in Wichita as practical, present my compliments to Earl Schaeffer, and ask him to fix it. He did.

Staging involved the same painful process as the Snow Provisional Group experienced at Grand Island a year before. The difference was that there were more bodies involved, we had our own airplanes, and we were being equipped and processed for a semi-tropical climate. The latter included briefings on malaria and cautions about leaving any skin exposed to mosquitoes. We were each outfitted with mosquito bars for our cots and netting to wear under our hats to cover our faces and necks. Any visions of living in shorts and sunning on tropical beaches vanished.

It was now the third week in September, and we were about ready to go, when we were stunned to receive a telecon addressed to General O'Donnell, signed "Arnold." It said that it had been determined that we were "deficient in high altitude formation training," and that all crews were to accomplish at least 20 hours at 30,000 feet or above before departing Kearney. Furthermore, we were then to proceed to our overseas destination in formation. Remembering my Great Bend conversation with General LeMay, I suspected that this was his work.

Rosie's reaction was to tell the well-worn story which ends "it tastes like horse shit, but it's good, it's good." In short, "It's orders, and we've got to do it."

On September 29, I reluctantly dispatched our first high altitude formation training exercise; two squadrons, 10 B-29s, and 120 crew members. A few hours after the first flight took off, a call came in from the base commander at Ellsworth AAF, 250 miles northwest of Kearney. He said two of our planes had collided in the air and crashed. Some of the occupants had bailed out. He didn't know how many.

It turned out that all the crew of one plane bailed out when their B-29 spun in 120 miles east of Ellsworth. Only three of those in the other plane made it out alive when their B-29 fell in pieces, 60 miles east of Ellsworth in the town of Philip.

This was a very bitter pill to swallow. Eight crew members dead, and two B-29s destroyed in a dangerous, unnecessary training flight. Forty-eight years later I had, as the last of the Mohicans, the bittersweet mission of dedicating a memorial statue to the crew members who lost their lives that day. All those higher on the totem pole—Generals Arnold, O'Donnell, and Ganey—had passed away.

After the tragic accident at Philip, we assumed that high-altitude formation practice for B-29s would be out. Fortunately, General O'Donnell agreed, and our first practice was our last. The matter seemed settled when, about a week after the accident, Haywood (Possum) Hansell, Commanding General of the 21st Bomber Command, commandeered 873rd Squadron Major Jack Catton's B-29 and crew, the first ready to leave Kearney. Catton later named his plane *Joltin' Josie*, "the Pacific Pioneer." This, on October 12, 1944, was the first B-29 to arrive in the Marianas. Catton was acclaimed as the pilot on this historic flight.

Colonel Ganey asked me to take the second single B-29 to go, and set up operations headquarters to handle succeeding arrivals. Finally on our way, we stopped first at Mather Field,

Sacramento, to clear with the Air Transport Command (ATC), which controlled all military ferry flights over our route. My old friend Colonel Bob Love was commanding officer of ATC's Pacific Wing, so I told him about our orders to fly to Saipan in formation. Bob said not to worry, that getting us there was his responsibility, and that ATC couldn't possibly handle formations of B-29s anyway. This took a load off my mind.

We departed Mather on the evening of October 13, 1944, passing over partly fogged-in Golden Gate bridge, and just at dusk, the Farallons, a string of small rocky islands 26 miles west of San Francisco. I remember thinking that this bird sanctuary and lighthouse might well be my last sight ever of the 48 states.

Nine hours later, approaching Hawaii, the rising sun behind us sparkled on Diamond Head. As we passed Waikiki Beach off our right wing, John Rogers tower cleared us for a right turn to land over seaplanes operating from Pearl Harbor where it all began. As we completed our turn, I saw bomb-damaged hangars and other buildings on the Naval air station. Final approach was quite bumpy for a B-29. I learned later that this was common because of the prevailing wind blowing over the mountain range northeast of the airport.

On the way over we had noted some minor malfunctions of our electronics systems that would take a couple days to repair. The local mechanics were delighted to see and work on this new equipment. We were delighted to see and work on Hawaii. The Air Corps had taken over a small resort hotel on the beach, and this forced layover seemed like a great time to learn

to surf. The native beach-boy instructor said that two days was nowhere near enough time, but that he could teach me the rudiments. Surfing there consisted mostly of dog paddling on one's stomach out to where the combers formed. This involved the use of muscles which, in my case, were not in condition for much of this new and strenuous exercise. My instructor did show me how to fall off in breaking surf so as to reduce the chance of being brained by the loose board. It was a pleasant, but brief, interlude.

Three days later we were off. Our next stop was Kwajalein atoll in the Marshall archipelago, 2,800 miles to the west. The only landmark on the way was tiny Johnson Island, 750 miles out from Hawaii. This pure white coral islet, surrounded by shimmering blue-green combers breaking over white coral reefs, measured only 600 by 3,000 feet. It had been made into a Naval airfield, equipped with a low-frequency radio beacon.

On the whole trip our navigator was busily giving us celestial fixes. I didn't let on that I was relying mostly on our ADF radio compass, which was usable for great distances over open water.

Our chart showed that Kwajalein was only the largest of nearly 100 close-spaced atolls, so about 12 hours out, we started straining our eyes for any signs of opalescent waves breaking over coral reefs. False sightings of land in the Pacific were apparently common, attributed to "coral eyes," but after a few false alarms, we identified some. Soon a lagoon full of ships, with a runway on the south side, came into sight.

We stayed at Kwajalein only long enough to service our airplane and its engines. It was a desolate place, with only

shell-shredded palm trees for foliage and the odor of death still in the air. It had been just a few weeks since the atoll was taken in fierce fighting.

On the last leg of our flight we passed over Eniwetok atoll, which was to become the target of atomic bomb tests four years later. Leaving Eniwetok astern, we noticed on our chart that the Pacific's intertropic weather front crossed our planned track and we began to wonder how we should deal with it. Those of us familiar with the turbulent South Atlantic front were unduly concerned. The Pacific front lived up to its name. We didn't even notice it.

Long before we sighted Saipan, we were given the once-over by a pair of P-47 fighters that suddenly appeared like ghosts out of the murky haze ahead. They waggled their wings at us as they disappeared in a climbing turn, and we were relieved to learn that someone was minding the store. We arrived at Saipan on October 17, 1944, four days by the calendar, 27 hours and 40 minutes elapsed flying time from Mather Field.

Our ground echelon, which had arrived by ship about a month before, had been getting things ready. They had erected a large Quonset hut for the 498th Headquarters and furnished it with an ample supply of chairs, tables, and benches. We still lacked blackboards, necessary for things like aircraft status reports, flights in progress, and mission briefings. There were no real blackboards to be found, so someone suggested painting plywood sheets with dull black

---

(above) As we neared Saipan, a pair of P-47 Thunderbolts emerged from the clouds to give us the once-over. These tough planes were the largest of all WWII single engine fighters.

paint. Since there was plenty of new plywood in the supply depot, I requisitioned enough for our needs, but was told, "Sorry, it's all reserved for the island commander's quarters under construction." I almost blew my top before our canny supply sergeant took me aside, said he and the sergeant in charge of the supply depot were good friends, and to leave it to him. We soon got our plywood "by moonlight requisition." I learned a valuable lesson. It's sometimes not so much who you are but who you know that counts.

I soon realized that almost everyone on Saipan was in shorts and short-sleeved shirts. I asked about malaria, and was told that the island had been thoroughly doused with DDT. There were no mosquitoes, and thus no threat of malaria. This was a dozen years before Rachel Carson's book *Silent Spring* sparked the movement to ban DDT, or the air offensive against Japan might have been more unpleasant for us than it was.

As more crews arrived, we began to mount limited real-life practice missions. For this we selected Truk, Japan's "invulnerable" island fortress, which had been bypassed in MacArthur's island hopping tactic. We mounted three high altitude formation bombing raids in close succession, the first on October 28. The airplane commander of one of the 20 crews scheduled for the third, November 2 mission turned up with a mild case of dengue fever. I was more than happy to be his substitute.

Truk, a small rocky island with a well-protected harbor and air strip, looked pretty harmless from 25,000 feet—that is until we spotted Japanese fighters coming up to meet us. However, none of them reached our altitude before we had dropped our bombs and turned for home. I suspect that they, outnumbered 10 to 1, were as nervous as we were on our first combat mission.

Our grand strategy for the war against Japan, dictated from Washington, was first to neutralize the Japanese air force by destroying its engine and propeller manufacturing plants, and then to go after airfields and industrial and urban targets. Special missions included mining the Straits of Shimonoseki so as to bottle up what was left of the Japanese navy in the Inland Sea; and dropping propaganda leaflets to the general population.

The Imperial Palace in Tokyo, the ancient capital of Kyoto, and the industrial-military city of Hiroshima were off-limits for any mission. The reason for the first two was obvious. We did not understand the third until much later on.

The target information supplied to us began with this summary comment: "There is no more important target in the Jap aircraft industry than the Nakajima engine plant at Musashino-Tama. This plant and the engine plant in Nagoya owned by the Mitsubishi interests together account for about 75% of total output for Jap combat aircraft." Located on the western edge of suburban Tokyo about 10 miles west-northwest of the Emperor's palace, Nakajima had been designated Target 357, destined to become three familiar digits.

It came as no surprise when our first serious strike against the Japanese mainland was to be aimed at Target 357.

(right) B-29 formations leaving on a bombing mission. Our first, and most important target was to be the Nakajima engine plant at Musashino-Tama, Target 357.

CHAPTER 16

MISSING THE TARGET

DATE	TYPE	MISSION	HOURS	TARGET	RESULTS	A/P CM
11/24/44	B-29	Bomb	17.3	357	Poor	Snow

As we approached our assigned altitude of 32,000 feet, sinuous white contrails formed behind the four engines of each plane, and scattered puffs of smoke appeared, flak from coastal anti-aircraft batteries. Tension increased as central fire control and our waist and tail gunners called in bogies all around the clock. Soon we spotted Mt. Fuji, a majestic, white-capped green pylon marking the start of our bomb run. From there until bombs away, the flight crew and especially the bombardier would have only one job—to put our bombs on target.

Five-thirty a.m., November 24, 1944. Every 35 seconds a B-29 of the 73rd Wing lumbered heavily into the air, aimed prophetically towards the rising sun—111 in all, divided into five independent strike forces of two squadrons each, all aimed at Target 357. General O'Donnell, with elements of the 497th Group, took the lead, followed by Colonel Wiley Ganey, Commanding Officer of the 498th. Each plane, with a design gross weight of 120,000 pounds, was overloaded by 10 tons to accommodate the necessary bombs and fuel. The single, 8,500-foot packed-coral runway was marginal for such an overload. Fortunately, the white knuckles takeoff was to the east where the terrain beyond the far end of the runway dropped off sharply to the blue waters of Magicienne Bay, 100 feet below.

Our takeoff procedure with these overloads was to keep the main wheels on the ground, lifting the weight off the nosewheels just short of the end of the runway. The plane could then be allowed to settle enough if necessary to pick up the airspeed needed for a safe climb. These takeoffs were reminiscent of the one I used back in 1928 to depart from the Plains of Abraham in Quebec, overloaded with Canadian liquor bound for dry Connecticut.

(left) Majestic Mt. Fuji marked the initial point of our bombing run on our first attack against Japanese military installations.

I went along on the mission as an observer with Major Walter Todd and his crew. The plan was to proceed individually at low altitude to our flight assembly point. This was far enough short of our IP (Initial Point), Fujiyama, to permit us to home on our leader by radio compass, form in squadrons, climb, and cross our IP at the assigned bombing altitude of 32,000 feet. The low altitude outbound had two advantages: it conserved fuel, and it reduced the chance of being picked up by radar from Iwo Jima or Japanese coastal picket ships.

We were to bomb our primary target visually, and if unable, to bomb our secondary, Tokyo's docks and waterfront, visually or by radar. About an hour out, Colonel Ganey radioed to say he had a runaway prop and was aborting. I was to take over as airplane commander of his flight. Our field order called for bombing on each flight leader (all bombs released when the flight leader dropped his), the successful tactic developed by General LeMay for B-17s in Europe. This switch made me responsible for the bombing success or failure of the 874th and 875th squadrons—not a happy prospect considering our different B-29 training.

The rest of the 1,250 mile flight was routine. While we climbed to altitude, the gunners exercised their hydraulic turrets, fired a few rounds to clear their guns, and all of us donned flak jackets, helmets, and oxygen masks.

As we approached our assigned altitude of 32,000 feet, sinuous white contrails formed behind the four engines of each plane and scattered puffs of smoke appeared, flak from coastal anti-aircraft batteries. Tension increased as central fire control and our waist and tail gunners called in bogies all around the clock. Soon we spotted Mt. Fuji, a majestic, white-capped green pylon marking the start of our bomb run. From there until bombs away, the flight crew and especially the bombardier would have only one job—to put our bombs on target. The gunners would have to worry about enemy fighters.

Our bombardier had already entered the trajectory characteristics of our bombs in the Norden bombsight. He now entered the temperature and radar altitude. The sight had fore-and-aft and transverse cross-hairs controlled by knobs. Its mechanism could be hooked up to the autopilot by the Automatic Flight Control Equipment (AFCE). Then, so long as the cross-hairs were centered on the aiming point, the Norden bombsight would fly the plane, correct for drift, open the bomb-bay doors, and release the bombs at the appropriate point.

At the bombardier's hand signal that he had the target on his cross-hairs, I engaged the AFCE, turning the controls over to the bombsight. I was occasionally able to spot the sprawling Musashino plant dead ahead, and in the distance, Tokyo, through several layers of scattered clouds. There were plenty of flak bursts and fighters around, but they were well below us, so at least completion of our first real mission seemed assured.

We appeared to be coming up on our target awfully fast, so I expected to hear our bomb-bay doors open. When they didn't, I banged the bombardier on his flak helmet. He had his eyes glued to the bombsight and was busily twirling its knobs. I asked if anything was wrong. He replied that he couldn't get the transverse cross-hairs to stay on his aiming point no matter

what he did. By then we were passing over our target, clearly too late to hit it. We decided to go for Tokyo's dock area, ahead and to our right. This required a right turn in formation, and at the rate we were covering ground, I was afraid we might have overflown Tokyo by the time we completed a normal turn, so I tightened it as much as I dared. Using occasional visual sightings of the city below, and a good radar picture of Tokyo's waterfront, we made a manual drop aimed at the docks. The rest of our flight released their bombs when we did. Because of cloud cover, none of our crews could tell where they landed.

My last view of Tokyo (this time) was as the brown-and-gray background for a fearless, twin-float Japanese seaplane trying valiantly to intercept us. It couldn't quite reach our altitude, stalling out each time it tried, ending up once upside-down, with both its pontoons pointing to the sky. I don't believe any of our gunners fired at it, it looked so helpless.

Although this was the first serious B-29 attack on Japan, it was a bit anti-climactic for us, second over the target. It had not been such a free ride for General O'Donnell. Befitting his rank, he led the first flight over the target and reported "heavy fighter opposition and moderate to heavy flak at the target and beyond." One bombardier was badly injured by a 20-millimeter shell, and two aircraft were sufficiently damaged by machine gun attacks that both the pressurization and oxygen systems failed.

Quoting from the secret post-strike analysis: "The lead flight was credited with five enemy fighters shot down and four probables. The second flight encountered only minor and inaccurate anti-aircraft fire and no fighter attacks whatsoever, although fighters were observed several thousand feet below the formation." Further from the report: "Strike photographs were obtained by all squadrons and were technically very good; however, either because of the excessively high ground speed, or because of too rapid turns after bombs away, none of the photographs . . . have been found to show any impacts. However, all films show bombs dropping, and . . . it is easy to determine

(above) Flak from enemy anti-aircraft batteries penetrating the clouds.

approximately where the bombs must have fallen." Probable impact locations listed were the heavily built-up area in the southeastern part of Tokyo, the dock area south of Tokyo, and well over Tokyo to the east.

On the long, slow descent home, throttled back to 180 miles per hour to save gas, we had plenty of time to think and talk about what had happened. Our first thought was malfunction of the Norden bombsight, but I couldn't help remembering the old maxim that a good workman doesn't blame his tools. Furthermore, the bombardier couldn't recall anything similar happening during his many hours of training.

We looked in the Norden manual for clues, and found that the bombsight was designed for limits of 45 degrees of crab, and 500 miles per hour of ground speed. I was sure that we had no appreciable crab on our bomb run. Our indicated air speed had been approximately 200 miles per hour, which, at 32,000 feet gave us a true air speed of 340 miles per hour. To exceed the bombsight's limits, then, would require a tail-wind component of more than 160 miles per hour. Since the Beaufort wind scale defines hurricane winds as those from 74 to 136 miles per hour, this didn't look like the answer.

At this point, our navigator said he could figure out our bomb-run ground speed. Using his drift-sight, he had recorded our times over the IP and Target 357. Our chart showed the distance to be 50 miles. The rest was easy. He came up with an astonishing ground speed of 550 miles per hour, giving us a tail-wind component of 210 miles per hour. We felt we now had the answer to our problem. We had encountered an unpredicted (and in fact unknown) weather phenomenon that our bombsight was not designed to handle. On the frustrating, eight-hour return flight, we had, in effect, discovered the jet stream.

It was not until many years later, when high-flying military and commercial jets covered the world's skies, that this meandering, shallow, invisible, river of high level, high velocity air was fully analyzed, understood, and given a name. We learned that its location, course and speed changed with the seasons and the weather pattern; that it could be an important tool in weather forecasting; and that knowledge of its daily location was an essential part of long-range jet aircraft flight-planning.

Because Saipan's single runway could handle fewer landings at night than in daytime, airplanes of the 498th Group were scheduled to go on to Guam if they had sufficient fuel. Interrogation facilities were set up at both places. Only eight airplanes made it all the way to Guam. We were one of them, after 17 hours and 20 minutes in the air. After our return to Saipan the next day, we found no evidence of hits by anyone on the primary target, with most bombs jettisoned over or beyond Tokyo. In most cases, the reason given was unfavorable weather. Two B-29s were lost, and 11 were damaged. A second strike against the same target was scheduled two days later. I was unable to sell my idea about the winds in time to affect the flight plan. Eighty-one planes took off; none of them even tried to bomb Target 357 because of "adverse weather;" one plane was lost and one was damaged.

(left) A bombardier's view of bombs dropping near our number one target, the Musashino aircraft factory. None of them will hit it.

Our weather officers remained dubious about 210 mile per hour westerly winds at 32,000 feet, but finally admitted that they didn't know much about high-altitude weather over Japan. The most obvious solution to the bombsight problem was to go in upwind, but the idea of being sitting ducks for anti-aircraft fire was not very appealing. Finally, we got permission from 20th Air Force headquarters to try it, at a lower altitude and at night.

On November 29, twenty-nine planes took off for individual night radar strikes against the waterfront industrial area of Tokyo to approach up-wind at 22,000 feet. My log lists 10 night instru-

ment hours of that 14 hour mission: 11 of us in each plane, cut off from the world, seeing nothing for 10 hours but our glowing, multi-hued instruments; the metronomic sweep on the radar scope; and, for a few of us, radar navigation and target charts. This was to be our first night strike in combat, our first by individual aircraft, our first to bomb the primary target by radar, and our first to bomb from as low as 22,000 feet—and, we thought, perhaps our last. But it was precisely what we had trained for.

Land-water boundaries are very sharp on radar, with water showing up black, and land white, so navigating our approach to

(above) This B-29 made it back to Saipan despite damage caused by a Kamikaze attack.
(left) High altitude formations drop their bombs together through smoke from previous strikes.

Tokyo was easy. A row of small islands ("Jimas" or "Shimas"), extends 150 miles south of Tokyo and lines up with the throat of Tokyo Wan (bay). The city sprawls on the north and west sides of the bay, with our target on the east-facing waterfront area. Leaving the last island, O-Shima, at bombing altitude, we got a beautiful radar picture, just like our target chart, of Uraga Strait, the bay, the Chiba Peninsula and, not quite so clear but easily identifiable, the built-up area of the city. Our plan was to fly up the middle of the peninsula, turning west in time to cross our IP, Iwaga Point, just south of Chiba, and make our 25-mile bomb run into the wind. If the wind was blowing 200 miles per hour from the west, as it had been during our attack on 357, the run would take us 25 minutes in straight flight at 80 miles per hour ground speed, directly exposed to Japan's heaviest concentration of anti-aircraft fire.

We were now at 22,000 feet heading north and still in clouds, with not even an occasional glimpse of ground or sky. Everything had gone like clockwork so far, and our spirits picked up when we realized that our slight crab to port was hardly consistent with strong westerly winds. Maybe we wouldn't be sitting ducks after all.

On a radar bomb run, an automatic camera takes pictures of the radar scope during the run and at the moment of bomb release. From these we could make a good approximation of bombing results. I figured our true airspeed at

(left) We used radar navigation charts like these to help reach our targets. We also had on-board radar, which gave us a picture that looked very much like this.

290 miles per hour and our ground speed at 210 miles per hour. This meant that we had a head-wind component of only 80 miles per hour.

When a fully loaded B-29 salvoed its bombs, as we did, the plane would jump several hundred feet. Just after we released our load, there was a loud explosion, apparently under our right wing. We were thrown into a steep left bank, and the clouds momentarily glowed greenish-yellow with what looked like summer heat-lightning. We recovered, and all crew members checked in by intercom. We had no reports of obvious damage, other than to our composure. We concluded that the Japanese either had a very lucky gunner, or at least one pretty good radar controlled gun sight—also, that we were fortunate to have dropped our bomb load just when we did.

Of the 29 planes that took off that night, 24 bombed the primary target by radar, one was lost (missing), and one was damaged in the right wing (us). Analysis of the scope photos suggested good results, which were confirmed by later reconnaissance. This exercise contained three obvious lessons: radar bombing of small area targets at night or in bad weather by individual aircraft was practical; the Japanese had some radar controlled anti-aircraft weapons; and winds over Japan didn't always blow 200 miles per hour from the west. Furthermore, this was our first successful mission. The first two high-altitude, visual, formation bombing-on-the-leader attacks had been complete busts so far as hitting the primary target was concerned.

(right) A mixture of delayed action high explosive and incendiary bombs headed toward the target.

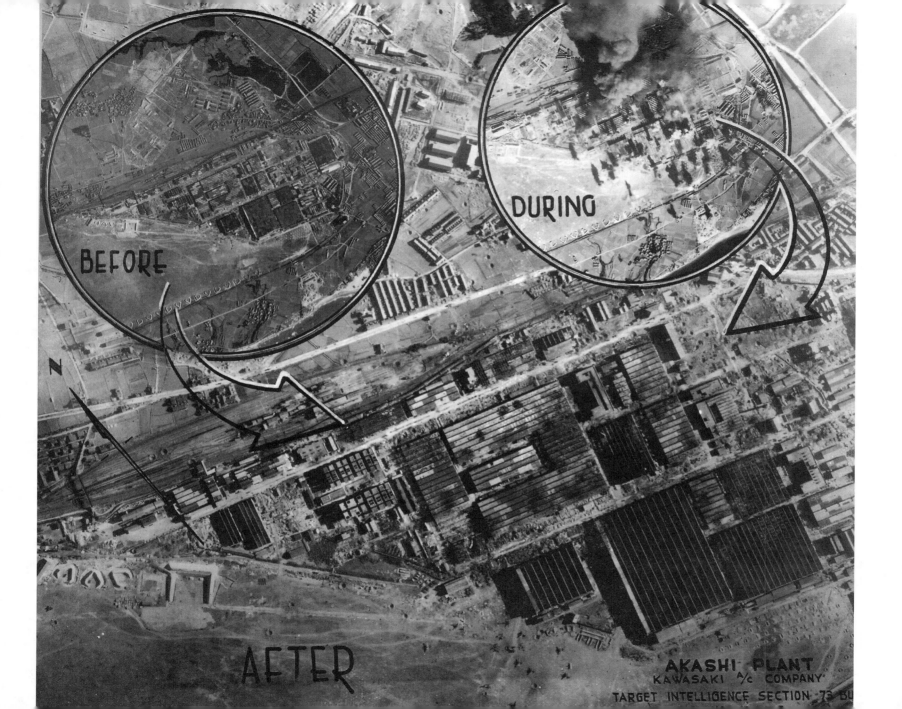

BEFORE

DURING

N

AFTER

AKASHI PLANT
KAWASAKI A/c COMPANY
TARGET INTELLIGENCE SECTION 73 BU

I hoped this would be enough to persuade Washington to authorize a good test of the tactics for which the 73rd Wing had trained. I should have known better. Our next Field Order, #7, for December 3, called for the same old thing against Target 357. Eighty-six aircraft were airborne; six were lost, including the one carrying the strike leader, Commanding Officer of the 500th Bomb Group, Colonel Richard King, and Wing Headquarters Colonel Brugge. Eighteen planes were damaged. The results were deemed "unsatisfactory on primary."

For the balance of December, six more high altitude formation missions attacked various targets, with mixed results. Two against Iwo Jima airfields, and another against 357, were adjudged poor. One against the Mitsubishi plant in Nagoya, Target 193, was "unknown," but two against the same target were good. The improvement could have been due to more experience, and to the fact that the Mitsubishi bomb run was south-to-north, and thus not as adversely affected by high winds. However, approach was up Nagoya Bay, which was so heavily defended it came to be known as Flak Alley.

The December 22 raid on Nagoya stands out in my memory. Our Wright 3350 engines had one bad habit: they occasionally swallowed a valve, but were considerate enough to warn the knowledgeable pilot that this was about to happen. The pilot controlled power with four throttles operated by his left hand. Just before a valve episode, the corresponding throttle would give a few kicks against one's palm. This happened to me just as we became airborne, so it was no surprise to hear a waist gunner call out on interphone, "Fire in number three engine." We got the gear up, number three cowl flaps closed, fire bottle pulled, and prop feathered in nothing flat. Now we had the ticklish job of flying over-loaded for several miles on three engines, barely clear of the water until we picked up enough speed to climb. I told the bombardier to prepare to jettison our load as soon as we reached a safe altitude. I was not ready for the outcry from my borrowed crew, many of whom wanted to keep going. I thought at first, "what dedication to duty," but then realized it was probably more a desire to be credited with a combat mission. Twentieth Air Force policy was to rotate crews home after 35 of them.

January 1945 was more of the same. Of six strikes, two on 357 were rated "poor" or "unsatisfactory." Only one, on the Kawasaki Aircraft plant in Akashi, was called good. Twenty-seven B-29s and their crews were lost, and 124 were damaged.

Early in the month, I drafted a letter for Colonel Ganey to General O'Donnell. It read: "Because of the probability that measurable results of the present air offensive against Japan by the XXI Bomber Command are not equaling the cost, recommend that either the basic strategy be changed, or that the tactics employed be altered to more effectively accomplish the apparent objectives of the present strategy. It is specifically recommended, therefore, that: Nightly attacks by a series of single aircraft be made on Tokyo, Nagoya, Kobe, and Osaka, dropping a mixture of delayed high explosives and incendiary gel bombs."

(left) "Before, During and After" photos like this one were supposed to boost morale by showing the crews what they were accomplishing. Although the results of this raid were considered good, the aircraft factory remained operational.

A-2
CENTER QUONSET
ASSISTANT CHIEF OF STAFF A-2
LT. COL. CROCKER SNOW
PHOTO INTERPRETATION   FLAK ANALYSIS

EAST QUONSET
TARGET INTELLIGENCE   TRAINING
ESCAPE and EVASION   FIGHTER ANALYSIS
RADAR INTELLIGENCE   MAPS and CHARTS

WEST QUONSET
ADMINISTRATION   HISTORICAL
BASE S-2   COUNTER INTELLIGENCE
MISSION REPORTING

On January 20, 1945, Major General Curtis LeMay replaced Possum Hansell as Commanding General of the 21st Bomber Command. Ironically, General Hansell had been Colonel LeMay's superior officer in the Eighth Air Force in Great Britain. From January 20 to March 9, we carried out nine high altitude formation strikes; four of them on 357, and two on 193. Bombing results were still poor. A slight improvement was probably because, beginning on February 4, the 313rd Wing on Tinian doubled our strength. We also started sending single flights ahead of the formations to report back winds and weather conditions. However, it was hard for me to see how any responsible commander, no matter how opinionated, could fail to realize that something was wrong with our tactics or execution.

During this period, General O'Donnell made some organizational changes that affected me. On February 13, 1945, Don Saunders replaced me as 498th Deputy, and Walter Todd as S-3. At the same time, I moved a little closer to the throne as A-2, assistant chief of staff, combat intelligence of the 73rd Wing. I was afraid at first that this would cut down my flying, but General O'Donnell was an understanding boss, as was his Deputy, Colonel Walter "Cam" Sweeney. My A-2 Section was responsible for target radar, counter intelligence, photo interpretation, flak and fighter analysis, escape and evasion, maps and charts, and mission reporting. It was obvious that frequent participation in combat missions would improve my performance in most of these disciplines.

I was fortunate enough to inherit an unusually competent staff, headed by Major Bill Beckett, enthusiastic tennis player, and in private life, president and owner of the Beckett Paper Company of Hamilton, Ohio. Our roster was well-spiced with academics and technical experts, who collectively did an outstanding job. They were pioneers in realizing that the orientation of streets, buildings, and the axis of attack had much to do with successful radar bombing. Among other innovations they devised simple, photographic mission reports called "See for Yourself," with before, during, and after aerial photos and interpretations. Posted in clubs and mess halls, these helped the troops see that their hard work was accomplishing something.

We were also responsible for preparing written reports for transmission through channels to Washington. My first one, on Mission 26 against Target 357, was terse. It said that no aircraft out of a total of 99 airborne bombed the primary target and four B-29s were lost. When my report reached the deputy wing commander, he suggested that I soften it a little, saying, for instance, that we were "unable to determine exact bombing results because of cloud cover."

I got the point. To avoid having my reports edited along the way, it was important to accentuate the positive. This practice is still SOP, "Standard Operating Procedure" in the Services as well as in most bureaucracies.

(left) **My highly qualified A-2 staff. I am standing in the middle.**

CHAPTER 17

HURRY UP AND WAIT

DATE	TYPE	FROM	TO	TIME	PILOT
2/10/45	B-24	Saipan	Iwo Jima & return	10 hours	Crocker Snow

From my vantage point, the display of force was awe-inspiring. As far as I could see were vessels of every size and sort. Even the distant horizon was serrated with the hazy shapes of ships. Almost every ship was on the move, with some of the multitude of wakes nothing but circles. In all, more than 900 ships and a quarter million men were poised to wrest the eight-mile square, pork-chop shaped island from its 20,000 defenders. I hoped this incredible fleet was as irresistible a force as it appeared to be.

War has been well described as "hurry up and wait," especially for those not busy with command or administrative duties. Air combat crews had several days "on" for a bombing run, and then several days off without much to do. To be sure, bombing missions were a major undertaking, and generally required crews to be functioning in stressful situations for a full two days on end with very little sleep. Most bomb crews went on one mission a week, with the remaining days to unwind and relax. These blocks of free time were probably necessary to make sure that everyone remained healthy, well-rested, and sane.

Fortunately for us, Saipan was a comfortable place to wait. The island was blessed with an ideal climate for recreation and relaxation. The winter wet season had average low temperatures of 70 with frequent showers and almost daily periods of sunshine, while the summer dry season had average highs of 85 with a daily shower. As a result, everything green grew like mad.

Saipan also had a special asset in a beautiful tropic beach, where blue-green combers full of multicolored fish broke over a coral reef just offshore. This was a fine place to kill time.

(left) The B-29 had plenty of space on the nose for imaginative murals, and just about every crew in the 73rd Wing had its own, talented artist, who turned each plane into a flying work of art.

Unfortunately, early in December several G.I.s drowned, carried out to sea by a strong undertow, so the island commander closed the beaches. This, on top of poor and costly bombing results, was terrible for morale, especially of combat crews.

My analytical approach to things came in handy. After some argument, I got permission to study the problem first-hand. Between the reef and the beach, the water was too shallow for swimming, but here and there were deep water gaps in the reef about 30 or 40 feet across. This is where the best swimming was. After sitting on the beach and watching for a while, I noticed that the water constantly breaking into the shallow lagoon between the beach and the reef didn't go back out the way it came in. Instead it went sideways and back out those deep water gaps. This created an outbound current that varied in intensity with the size and frequency of the breaking waves. I theorized that on the days of the drownings, there had been an unusually heavy onshore surf, and that the victims had been unable to buck the current while trying to make it back to the beach in one of the deep water channels. I further theorized that, had they only swum parallel to the beach

just outside the reef, the incoming surf would have brought them home.

To test my theory, I arranged to have a manned rubber boat stand by, put on heavy sneakers to protect my feet from the coral, and headed out one of the more popular gaps. There was only a moderate sea running, but even so, I couldn't swim straight back against the current. However, after swimming parallel to the reef for a few yards, it was no problem to reach it, and to wade from there to the beach. With this information and a promise to publicize it, together with a caution against swimming at all with a heavy sea running, we reopened the beaches.

When our idle crews were not taking advantage of our lovely beaches, they might be found engaging in other creative pursuits, such as decorating the B-29s with imaginative and elaborate nose art. It had early on become standard practice to mark bombers and fighters with tallies (often in the shape of little bombs) to symbolize each successful mission flown. Besides these marks, B-29s had lots of space up front for artistry, and there seemed to be a number of talented and ambitious artists in the 73rd Wing. The planes sported their decorations

(above) Saipan's coral beaches were initially closed to swimming because of a dangerous undertow that had carried several G.I.s out to sea, where they drowned. After I discovered how to beat the strong, outbound current, we reopened the beaches.

with great pride. These were usually in the form of voluptuous females with names like *Supine Sue, Adam's Eve, Celestial Queen,* and *Dina Might.* The ladies were depicted in various sultry poses and states of undress. We also had planes that showed cartoon characters, such as Bugs Bunny and Woody Woodpecker.

Although nose art was a morale booster for the crews, it was not universally appreciated. In July 1945, some visiting bluenose (perhaps a member of Congress from the Bible Belt, or a cleric of some sort) objected, and asked to have the paintings removed. What a terrible impression it would create if a B-29 with a risqué decoration were forced to land in Japan, he said!

Whoever opposed the nose art, he must have been pretty important, because we got orders, straight from Washington, to have all the decorations removed. We were pretty busy at the time and never got around to it.

Before the war, Saipan was a Japanese sugar-producing center and a military base. American

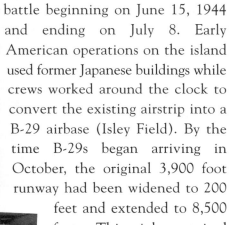

forces took the island in a 24-day battle beginning on June 15, 1944 and ending on July 8. Early American operations on the island used former Japanese buildings while crews worked around the clock to convert the existing airstrip into a B-29 airbase (Isley Field). By the time B-29s began arriving in October, the original 3,900 foot runway had been widened to 200 feet and extended to 8,500 feet. This job required moving 4 million cubic yards of coral.

In November, nearly all of the 73rd Wing was stationed on Saipan. The 1,300 members of the wing at first lived in tents. Later, many moved to more permanent barracks. Life on Saipan was relatively comfortable. We were supplied with ample food and drink by ships, which also brought us the latest American movies, shown every night at the cinema and bar. Other

pastimes included playing cards at the O's Club. Hiking through the countryside was not always a good idea, however, despite the undeniably pleasant scenery. The massive spraying of DDT on the island had killed all the malaria-carrying mosquitoes (and most other bugs), but it had no effect whatever on a particularly vicious species of indigenous hornet. These little devils had a sting that would not soon be forgotten by anyone who accidentally encountered a nest.

Although for the most part, our down time on Saipan was tranquil and even pleasant, we were not entirely out of the war zone, especially in the first few months. Saipan was some 1,200 nautical miles from mainland Japan, but only about half as far from islands still under Japanese control. The most important of these enemy territories was Iwo Jima, a mere 623 miles away over the water. Occasionally, Japanese planes from there would strafe us with machine gun fire. Their targets were generally our B-29s, not those of us who flew them. We would often hear the Japanese twin-engine light bomber Bettys and Zero fighters sweeping in at night, shooting constantly. By the next morning, we would find many of our parked B-29s damaged, disabled or destroyed. The last large-scale air attack happened on Christmas night, 1944, when Japanese fighters slipped under our radar and destroyed one B-29 and damaged 14 others, 3 of them beyond repair. Early in my stay, I remember one night when the gun fire came a bit closer to home. I was still living in a tent at the time. That night, a Japanese raid strayed from the airplane hard-stands, and I could hear shots spraying the ground all about me where I lay.

Keeping our B-29s in fighting shape was a round-the-clock undertaking in the first place. Having Japanese fighters shell them at night as they stood parked on the runway was obviously not to our advantage. Iwo Jima would be a major asset for us if we could capture it. Not only would we be spared nighttime enemy strafing, we would also have a place to land damaged B-29s if they could not make it all the way back to Guam, Tinian or Saipan. Finally, bases on Iwo Jima would enable us to use shorter range fighters, such as P-51s, to protect us on our missions against the mainland. Taking Iwo Jima started as a goal, and became a priority.

On January 14, 1945 the 498th provided three B-29s to convoy two flights of P-38s to Iwo. The mission was for one flight to take low-level aerial photo maps of the east and west shores to be used to plan landing operations, while the other strafed the airports and gun emplacements. We were to coordinate this operation with a high altitude bombing attack by B-24s and shelling by a Navy task force.

One B-29 never got off the ground, and the leader in the second B-29, Colonel Ganey, had radio trouble that made it impossible for him to communicate with the fighters, although he was in contact with me in the third Superfort. As deputy, I once again took over the lead. After topping a front, we made the last 150 miles "on the deck" (as low as possible and under enemy radar) and achieved almost complete surprise. On the way out, Ganey and I agreed that I should orbit just off the east coast of Iwo to help any P-38s in trouble, while he would wait

(left) Our base at Saipan. (top) Headquarters for a group. (bottom) A typical tent.

for the bulk of the fighters at our preplanned rendezvous, nearby Minami Jima. While orbiting, I took movies of the action while at the same time flying the plane. The pictures were a bit jumpy, due perhaps to some of the flak we were getting from shore batteries. Here are some excerpts from my mission report:

> **Attack Results:** B-29s observed two substantial fires at the approximate location of airfields 1 and 2, also extensive 50 caliber and 20mm impacts on or about a trawler south of the volcano (Suribachi) and a large armed vessel in the southeast harbor. Fighters report one Zeke parked between airfields exploded and two adjacent fighters damaged. Nick destroyed in air, ammunition dump set fire with resulting

exploding phosphorus bombs, small vessel forced to beach, two small fires started fore and aft of bridge of large vessel, which was unloading into lighters and many persons seen to jump from large vessel into the water.

> **Enemy Activity:** Intense light flak both from shore installations and naval vessels in southeast harbor. A few heavy flak bursts observed by crew members of the lead B-29. One P-38 lost half its horizontal stabilizer. The damaged P-38 together with two others was escorted home immediately after the attack. All aircraft returned safely.

> **Remarks:** The fighter organization reported the mission very satisfactory from its standpoint.

(above) At night, Japanese fighters tended to avoid our living quarters, strafing instead our parked B-29s, often damaging them beyond repair.

The only thing I refrained from setting down in my official report was the hell of a time I had all the way home keeping the fighters, including the one with half his tail shot off, from attacking every ship they spotted. I was pretty sure all the ships we passed on our way home were U.S. air-sea rescue vessels. I began to understand why I had been considered too old to command a fighter group in combat.

Our initial attack on Iwo was just a preview of what was to come two weeks later, in the bloodiest and most difficult battle of the Pacific war. On February 10, the Navy began to gather in the waters south and west of Saipan, preparing for an all-out invasion. I went aloft to observe in a borrowed B-24, taking movies of the panorama of power spread out on the grey, choppy waters.

From my vantage point, the display of force was awe-inspiring. As far as I could see were vessels of every size and sort. Even the distant horizon was serrated with the hazy shapes of ships. Almost every ship was on the move, with some of the multitude of wakes nothing but circles. In all, more than 900 ships and a quarter of a million men were poised to wrest the eight-mile square, pork-chop shaped island from its 20,000 defenders. I hoped this incredible fleet was as irresistible a force as it appeared to be.

Nine days later, on February 19, our Army, Navy, and Marine Corps began the successful invasion of Iwo Jima. We provided indirect support with maximum-effort strikes against

(right) Our Navy attacked Iwo Jima with over 900 ships, an awe-inspiring show of force.

the mainland at the same time. While we bombed and strafed from the air, our ground and sea forces attacked, only to be ferociously repelled by the defenders, who were dug into numerous caves on the lava and tufa island. The battle lasted 26 days and cost our side over 5,500 dead and more than 17,000 wounded, with some infantry battalions recording 100% casualties.

Although Iwo Jima was not considered secured until March 16, 1945, on March 10, a battle-damaged B-29, returning from one of our low level night fire bombings of Tokyo, made a successful emergency landing there. By April 7, we were being supported over Japan by P-51 fighter cover based on the island. For the remainder of the war, Iwo Jima was important to us both as a base and as a place to land our damaged planes. We tried not to overcrowd it, however. We had a rule that if a B-29 was flying home with two operational engines, it was to proceed on to Saipan rather than stop at Iwo.

The last few weeks of March were comparatively quiet. I made several administrative flights to Iwo to coordinate our intelligence activities with the fighter command there. The northern Marianas, directly en route, included many small volcanic islands, densely covered by what looked like spruce, rising sheer green for hundreds of feet out of the blue Pacific. Often, usually in the early morning, their peaks would be topped by a nun's cap of white cloud while all about was clear. I thought, with the climate and beautiful surroundings, what great vacation country this would be in peaceful times. As it turned out, after the war, Isley Field became Saipan International Airport, and the Marianas became a favorite resort area for Japanese honeymooners.

My brief break gave me a chance to investigate the theory that Amelia Earhart had landed on Saipan and been put to death by the Japanese. When our forces took the island in the summer of 1944, the native Chammoros were rounded up and put in prison camps. We soon found them to be friendly, honest, and excellent artisans and farmers. As they returned to their natural ways, we gave many of them work, in the course of which they picked up a smattering of English. None that I talked with could recall any substantiation of this particular theory of Amelia Earhart's disappearance.

(left) The bloody battle for Iwo Jima began with naval shelling and aerial bombardment, followed by hand-to-hand fighting before the island was secured. Suribachi—where the Marines planted the American flag after our victory—is in the foreground.

CHAPTER 18

THE AIR WAR HEATS UP

DATE	TYPE	MISSION	HOURS	TARGET	RESULTS	A/P CM
04/12/45	B-29	Bomb	14:30	357	Excellent	Crocker Snow

One hundred and nineteen B-29s flew towards the Nakajima Aircraft Factory, Musashino plant, covered by 93 P-51s from Iwo Jima. Our altitude was 15,000 feet, and we flew by daylight. We approached the largely undamaged plant and dropped our bombs. Ninety four planes hit the target. Much of the factory was destroyed—the Musashino Plant was finally out of business.

On February 26, 1945 (which was, coincidentally, my 40th birthday), General LeMay summoned key officers from each of the three wings then in operation, the 73rd, 313th, and 314th, to a conference at his headquarters in Guam. I'll never forget his remarks. He said that after observing our operations for a month, he had concluded that we were going about it the wrong way. What worked in Europe for B-17s wasn't working in the Pacific with B-29s, and it was time to try something new. We were to prepare for a series of maximum-effort night incendiary strikes by individual aircraft against Japan's major cities: Tokyo, Nagoya, Osaka, and Kobe.

This was the basic tactic the 73rd Wing had wanted to employ from the beginning. LeMay's innovation was to increase bomb loads by eliminating both waist gunners and all gun ammunition except for that used by the tail gunner. This was to be the first phase of a new strategic plan to burn Japan's cities, instead of concentrating only on military targets. The scientists and P.h.D.s of the Joint Target Group had concluded that the papier mache buildings characteristic of Japanese cities made them extremely vulnerable to fire bombing. Once started, fires would feed on themselves, creating fire storms with high winds to spread the flames—more bang for the buck

(left) In the spring of 1945, we stepped up our bombing program. On March 4 the last high altitude, daylight formation of the war attempted to hit the Musashino plant. Results were termed "unknown."

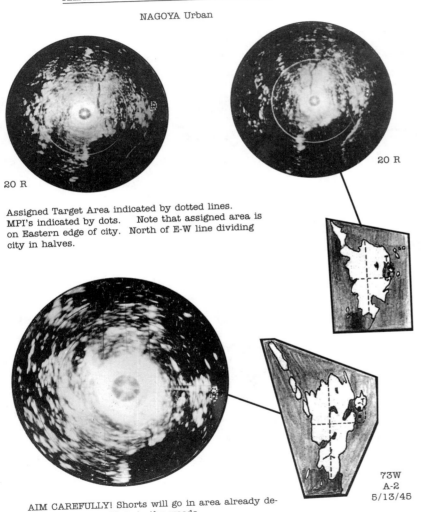

RADAR TARGET IDENTIFICATION STRIP   NO. 1

NAGOYA Urban

20 R

20 R

Assigned Target Area indicated by dotted lines.
MPI's indicated by dots.   Note that assigned area is
on Eastern edge of city.   North of E-W line dividing
city in halves.

73W
A-2
5/13/45

AIM CAREFULLY! Shorts will go in area already destroyed. Overs will go in the woods.

than with the earlier use of high explosives.

This was, of course, an attack against the entire population. The technology for destroying selected buildings or
specific bridge abutments with "smart bombs" was still
decades away. In the 1940s, once the bomb left the carrier,
its trajectory could not be changed.

On March 4, 194 B-29s engaged in the last high-altitude daylight formation mission of the war: their target,
357. No aircraft reported bombing the primary. Results
were euphemistically termed "unknown." *Sic transit gloria*
LeMay's way, I thought. From then on a majority of the
missions were carried out at night, and all at medium-to-
low altitudes.

Because of the 73rd's unique experience in radar
bombing in combat, we were selected to prepare target
information and optimum axes of attack for LeMay's
night blitzes. All we had to do for our first objective,
Tokyo, was duplicate the radar charts and routes successfully used in Mission 9, our November 1944 night radar
strike. Major Danny Farmer, our A-2 radar expert,
arranged for pre-strike radar briefings. Besides the 73rd's
161 aircraft, the 313th and 314th Wings together provided 173 more.

Similar strikes on Kobe, Osaka, and Nagoya followed every second day, with equally good but
expensive results. 15.8 square miles of Tokyo, 2.9 of
Kobe, 8.1 of Osaka, and 5.1 of Nagoya were destroyed,
with five B-29s downed by enemy action. Nineteen

more were lost for "other" reasons, 13 of these on the Tokyo raid. An average of 320 aircraft out of an average of 378 on hand took part in five missions in 11 days, a remarkable achievement. The maintenance crews deserved and got great credit for this, as did General LeMay.

After this, the next four weeks were comparatively tame, with many smaller missions flown by individual wings, mining harbors and straits in Japan and Korea, and bombing military airfields. Our losses were low because our daylight raids had regular P-51 fighter-cover from Iwo, and our results improved all the time. The lull gave us an opportunity to devote our attention to the stubborn problem of our number one target, 357, the Nakajima engine plant, still intact after 10 maximum-effort high altitude formation strikes between November 24, 1944 and April 1, 1945.

On April 4, I presented our recommended solution (low-to-medium-altitude daylight raids) to General O'Donnell. I was afraid of the NIH (not invented here) syndrome peculiar to bureaucracies, whether governmental, military, or business. Unless a new idea comes from the top, or can be made to appear

so, it may not get very far. For once, my pessimism was unwarranted. Although Bom-Com didn't go all the way, we got most of what we wanted.

On April 7, the 73rd Wing was authorized to make two medium-altitude daylight raids on Target 357, the first from 20,000 feet, and, five days later, from 15,000 feet. I hitched a ride on the second raid. One hundred and nineteen B-29s of the 73rd Wing took off. Of these, 94, covered by 93 P-51s from Iwo, hit the target. Post-strike reconnaissance photos showed 63% of the Nakajima Aircraft Engine Factory, Musashino plant, destroyed—enough to put it out of business. Losses for the first raid were three B-29s and 33 crew members, none of either for the second, thanks in part to fighter cover. Three planes, 33 crew, and target eliminated. Compare this with the preceding 10 missions against the same target: 40 B-29s, 440 crew members lost, and no significant damage to Target 357.

While the April 12 mission was underway, word came that President Roosevelt had died in Warm Springs, Georgia, and that Harry Truman had been sworn in as his successor. This bulletin was shortly followed by a long message, "SPECIAL

(above) **Bombs ready for loading into a B-29's bomb bay.**

243

GUIDANCE ON PRESIDENT ROOSEVELT'S DEATH," addressed to all U.S. commands. We were told what to stress and how to do it in great detail, starting with, "Naturally we should, for the next 24 hours, treat the President's death and Truman's inauguration as the most important news in the world." The guidance closed with this interesting bit, "You should suspend all light music (Yankee Doodle included)."

This was, of course, world news, but to me the news that we had finally succeeded in destroying our most important Japanese military-industrial target was at least as significant.

On April 30, another bulletin informed us that Adolf Hitler had died in Berlin. It ended with the perceptive forecast, "Note: There will be quite a few bulletins today." The prediction was to expect a speedy end to the war in Europe, which would be great for us. Until now, the war against Germany had had first priority in men and matériel.

A week later Germany surrendered unconditionally to the Allies. At that time, our bomber fleet numbered about 500 B-29s. By the end of July, it had doubled, leaving little doubt in our minds that the end of the war was near. It was only two years earlier that Roosevelt and Stalin had apparently believed that a joint effort, supported by 100 heavy bombers operating from Vladivostok, would have defeated Japan.

With the end of the war in Europe, we could also hope that the Russians would soon join our efforts. Back in February, Stalin and Roosevelt had met at the Yalta Conference, where Stalin had agreed to join the Allies against Japan "in two or three months after Germany has surrendered."

Although the exact timing of the Russians' entry into the war was considered secret, the fact that they were expected to join us was not. Stalin's agreement with Roosevelt, in fact, made it advantageous for Russia to declare war against Japan, since by the terms of the Yalta agreement they would then get control of Sakhalin Island and islands near it, gaining a sphere of influence in Manchuria, which they desperately wanted.

On May 25, 474 aircraft struck Tokyo at night, dropping hundreds of incendiaries such as high phosphorus E-48s, mixed with occasional delayed-action high explosives to discourage fire fighting. Assigned bombing altitude was 13,000 feet, and results were excellent, raising the total area of the city destroyed to 56.3 square miles.

Unfortunately our losses were the highest of the entire campaign, with 27 B-29s missing. The intelligence analysis in our May 28 memorandum suggested air-to-air bombing, some by our own B-29s. This was not surprising. Over 300 B-29s took off into the night with the same assigned altitude. Some pilots, probably trying to improve their odds for survival, flew several thousand feet too high and dropped bombs on their unsuspecting compatriots.

Several days after the Tokyo raid we tested the "friendly fire" hypothesis by dropping E-48 incendiary clusters off the Saipan shore at night. Most of the combat crew members observing the drops agreed that the flashes of light looked like those they had seen over Tokyo.

(right) A mixture of high explosive and incendiary bombs hit the Tokyo area at night.

Our prime Japanese military-industrial target was now out of commission, its navy either destroyed or immobilized, its major cities and industries destroyed. At the same time our Air Force had grown from 111 B-29s during our first raid on Tokyo to eight times that many by June, with crews to fly them transferred from the European theater of operations. With these beefed-up forces, we now turned our attention to the smaller cities where civil manufacturing companies had been pressed into service to make the weapons of war.

We used novel tactics made possible in part by dramatic reduction in enemy defensive action, and in part by our own augmented numbers. We would choose five or six smaller cities for simultaneous night radar attacks. We then dropped leaflets the day before, naming these cities plus an equal number of others, announcing that we would bomb half the list that night.

One I remember for a special reason was the Japan Musical Instrument Company in Hammamatsu on the south coast of Honshu between Nagoya and Tokyo. This factory made most of the propellers used on Japanese military aircraft. On January 18 we had hit this factory as a secondary target in a raid aimed at Target 357. Post-strike photos showed the propeller factory badly damaged and most of the urban area burned out. On June 17, a second raid finished off the job. Although logic would dictate that Hammamatsu was no longer a threat, it made the hit list again late in June.

I was summoned to Guam along with General O'Donnell, Colonel Sweeney, and Colonel Sutherland, deputy chief of staff operations, for a meeting with some Navy brass. The Naval officers explained that they had set up an important operation and they wanted to coordinate with us to avoid shooting at any of our B-29s or having any of our bombs dropped on their ships. They wanted a B-29 officer to work with. This officer could only pass on such details of the plans as were absolutely necessary at the appropriate times.

The ranking mariner looked at Rosie O'Donnell, who thought for a moment and turned to his deputy, Cam Sweeney. When Sweeney turned to Sutherland, I quickly looked the other way. But no luck. Being low man on the totem pole, I got the job. As it was explained to me, the Navy planned to use their big guns and, for the first time, shell an important target on the Japanese mainland. For propaganda purposes they wanted a location in the Tokyo–Nagoya area, so that as many people as possible would know that the heart of the Empire was within range of our battleships. In the middle of July, Admiral Bull Halsey's Third Fleet would attack Hammamatsu.

Naturally, I explained that we had already hit Hammamatsu twice, that I took part in the second raid just over a week before, and that there was nothing much left for the Navy to shell. This didn't bother them a bit. What they needed was a city of some size and military importance, near the ocean, with deep water close to shore, and lightly defended with shore batteries. Hammamatsu was the only place that filled the bill.

The entire operation was cloaked in secrecy. As B-29 coordinator for the effort, I was the only one in the 20th Air Force

---

(right) Toyama after the bombing. Over 99% of the urban area was destroyed.

to know the details. During the weeks that the Navy was preparing for this mission, I was forbidden to fly over Japanese territory, for fear that if I were captured, the Japanese might have gotten the information out of me through torture. My interpretation of this order permitted me to fly one "superdumbo" mission during the Navy's attack.

We used to get thin paper editions of the U.S. news magazines and newspapers (without advertising!), and I remember reading feature stories of how, on July 10, Admiral Bull Halsey's Third Fleet had sailed close enough to the heavily defended Japanese shore that its guns destroyed a vital military factory.

With our expanded B-29 force we continued to bomb cities designated by the Joint Target Group in Washington, still avoiding Kyoto, the Emperor's Compound in Tokyo, and the military-industrial strong point, Hiroshima. During this time, most of us in combat intelligence thought it virtually impossible for Japan's military to survive as an effective fighting force. True, there was still the Japanese empire's three million strong, well-equipped and unbloodied army, along with over 9,000 planes and pilots willing to fly Kamikaze missions. However, we couldn't believe that any sane U.S. commander would, under the circumstances, give the army a chance to fight on its own turf by invading Japan.

We were therefore satisfied that our mission, born on January 10, 1944, in Salina, Kansas, would soon be accomplished; that for the first time in history a major war would be won primarily by air power; and that unjustly-martyred General Billy Mitchell's military philosophies would soon be vindicated. Japan, had, in fact, been reduced to her knees, all from the air. All that seemed left were the formalities of surrender. Despite the fanaticism of the Japanese military, the country would surely not be able to hold out much longer.

Some of our reconnaissance aircraft were specially equipped to monitor Japanese radio communications and domestic broadcasts. About the middle of July, we began picking up transmissions which we interpreted as requests for Russia, the only major country still neutral, to find out U.S. conditions for ending the war. We were not surprised by these overtures. In fact we were convinced, both from photo interpretation of the

(above) General Emmet "Rosie" O'Donnell, commanding general of the 73rd Wing and my commanding officer.
A West Point varsity football star, he turned out to be a top pilot and combat commander.

damage we were doing, and because of the weak response to our recent bombing raids, that the Japanese knew they were licked and wanted to salvage what they could. It appeared that what they wanted most was assurance that their emperor would not be harmed.

The Russians did not pass along the Japanese requests, apparently preferring to wait for a complete Japanese collapse, when they could pick up Manchuria on the cheap. We learned, again from intercepted and decoded radio exchanges, that on July 24, Russian employees at the embassy in Tokyo would leave for home from Sakata, on the Sea of Japan.

Since it seemed to me that the war was essentially over, I wrote a letter to General Rosie O'Donnell asking to be relieved of my duties so that I could return to home and family. I had not seen Jan and the children for a year and a half.

O'Donnell wrote back to say that my early release would not be possible because such releases for senior staff officers had been placed on hold, and that I should relax and enjoy myself. I did not know that the most dramatic part of the war was still to come.

(right) By July, 1945, our bombing missions were so successful most of us in combat intelligence realized the war was essentially over. It was only because Russia refused to pass on Japan's surrender pleas that we were still fighting,

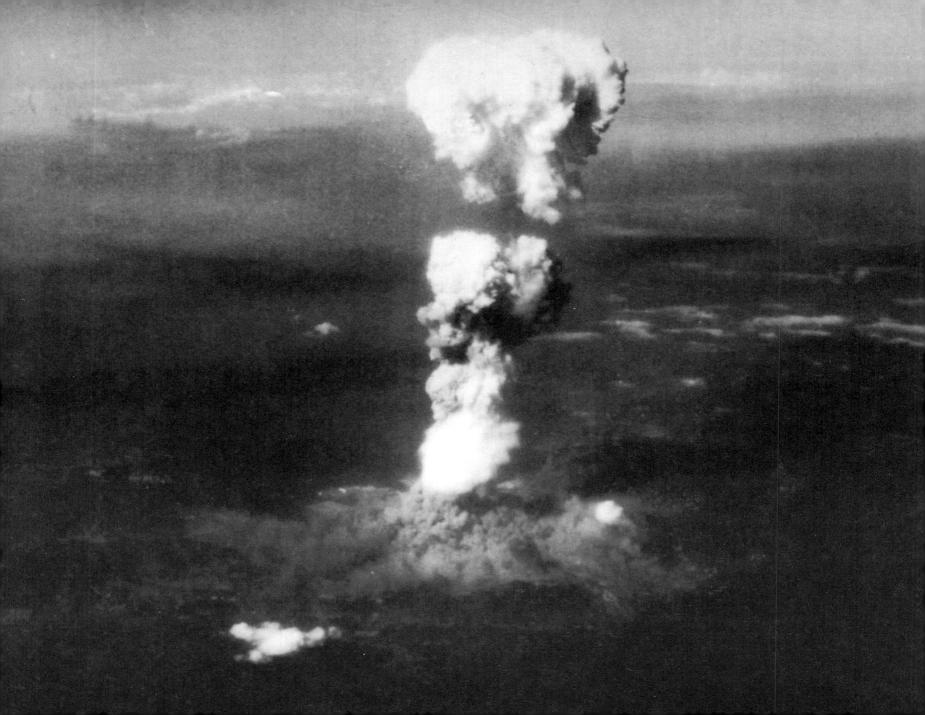

CHAPTER 19

ATOMIC BOMBING

DATE	TYPE	MISSION	HOURS	TARGET	RESULTS	OBSERVER
8/8/45	B-29	Propaganda	14:50	Tokyo–Nagoya	Good	Crocker Snow

"EVACUATE YOUR CITIES NOW!!"

So began the leaflet that we dropped over Japanese cities, the day after the blast at Hiroshima. We flew at a variable 25,000–30,000 feet between broken clouds above and below us, releasing our leaflet-laden bombs near the centers of densely populated Nagoya and Tokyo. Our route was the well-travelled one from the Chiba peninsula upwind over Tokyo direct to Nagoya. On the whole trip we saw neither enemy aircraft nor anti-aircraft fire.

In the middle of May, 1945, advance elements of the 509th Composite Bomb Group began arriving at Tinian. This was a self-contained unit commanded by Colonel Paul Tibbets, and attached to the 313th Wing for organizational purposes only. Its single combat squadron, the 393rd, was under the command of my old friend from the Massachusetts Air National Guard, Major Charles Sweeney.

The 509th had a separate operating area that was fenced off and out of bounds, except for specially authorized people. This secrecy aroused a fair amount of curiosity, which, for most of us, was not satisfied until August 7. However, I became involved early on because the 509th needed advice and information on possible practice targets. I was informed that they wanted to test-drop some heavy, odd-shaped high explosive bombs to compare their actual trajectories with their theoretical ones, and do some good with them while they were at it.

We were happy to oblige, and supplied them with a list of nine lightly-defended strategic targets for their experiments. On July 24, the 509th flew special missions with 10 B-29s. Two bombed the Sumitomo Aluminum Company. Single aircraft hit

(left) The first atomic bomb explodes over Hiroshima, ushering in the nuclear age and changing the geopolitics of war forever.

the rest of the targets. The results were mostly excellent.

My curiosity about the 509th remained unrelieved until late July, when General T. F. Farrell arrived from Washington. General Farrell's job was to carry out a program of psychological warfare in connection with a still top secret weapon, and I had been assigned to work with him. The 509th's mission, said General Farrell, was to deliver one, or possibly two, super bombs that had been under development for several years. Only one had been completed and exploded experimentally on a tower at the Alamogordo testing grounds in the New Mexican desert on July 16. Although the bomb in this test had performed well, no such bomb had ever been dropped from a plane, and no one was certain that it would explode if it were, or what kind of damage it would do, if any.

The general's first task for us in Combat Intelligence was to increase the delivery by air of propaganda material. We were to flood Japan with a series of leaflets describing what was happening in the war and outlining our terms for surrender. Our purpose was to show the people that their country's position was hopeless, persuading them to bring pressure on the emperor to surrender and halt the needless slaughter. We had already started combination weather observing and leaflet dropping

sorties in June, with 103 flights for the month. We upped this to 687 flights in July, and continued at about the same rate.

One of my favorite soft sells, distributed in June, had on one side a counterfeiter's dream of a 10 yen note, with a message on the other side. This, roughly translated, said "In 1930, when the gumbatsu had not yet started the war in China, you could buy the following items for ten yen: 25 sho of good rice or material for a summer kimono, or two bags of charcoal. Today, after waging three years of hopeless warfare against the world's greatest powers, you can buy the following for ten yen: 1.2 sho of good rice on the black market or small amount of charcoal if you can get it, cotton material, nothing. This is what your leaders call co-prosperity."

I didn't know until after the event that two "super bombs"— they were, of course, atomic bombs—the only ones in existence, had been delivered to Tinian, one by ship on July 26, the other by B-29 on August 2. Both bombs were designed to be armed before takeoff, so completion of their missions was non-negotiable.

Events followed quickly after the delivery of the bombs. About the first of August we had started dropping a message in Japanese from President Truman describing his conditions for surrender. It began, "The following are our terms: We will not

(above) Men listening intently at the briefing before the Hiroshima strike.

deviate from them; there are no alternatives. We shall accept no delay." The leaflet went on to detail the eight points of the Potsdam Declaration.

Truman meant what he said, and on August 7, 1945, we dropped the first atomic bomb on Hiroshima, a manufacturing center with a population of 334,000 on the southern coast of the main island of Honshu. Photo reconnaissance showed that 60% of the city's roof area was destroyed. Japanese radio reported nearly 80% casualties in the awesome explosion.

Because of my involvement in both propaganda and damage assessment, I was invited to sit in on the closely-restricted post strike interrogations of the crews. Except for one bending of the rules that especially interested me, and some unusual maneuvers when the bomb was dropped, the first, four plane mission itself was routine. It consisted of the bomb-carrying *Enola Gay*; the *Great Artiste*, an instrumented plane to record shock waves and other phenomena; *Number 91*, the photo plane; and *Top Secret*, a standby waiting on Iwo Jima with cameras and recording instruments in case of trouble with either the *Great Artiste* or *Number*

91. The weather at the target was reported and found to be good, with less than $3/10$ cloud cover. When the bomb left its bay, all the planes did instant steep diving reverse turns to avoid the expected blast. When the explosion came, 1800 feet in the air as planned, crew members reported extreme turbulence from shock waves for a few seconds.

The bent rule: Navy Captain William Parsons, involved with the atomic bomb project since the early days of Los Alamos, was responsible for arming the bomb just before takeoff. One night, as he watched B-29s of the 313th Wing depart Tinian's North Field on a conventional bombing mission, he saw several planes splash in the ocean immediately after takeoff. This was an all too common sight from my quarters across the channel from North Field on Tinian. I remember watching the B-29s crashing into the water, and wondering why the 59th and 313th Wing on Tinian didn't follow the example of the successful takeoff procedures we used on Saipan. We would hold the planes on the runway until it ended at the hundred foot drop to Magicienne Bay. Overloaded as we nor-

---

(above) We dropped this facsimile of a 10 yen note over Japanese cities. It had a message on the other side, with a persuasive argument to convince the people of Japan that they were losing the war.

mally were, we had plenty of room to let the plane settle a bit and pick up speed before starting our climb. Fifty years later, Major Chip Collins, who had been a B-29 pilot on Tinian and later wrote the Ninth Bombardment Group history, explained to me that Tinian's runway only had a three foot drop from the end of the runway to the water.

Captain Parsons realized that if a B-29 carrying an armed atomic bomb splashed on takeoff, tens of thousands of Americans on Tinian and next door Saipan might be killed. With the concurrence of Colonel Tibbets, Parsons went along on the first mission, arming the bomb in the air when the plane was

well clear of the Mariana islands.

On August 8, the day after the Hiroshima strike, Russia announced plans to join the fight against Japan the following day. Shortly after this, we delivered another leaflet message, which started out: "EVACUATE YOUR CITIES NOW!! Because your military leaders have rejected the 13 part surrender declaration, two momentous events have occurred in the last few days. The Soviet Union, because of this rejection on the part of the military (sic) has notified your Ambassador Sato that it has declared war on your nation. Thus, all powerful countries of the world are now at war against you. Also, because

(above) North Field at Tinian, home of the 509th Composite Group. During my stay at Saipan, I often saw overloaded B-29s struggling to take off from these runways, only to crash in the water. No wonder Captain Parsons decided to arm the atomic bomb after the plane was airborne.

of your leaders' refusal to accept the surrender declaration that would enable Japan to honorably end this useless war, we have employed our atomic bomb."

Itching to become more involved and "see for myself," I arranged to sit in the right front seat of one of the planes distributing this latest advice to the people of Japan. Our prospective readers resided in the densely populated Tokyo and Nagoya metropolises; our route was the well-travelled one from the Chiba peninsula upwind over Tokyo, direct to Nagoya. We flew at a variable 25,000 through 30,000 feet, mostly between broken clouds above and below us, and released our leaflet-laden bombs near the centers of both cities. On the whole trip

we saw neither enemy aircraft nor anti-aircraft fire. This confirmed recent similar reports that suggested Japan was saving its meager remaining air defenses to oppose the expected invasion.

The second atomic strike, on August 9, was not as straight-forward as the first. The airplane commander, Major Charles Sweeney, could not use his familiar, specially instrumented B-29 in which he had flown for the Hiroshima strike. He had to borrow an unfamiliar B-29 named *Bock's Car*. His primary target was Kokura, a rail and industrial port of 290,000 on the Straits of Shimonoseki. Reported as clear by a preceding weather plane, Sweeney took off for a designated rendezvous on the way out with his photo and instrumented planes. When he arrived at the

(above) **The distinctive mushroom cloud rises from the Hiroshima blast.**

rendezvous, the *Great Artiste* was already waiting, but there was no sign of the photo plane. After circling for 45 minutes, while burning precious fuel at the rate of 800 gallons per hour, Sweeney headed for Kokura to find it obscured by scattered clouds and blowing smoke from nearby Yawata, earlier hit by conventional incendiary bombs.

The bombardier made several passes, but was unable to see his aiming point. Since orders ruled out radar bombing except as a last resort, Sweeney, knowing he now carried the only atomic bomb in existence, headed for his secondary target, Nagasaki, which was also covered by a broken cloud deck. At first the bombardier was unable to spot his aiming point, but, after several attempts he did get it in his Norden bombsight long enough to drop the second bomb. By that time, *Bock's Car's* fuel gauges showed only 300 gallons remaining of the 7,400 gallons of fuel it had started with. This was not nearly enough to get back to Tinian, or even to Iwo Jima. The only possible alternative (and by the book they couldn't make it) was Yontan field on the recently captured island of Okinawa, 400 miles southwest of Nagasaki. Sweeney landed there with only seven usable gallons of fuel left in his tanks.

Nearly a half century later I spoke to Charley Sweeney, now

an active retired general, to ask him his thoughts about the atomic bombing missions. He told me that his involvement with the nuclear experiment began in the spring of 1944, when, with his friend and mentor Colonel Paul Tibbets, he helped organize the 509th Bomb Group at Wendover Army Airfield in Utah. They soon moved to Eglin Field in Florida, where scientists had the job of fitting the trajectories of 10,000 pound, concrete-filled bombs dropped from 30,000 feet and above to the Norden bombsight. (This corrected what I had been told about the purpose of the practice flights of the 509th when they first arrived at Tinian.)

While at Eglin, Sweeney gave General Curtis LeMay lots of left-seat pilot time in B-29s, including three-plane formation flying at high altitudes. I'll bet my shirt that this was right after LeMay visited the 498th at Great Bend to see what our B-29 training philosophy was.

In September 1995, General Paul Tibbets wrote me "LeMay was in Grand Island for a week to become familiar with the B-29 before going to Guam to take command. He was so frustrated with the inability of the airplane to fly formation at high altitude that he asked General Frank Armstrong (my boss) 'What am I to do with such an airplane?' Frank said he did not

(above and right) We continued dropping leaflets over Japanese cities to intensify civilian fears of our bombs.
Often depicting graphic scenes of death and destruction, these leaflets, combined with the very real
devastation caused by conventional and nuclear bombs, must have been horrifying to the civilian population of Japan.

know. I told LeMay that I would fly at low altitude at night and drop fire-bombs. LeMay looked at me and said 'You're crazy as hell'—a statement for which he apologized when I went to Guam to brief him in May of 1945."

Those of us in combat intelligence were perhaps the first to comprehend the enormity of the physical destruction caused by only two bombs. Of course we had no conception at the time of the human consequences, nor did any of us even come close to understanding how utterly this breakthrough in the physics of the atom would change the geopolitics of war, the peacetime production of energy, and the practice of medicine. For us on the front at the time, it was just a much bigger bang.

The general state of confusion on August 10 is exemplified by two teletype messages, the first one received at 13:36 Zebra (Greenwich Mean Time) calling for business as usual, and the second at 14:07 Zebra scrubbing all missions except weather and photo. Meanwhile, at 12:38 Greenwich time, my office picked up a trans-

BWPL 15 AUG.45 G550I - V DAY PARTY
EN. O'DONNELL'S QR'TS   SAIPAN

lation of an intercepted last gasp radio transmission, which initiated with Japan and was addressed to Sweden. The Japanese were asking Sweden to inform the Allies that they were willing to surrender unconditionally as long as they could keep their emperor. Considering the number of places this transmission must have been before it got to me and was passed along, what with decoding and translating, it seems probable that the request was delivered to Sweden before the Nagasaki bomb was dropped.

But even after Nagasaki our job was not yet done. For the next five days, our bombers went back to business as usual. We continued incendiary attacks on small urban areas, and even took a last whack at Target 357.

On August 15, 1945, Japan's Emperor Hirohito announced his unconditional surrender. On the same day we dropped our last bombs on the small city of Isasaki. It was the 20th Air Force's 330th combat mission of the war.

With, I suspect, a lot of fingers crossed, arrangements were made for a formal signing of a surrender agreement on the U.S.S. *Missouri* in Tokyo Bay on September 2. As a precaution, the 20th Air Force was ordered to prepare for a maximum effort, fully-armed show of force over the ceremonies. Organizing the intelligence portion of the 73rd's part in this operation was sufficiently routine so that most of the ensuing weeks were, for me, a time of ambivalent retrospection and mixed emotions.

Like the rest of my colleagues in combat intelligence, I was satisfied that the war would soon have been over anyway, and I

(left) On August 15, Japan announced its surrender. We held a V.J. Day party in General O'Donnell's quarters.

couldn't help wondering if the atomic bombs had really been necessary. Looking back, I remember favoring anything that promised to speed up the end of the war. However, I have never thought an invasion of Japan would have been required, even without the atom bombs. In fact, more recent controversy notwithstanding, the opinion that the atomic bombs were not essential to our victory was pretty generally shared by just about everyone seriously involved in military analysis immediately following the war. A July, 1946 U.S. Strategic Bombing Survey entitled "Japan's Struggle to End the War" reports that Japanese leaders themselves discounted the atomic bombs as reasons for surrender:

> The Hiroshima and Nagasaki bombs did not defeat Japan, nor by testimony of the enemy leaders who ended the war did they persuade Japan to accept unconditional surrender. The Emperor, the Lord Privy Seal, the Prime Minister, the Foreign Minister and the Navy Minister had decided as early as May of 1945 that the war should be ended even if it meant acceptance of defeat on allied terms. . . . The impact of the Hiroshima attack was to bring further urgency and lubrication to the machinery of achieving peace. . . .

Of course, neither an invasion nor the atomic bombs would have been necessary had Stalin passed Japan's many requests for surrender conditions on to us. As usual, Stalin placed his expansionist aims ahead of the welfare of countries that had, at great cost to their people, saved Russia from defeat by Germany. Although at Yalta, Stalin agreed to join the war against Japan, he held off as long as possible, with no regard for his supposed allies. It is beyond me why Truman didn't save the atomic bombs until after Russia joined us in the war as Stalin had promised. If we had had access to Vladivostok, we could have poured thousands of B-17s released from Europe into a base within easy range of attack on Japan. With B-29s continuing their deadly attacks from the south, and B-17s from the north, and the request through Sweden for surrender terms on the table, Japan could not have continued to fight effectively for long and the atomic bombs may never have been necessary.

Nothing, however can detract from the amazing job done by the scientists and technicians who designed and built the bombs, nor from the patriotism, expertise and courage of the B-29 crews who delivered them. They were only obeying the orders of their Commander in Chief.

CHAPTER 20

COMING HOME

DATE	TYPE	PURPOSE	FROM	TO	HOURS	PILOT
8/28/45	B-29	Ferry B-29	Saipan	Fairfield Field	29	Crocker Snow

We departed Kwajalein about midnight, flying under the stars. Halfway to Hawaii, we met the sun rising dead ahead out of the limitless sea into a cloudless sky. The same sun, I thought, right now was at its zenith at home, shining down on my wife and children. Landing at John Rodgers Field on Hawaii was almost a repeat of a year before, with the same bumpy approach. On final, Pearl Harbor, off to our left, looked about the same as it had when I left it.

After the Japanese announced their plans to surrender, my job was to organize the intelligence portion of the formal signing ceremonies on the *U.S.S. Missouri*. A simple task, it was easily completed well in advance of the September 2 event.

I had just signed up to fly one of the B-29s in our triumphant show of force over the ship, when a notice crossed my desk that crews were needed to fly two war-weary B-29s back to the States. These were planes that had flown so many hours they required complete overhauls in maintenance depots. I held onto the notice, intrigued by the possibilities it presented me.

Here, on the one hand, was a chance to enjoy an uncontest-ed, leisurely sightseeing cruise over familiar territory that had heretofore been strenuously defended against such incursions. This would include the opportunity to inspect the damage to some of our targets at close range as well as the chance to partic-ipate in a flying celebration of the victory we had worked so hard to achieve. There, on the other hand, a unique chance to get home in a hurry after four long years of war.

Home and family won out, although I sometimes regretted missing the opportunity to see Japan in ruins, just as I regretted not having taken advantage of Ben Giles' earlier gift of a tour of the world at war. Seventy-third Wing Special Order Number

---

(left) **The B-29 won the war against Japan, making the Pacific conflict the first major war ever won without a ground invasion.**

230, dated 27 August 1945, designating me "AP Cmnder of War Weary B-29 AP Ser No 42-24601," instructed me to deliver the plane to Hamilton Field, California. Wasting no time, my crew and I departed Saipan early on August 28, landed at Guam to join the Air Transport Command system, and flew on to Kwajalein, where we gassed up.

We started in Saipan with a full crew of 11, a number that expanded exponentially at Kwajalein. This small atoll was short on air or sea transportation anywhere and long on G.I.s hitchhiking home. Operations asked if we had any room. I figured that without bombs and ammunition, even our tired plane would carry the weight of any extra bodies we could squeeze in. We agreed to take a couple of passengers in the already crowded nose and as many in the waist as its present occupants felt they could handle. My only condition was that base operations, not I, would choose among the scores who would give their eye-teeth for the ride. I don't remember how many made the list, but I do remember how happy and grateful they all were.

We departed Kwajalein about midnight, and halfway to Hawaii met the sun rising dead ahead out of the limitless sea into a cloudless sky. The same sun, I thought, right now was at its zenith at home, shining down on my wife and children. Landing at John Rogers Field on Hawaii was almost a repeat of a year before, with the same bumpy approach. On final, Pearl Harbor, off to our left, looked about the same as it had when I left it.

While waiting for our plane to be serviced, I called a Harvard classmate, Charlie Henderson, who was stationed on Hawaii as deputy director of civil defense. He invited me to lunch at his home, and, assuming rightly that I had been deprived of some of the finer things of life, asked what I would like most. Fresh, cold, real milk, was my response. I must have guzzled several quarts straight, and for quite a while afterwards couldn't even think of milk without feeling ill.

For the next leg of our flight we were routed northeast of San Francisco to Fairfield Field (now Travis), the Air Transport Command's Pacific passenger terminal. When we first saw the mainland ahead, the city lights still on in the early dawn, we got quite an emotional charge. After we landed I took a picture of the many happy faces of my passengers lined up in two rows along the fuselage.

Next, we went through an informal combination customs and personnel processing setup. I had a footlocker aboard crammed with memorabilia of the 498th Group and the 73rd Wing. These consisted of numerous photographs, reports and letters as well as the almost mandatory Samurai swords, bought from a Marine on Iwo Jima. I also had a Certificate of Inspection, signed by the Summary Court Officer of the 73rd Wing, testifying that he had inspected my footlocker and it contained no unauthorized military trophies or government-owned property. Equipment issued to me was separate, including my parachute, oxygen mask, hack watch and side

---

(left) I signed up to deliver this war weary B-29 back to the U.S. Every available space
was soon occupied by G.I.s happy to be in the States at last.

FRIDAY, SEPTEMBER 7, 1945   THE BOSTON DAILY GLOBE

Hamilton Hero, Home, Says B-29s Knocked Out Japan

By TED ASHBY

HAMILTON, Sept. 6—Tall, lithe Lt Col Crocker Snow stretched at full length in a deck chair on the lawn at his home here. A week ago he had been at Saipan, from where on Nov. 24, 1944, he had led a cluster of strategic bombers on the first flight of B-29s over Japan —a Japan, by the way, that knew the planes were coming.

He let his mind travel back four years to the pre-Pearl Harbor weeks when he assisted in establishing the keystone of the North Atlantic ferrying route of fighting planes for Britain. It was in September, 1941, that the Federal government, needing his knowledge of airports and flying, got him to go into the service. And from the ferrying route set up then has developed the Army's gigantic Air Transport Command.

If you would let the lieutenant colonel get away with it, he would describe that historic flight over Tokyo in two words: "Pretty soft." Actually, those in the 95 planes comprising the flight knew almost nothing about what they would encounter. No weather information. No estimate of what opposition would be encountered. The planetary winds would be blowing from west to east at about 31,000 feet. That's about all they knew.

Flak and Fighters Came Up

"I was listening on the radio on the way in," said Snow. "I could tell by the excited Japanese voices when we had been discovered. Then their radios went off the air. Quite a number of Jap fighter planes came up. And they sent up a lot of flak. Most unusual sight, probably, was a Japanese seaplane trying valiantly to reach our height. The Japs obviously were surprised at our height and speed. Their planes couldn't reach us. And the flak was ineffective. We didn't lose a ship nor a man."

Col Snow says the B-29 is the greatest ship of the war, better than anything any other country had.

"I suppose," he commented, "that there will be some 'who won the war' talk now. But the B-29 knocked out Japan."

Take that incendiary bomb raid

ON NORTH, NOT PACIFIC, SHORE—Leader of the first flight of B-29's over Japan, Lt Col Crocker Snow is shown with his family on the lawn of their Hamilton home. Left to right are Mrs. Janice Snow, holding Crocker Jr.; Donald, Col Snow and Patricia.

on Kobe, if you would like to know what the Hamilton officer means about the B-29. "We flew planes 3200 miles," Lt Col Snow began. "It would have taken 800 B-17s to carry the number of tons of bombs we carried. And the B-17s wouldn't have been able to fly that far. The average distance we flew on bombing missions was equal to that from New York to Paris. With crews consisting of men recently drug clerks or, maybe, farmers, flying bombs and ammunition in this highly technical piece of machinery, our record of losses would compare fairly favorably with that of a commercial air line flying from New York to London."

He Knew Too Much

Around last May, Lt Col Snow was "grounded" for a very unusual reason. He knew too much. And he was among those no longer permitted to fly over Jap territory because of the "unusual" methods the Japs have of getting information from captured flyers. So he became combat intelligence officer after 15 missions, 12 of them over Japan. He did have a few "business trips" over Iwo Jima while the Japs still held it.

Asked whether, while on duty at Saipan, he ever heard reports that the Japs might have been responsible for the disappearance of the late Amelia Earhart in that area, Lt Col Snow commented: "It's possible, I suppose, but surely there is no direct evidence of it. I do know, or have heard, at least, that several persons who landed there after being shipwrecked never were seen again. One, as I get it, was an American naval officer."

Lt Col Snow's final mission probably was his most enjoyable one. The 155-pound, tanned former director of the Massachusetts Aeronautical Association flew a B-29 from Saipan to San Francisco, hopped a ride to Mitchel Field at New York, borrowed a plane there and flew it to Cape Cod. There he was met by his charming wife, Janice Vaughn Snow, and his three children.

---

arms. Those in charge didn't even bother to look at the footlocker, and no one would accept and give me a receipt for the other stuff. The attitude was: "The war's over, do what you want with it," so I made arrangements to ship it all home.

Learning that Bob Love was still running ATC's Pacific Wing at Hamilton Field, I called to see if he had any planes going east with an empty seat. He did: a new Lockheed Constellation, leaving Hamilton in two hours non-stop for Mitchell Field on Long Island. The only hitch; orders waiting for me at Fairfield were to deliver the B-29 to the depot at Enid, Oklahoma. Fortunately however, my co-pilot, Major Jim Hamilton, was also a qualified B-29 airplane commander, and Enid was on his way home. Some expedited paperwork, and the airplane became his responsibility.

I got a lift on a C-47 to Hamilton Field, thence to Mitchell Field, where I borrowed a C-45 and flew to Otis Field on Cape Cod, landing there at about noon on August 31. From Saipan to Cape Cod in three days, using four different airplanes—it must have been some kind of a record. My log book shows 30 hours and 45 minutes pilot time for the trip, not counting California to New York when I was nothing but a somnolent passenger.

(left) After four years, I was happy to be back home with my family.

During the war, Jan sold our place on Buzzard's Bay and moved the family to Hamilton, on Boston's North Shore, which was where Jan's family lived. When I called her from Mitchell Field on Long Island and said I was on my way to Otis, we had a race to see who could get there first. It was almost a tie. I finished my long trip home in a Ford beach wagon surrounded by boisterous children. It was hard to tell whether they were more interested in home affairs or in B-29s.

It was not long after I arrived home that Emperor Hirohito signed Japan's formal surrender on board the *U.S.S. Missouri*. The event was, of course, front page news. In a sudden, anticlimactic end of the greatest war in history, with hundreds of fully armed B-29s from Saipan, Tinian and Guam circling guard over Tokyo Bay, the Japanese empire surrendered unconditionally to a country that had been emotionally prepared for the bloodbath of a ground invasion of the Japanese mainland. For the first time in the history of the world, a major nation had been conquered without a ground invasion.

In reading some of the many different accounts of World War II, I am often shocked by how far some writers are willing to stray from the known facts, or to invent new ones to make their stories more saleable or appealing. Part of the reason for this kind of fabrication comes from igno-

(right) B-29s fly over the *U.S.S. Missouri* at the formal signing of surrender in Tokyo Bay. I sometimes regretted not staying in the Pacific to take part in the ceremony.

rance, part from self-aggrandizement, and part from the tendency, which I have often seen in the military, political, and corporate bureaucracies, of accentuating the positive. Still another reason why accounts of various events in the war do not correspond with each other is poor record-keeping on the part of the military itself. I had often read that the U.S. military seldom learned from previous wartime mistakes. Perhaps this is because many essential records are not preserved. My footlocker, for instance, contained original reports, memos and the like probably not available anywhere else.

This fact was brought home to me soon after I returned from my tour of duty. By April 1946, I had gone back to my rewarding prewar job as Massachusetts Director of Aeronautics. There I found the most pressing problem to be lack of capacity at Boston's airport (soon to be named, for no obvious reason, the General Edward Lawrence Logan International Airport, after an infantry general). Bedford Airport, currently leased by the military as the site of Hanscom Field, was badly needed as an overflow for Boston. Since my old Air National Guard friend Colonel Charles Wooley was on active duty in the Pentagon in

(above) Members of the Massachusetts Aeronautics Commission. Back row: Jack Hartt, Frank Sweeney, Bill Lewis, Joe Wallis, Red Bank. Front row: Esther Patras, Wilhelmina McGaffigan, Lilian Carbone.

charge of base closings, I made a date with him to discuss the possibility of using Bedford for civil purposes prior to the termination of the lease.

When I flew down to Washington, Charley gave me more than I expected: a temporary permit for the Aeronautics Commission and its invitees to use the airfield, a couple of vacant hangars and a small office building. Early termination of the military lease, he said, would require state legislation.

Leaving the Pentagon on my way home, I ran into Kenny Bergquist (now General Bergquist), who had been A-3 operations of the 73rd Wing when I was A-2. Asking me if I had some time to spare, he escorted me down to the secret bowels of the building. Here, he explained that he had recently been given a new job: the responsibility for preparing radar target tactics and charts for critical objectives in possible adversary countries. Russia was the prime target.

He said he remembered that our A-2 Section had successfully pioneered in this field, but, although he had scoured the military archives for a record of what we had accomplished, he could find nothing. I described the bare bones of our system,

referred him to Major Danny Farmer in Lafayette, Indiana, and headed home.

In April, 1951, I received a long letter from Lieutenant General R. K. Nugent, Deputy Chief of Staff, Personnel, United States Air Force. It discussed the uncertain state of peace in the world, saying,

Even if one doesn't consider the action in Korea a major war, there is no denying that a general war could be precipitated at almost any time by forces entirely outside our own control. The kind of planning we must do not only calls for mobilization of numbers of people and of industrial production, but also for the mobilization of 'know-how'. In order to learn where to look for the high-level 'know-how' which will be needed to make certain of winning this war which is not yet a war, all our general officers were requested to draw on their recollections and furnish the names of individuals who had performed outstanding service during World War II, and who, since separation from Service, have assumed real responsibilities and distinguished themselves in civil life.

The Chief of Staff has directed me to inform you that your name appears on that special list.

(above) General Curtis LeMay was often credited with developing the ultimately successful tactics of using the B-29 as a self-contained fighting machine. In fact, it was LeMay who initially ordered us not to use the B-29 this way, favoring instead the high altitude formations that were successful with B-17s in Europe, but a disaster with the B-29.

Despite these expressions of interest in WWII experience, misinformation still abounded. For instance, the December 1964 issue of the magazine *Air Force* contained an article entitled "How the Superfortress Paced the Attack Against Japan." The piece started out by accurately describing how ineffective the B-29 effort had been for its first four months, and then came up with the following half truth,

> Throughout this early period the Command adhered to the time-honored Air Force doctrine of high-altitude daylight precision bombing. Although successful in Europe, this approach failed to achieve significant results. . . . The period (beginning March 9, 1945) was one of tremendous success. . . . A key factor was the change in tactics inaugurated by General LeMay. . . .(he) decided to launch a series of low-level incendiary night attacks against four principal cities . . . Tokyo, Kobe, Nagoya, and Osaka. . . . An important change in tactics involved the decision to attack individually rather than in formation.

I knew, of course, that LeMay didn't deserve credit for originating our ultimately successful B-29 tactics against Japan, which first had been recommended in my study of B-29 capabilities back in January 1944. This concluded that, with the latest in radar for navigating and bombing, but poor outside visibility, the B-29 would be best used with individual flights at low altitudes, using darkness and bad weather for defense. General O'Donnell had agreed and directed me to prepare a training plan. Essentially the same tactics were later adopted by the other wings as they arrived at Tinian and Guam. However, LeMay does deserve credit for eliminating the weight of defensive ammunition to accommodate more bombs.

I wrote a letter to the magazine, to set the record straight, with copies to Generals Hansell, O'Donnell, and Ganey.

The article's author never answered my letter. General Hansell did at length, thanking me for my letter which he said was "a real contribution and a very valuable expression of 'the view from another vantage point.'" He also took much of the responsibility for the high altitude formation flying, while admitting that others besides myself had argued against it.

In recent years, people have expended much time and ink debating what would have happened if we hadn't dropped the atomic bomb. Perhaps we should also debate what would have happened if we had followed our low altitude, nighttime B-29 tactics from the beginning. In our first four months of high altitude bombing, we dropped 6,645 tons of bombs and used up 25 million gallons of gasoline, but destroyed only 1.1 square miles of urban territory in Japan. We lost 69 B-29s, damaged 229 others, and 624 crew members died. By contrast, in the month of March alone, using the tactics we had trained for almost 15 months earlier, we destroyed 33.3 square miles, losing only 22 B-29s and 154 crew members— many were picked up by our air-sea rescue crews. How much sooner would Japan have fallen had we initiated these successful tactics four months earlier? How many lives would we have saved?

Of course, another "what if" is even more interesting. What if Stalin had not reneged on his 1943 promise to let us use bases in Vladivostok from which to carry out our war against the Japanese? We would have been able to bomb Tokyo with B-17s instead of waiting almost two years for a bomber with sufficient range to strike at the mainland from the Marianas. And then, too, what if Stalin had passed along any of the many requests he had received from the Japanese, asking for our terms for surrender? It seems likely that in either of these two cases, we would never have had a chance to drop the atomic bombs. The war would have been over months, or even years before the first two were ready to go.

One of my most poignant wartime memories is of a letter mailed from England on December 30, 1943 to me at Presque Isle, which I had left a year before. From there it followed my tracks like a faithful dog via the 46th Training Wing, Dalhart, Texas, the 20th Bomber Command, Salina, Kansas, the 73rd Bomb Wing, Colorado Springs, Colorado, and finally caught up with me at the 498th Bomb Group in Great Bend, Kansas in the summer of 1944.

The letter was from Lieutenant Leo C. Lewis, of the 331st Squadron of the 94th Bomb Group. Leo had been my favorite B-17 pilot in the Snow Provisional Group.

In his letter he wrote that "good training over there in the States is just plain life insurance over here in combat," and went on to say "Our Provisional Group, thanks to you, did receive better, far better training than some of the crews that have been arriving here in the E.T.O., but there are still things the fellows should have literally pounded into them. Would like to be in a position to write you a few pointers if you are still handling training groups."

Touched, I wrote back, asking for his advice, but never heard from him. As it turned out he never got my letter. After the war, I often thought of the members of my first combat command. Daring to hope Leo had survived the war, I decided to find him. It took quite a while, but I finally discovered that he was commanding officer of SAC's 28th Bomb Wing at Ellsworth Air

(above) Generals O'Donnell, Harmon and Hansell. "Possum" Hansell later took much of the responsibility for the use of the B-29 in high altitude formation attacks, acknowledging that many of us flying the planes had argued against it.

Force Base in Rapid City, South Dakota. We corresponded extensively, swapping war time experiences, including the argument over B-29 tactics. He said that General Power, his commanding officer in Guam, agreed with me.

I learned that many of my Dyersburg Group had ended up in the 94th Group in England, but that few had survived the toughest part of the war against Germany. It was only after Leo had retired that I at last visited Ellsworth in 1989, on a Memorial Day mission to honor the men who had died in the training accident at nearby Philip, 45 years before.

My last significant reprise of the war came in 1975, engineered, I suspect, by my son, Crocker Jr., who by then had spent two years in Tokyo as the *Boston Globe*'s first foreign correspondent in Japan. A Japanese TV crew asked to interview me for a documentary about the air war against Japan. The set was outside my office at the Boston airport under a pine tree, planted when the airport was run by the Boston Parks Department, and gnarled by 50 years of airport effluvia. It was the only place around that looked at all oriental. The hardest question they asked me was how I felt unloading tons of high explosives and fire bombs over Japanese cities. Did I hate the Japanese people that much?

My answer was then, as it remains, that in the heat of battle I never even thought about it. All my thoughts and energies were devoted to hitting the target, and then getting the plane and its crew safely back to Saipan.

No, I said, I never hated the Japanese, especially in view of acts of extreme bravery that I witnessed. I recalled one especially, when three Zeros (single-place fighters) from Iwo attacked our flight line at Saipan, and, with every gun on the island firing at them, they twice, after strafing our parked B-29s, flew a couple of miles out to sea to reform, bored in for the third time, and were finally shot down. One of the pilots bailed out, but as he parachuted helplessly to earth, he was finished off in the air by our callous ground machine gunners. It was hard not to admire the kind of courage the Japanese pilots must have had, knowing that they would not make it home alive, and yet completing their mission anyway, dedicating their lives to their country.

(left) As Massachusetts Director of Aeronautics, I stayed intimately involved with aviation.

EPILOGUE

Oft expectation fails/And most oft where most it promises

All's Well That Ends Well, William Shakespeare

The fall of 1945 was an exciting time for America. The war, which had so completely occupied the country's collective consciousness for the past four years, was finally over. To me, our success had been, above all, a vindication of General Billy Mitchell, who had suffered so for his advocacy of air power. But beyond the vindication of Mitchell and his prophecies, it was clear that we had at last learned how to use the world's unlimited airspace for the benefit of all mankind. Our long-range intercontinental bombers had conquered all the oceans with routine non-stop flights. Our military transports had created a new, polar bridge of air between the Pacific rim and Europe, besting the problems of arctic weather and navigation.

It should, I thought, be easy to design passenger and cargo planes to do the same. Our single-engine, single-pilot fighter planes, operating from the island of Iwo Jima, flew as many as 1,300 miles to Japan and back protecting the B-29s. These planes could be prototypes of high-performance, reliable, small aircraft for sport as well as for private and business travel. It seemed that those who could afford it would be able to pass up the slow boat to China, and the ever more congested highways, to travel in the unbounded air. A new age of transportation was dawning, and planes, I thought, were finally going to become a normal part of most people's lives.

Apparently a large percentage of Americans shared my sentiments. Only two and a half months after VJ Day, a national aviation conference convened in Oklahoma City. President Truman set the tone there, saying, "In the global war which ended with the unconditional surrender of the last of our axis

---

(right) Here Jan hands me a cup of tea as I sit in the cockpit of my Navion. After the war, it seemed that airplanes might finally come into their own as a means of personal transportation.

foes, aviation came into its own. It underwent a complete evolution in the six years that lay between the beginning of the war and the collapse and capitulation of Japan. We are now looking at the future—a future of peace—during which aviation will achieve its greatest development and expansion and play a role of incalculable importance."

During the years immediately following the war there was a great surge of public interest in flying engendered by the exploits of military aviation, and fueled by discretionary money. The demand for private planes was further stoked by the federally-funded Veteran's Flight Training Program, which spawned dozens of new small flying schools. Unfortunately, with this free ride, the beneficiaries were not always serious about following through on flying as a new profession, nor did most of them want to buy planes. The greater part of the new schools soon folded.

In 1946, the Curtis Publishing Company, a customer and observer of pre-war civil aviation, conducted an aviation survey published in their *Saturday Evening Post*. The survey revealed not only that Americans were well aware of the importance of air power to our military security, but also that they expected airline travel to become routine. They also considered the possibility of personal air transportation to be not just intriguing but distinctly possible.

Unfortunately for airplane manufacturers, who might have been able to capitalize on this post-war bonanza, those interviewed also displayed a lack of understanding of the problems in owning planes. They expected too much for too little, and, the survey counseled, needed to be educated about airplanes if the private plane boom was ever to develop.

The survey went on to suggest that "In the foreseeable future, the airspace for planes appears unlimited. Ground space, however, for privately operated planes, is inadequate. Even now few cities have made provisions for the automobile age. No cities have as yet made enough provisions for the air age. . . A concerted and continuous effort by the entire private plane industry should be directed towards development of adequate ground facilities throughout the entire United States."

This is still true. I participated in enough of the early development of private, commercial and military aviation to recognize both its enormous potential and the gap that often exists between expectations and reality. Although I certainly hoped that postwar production would continue to supply a growing market both for aircraft and airports, I felt that there were difficulties ahead for both.

These caveats notwithstanding, the Curtis survey optimistically predicted that over one million private planes would be in operation within 15 years. At the same time, *Fortune Magazine* ran a story entitled "New Planes for Personal Flying," in which it invited readers to "shop around, to sample the promised millennium of fewer training hours, easier flight tests, foolproof planes and lower prices."

Initially, there was a boom in civil plane production. Boeing, Douglas and Lockheed were well-positioned to accommodate the market for commercial passenger and cargo planes. It was not so easy, however for the manufacturers of fighter and training planes to beat their swords into marketable plowshares. North American, builder of the best World War II U.S. fighter plane, the P-51, was a case in point. Relying probably on optimistic forecasts like that published by the *Saturday Evening Post*, company president Dutch Kindelberger decided to use his partially idled factory to design, build and market a lower cost, lower power, four-place version of the P-51 called the Navion.

I bought serial number 4-106 on March 3, 1947, paying just over $7,000 for it. A friend of Dutch's reportedly said he wanted to buy one of the new planes but couldn't afford the price. Reminding Dutch of what good pals they were, the friend asked if he could have one at factory cost. "Absolutely," said Dutch. "Just send me a check for $27,500 and you'll have the next one off the line."

Republic, manufacturer of our second most popular WWII fighter, the P-47, retooled to build a four-place amphibian, the Seabee, Percy Spencer's prewar design. This probably cost Republic more to build than the Navion cost North American, but their price was about the same. Both companies were gambling on vastly increased volume to bring production costs down.

(right) The Curtis aviation survey asked a broad sample of people for their opinions about air travel and airplane ownership. Most had a positive attitude towards aviation.

ASKED ONLY OF THOSE (14.2%) WHO HAVE TRAVELED BY AIRLINES—

DO YOU LIKE TO TRAVEL BY AIRLINES?

PER CENT ANSWERED <u>YES</u>

TOTAL	. . . . .	95.5%
MEN	. . . . . .	95.8
WOMEN	. . . .	94.9
URBAN	. . . .	95.6
RURAL	. . . . .	95.2

IF YES, WHY?

	SPEED	COMFORT	CONVENI-ENCE	NOVELTY AND SIGHT SEEING	CLEANER, MORE PLEASANT	SAFETY, BETTER PLANES	MISCEL-LANEOUS
TOTAL	84.3%	32.0%	24.1%	21.7%	18.6%	8.4%	2.7%
MEN	86.2	31.6	25.2	17.3	16.3	9.8	3.3
WOMEN	81.2	32.8	22.2	29.4	22.5	6.1	1.9

IF NO, WHY NOT?

MAKES ME SICK OR NERVOUS	AFRAID TO FLY	PREFER OTHER WAYS TO TRAVEL	JUST DON'T LIKE IT	MISCELLANEOUS
30.6%	28.6%	16.3%	10.2%	18.4%

The third plane in this class (low-wing retractable landing gear monoplanes), Beech's Bonanza, is the only one still being produced by the same company. Considerably modified, and equipped with the latest electronics, today's version sells for about $150,000. Half of the increase is the cost of product liability insurance, which has decimated (except for corporate jets and prop-jets) a once thriving U.S. industry.

The post-war aviation boom in private aircraft proved to be extremely short-lived. Production of personal aircraft dropped from a high of 34,568 in 1946 to 3,391 in 1950. Through the next decades, we experienced a slow recovery. In 1978, 18,000 general aviation aircraft were built and sold by U.S. companies, many of them going abroad. However, by 1992, for the first time since WWII, production dropped below 1,000 to 899. Over 18,000 jobs were lost and several companies went out of business, due in great part to the fact that tort lawyers could sue a manufacturer, and win, on product liability claims, even when the injured pilot operated a perfectly good plane in a stupid or irresponsible manner. It was not until 1994 that there was a turn for the better, due mostly to the efforts of Senator Nancy Kassebaum and Representative Dan Glickman of Kansas, who helped pass a bill limiting these outrageous lawsuits. During these times of great difficulty for the American general aviation aircraft manufacturing industry, Canada, France, and Brazil took up the slack and created thriving industries selling private planes to American customers. We may never regain our domi-nant position in general aviation manufacturing: U.S. tort lawyers have, in effect, killed our golden goose.

Fortunately, commercial aviation has done much better. After the war, the scheduled passenger-carrying airlines behaved much as predicted by the Curtis survey. In 1946, the U.S. domestic air carriers produced, in round numbers, 5.9 billion revenue passenger miles. Five years later, the number had nearly doubled, to 10.6 billion. Today, airlines count their customers by the hundred millions: a one hundred-fold increase from the number of passengers they flew in prewar days. Not only a major means of transportation, the airlines are also huge, and complex businesses, made difficult by conflicts of interest between those who live near airports and those who use the planes, as well as ground and runway space limitations, and bureaucrats, who, although many know nothing about aviation, are often called upon to make rules for those of us who do.

I became a bureaucrat myself, although one, I trust, who knew what he was doing. When I returned to private life, I went back to my job as Massachusetts Director of Aeronautics where I served until my retirement in 1976 under eleven different governors, five Democrats and six Republicans. However, my role in the creation and administration of aeronautics law was not confined to Massachusetts. In 1969, Massachusetts Governor John Volpe moved to Washington as President Nixon's Secretary of Transportation. Public Law 31-258, enacted in 1970, called on the President to appoint an Aviation

(right) Commuting to work in the Navion. I bought this plane (which I still have and fly today) in 1947 for just over $7,000—about $20,000 less than it cost North American to build.

Advisory Commission of nine experts to advise the President and the Congress on aviation's future. It appropriated three million dollars for expenses with a deadline of three years. I still can't get over my surprise when the President appointed me chairman. This was probably due to Volpe's influence.

With offices in Washington, and a technical staff of 14, we completed our task eight months ahead of schedule, and returned part of our three million to the treasury. Our report to the President and the Congress, entitled *The Long Range Needs of Aviation*, is 105 pages long, with eight pages of recommendations, among them the establishment of a new job in the Transportation Department, Under Secretary of Aviation, with responsibilities over the entire civil aviation industry.

Our commission report also contained a number of specific suggestions for the reduction of noise and pollution around airports, as well as how to alleviate airport congestion and the economic difficulties of the airline and aircraft industries. Perhaps most controversial, we recommended a much larger role for the pilot in air traffic control, known as "distributed management," in which the pilot, supplied with the same radar information as the ground controller, participates actively in navigation, station-keeping and collision avoidance.

We delivered our report on January 3, 1973. President Nixon acknowledged its receipt promptly in a short, upbeat note to me in which he promised that "it, and the supporting information [which he understood was] to follow, will be studied

(left) My daughter Trish cutting the ceremonial ribbon for United Airlines' new Mainliner Service between the East and West Coasts.

carefully within the Administration in the months ahead." Since almost all of our recommendations required Congressional action, or action by a federal agency responsive to the President, and since Nixon had been re-elected in a landslide less than two months before, I figured that we were home free.

When I took the supporting material to the White House with hopes of prompt action, however, I was told to forget it. By then, the President was in big trouble with the beginning of the Watergate scandal. My contact's advice was that I might as well prepare to carry the torch myself.

In some ways the subsequent history of the AAC resembled that of my work in WWII. After Japan surrendered, no one seemed to care about our hard-earned wartime knowledge. After Watergate broke, our commission lost its rudder. When we closed our Washington office, no one seemed interested in our voluminous files. I had them packed in the luggage compartment of the Navion, and they are now in my cellar in Ipswich. Despite the loss of our political connection, I was determined that our commission work would not be wasted.

In the following years, we had a great deal of support for our reforms from the aviation press, as well as many individuals in the Federal Aeronautics Administration and others connected with the aviation industry. Airport and other local officials picked up our advice about noise control; and, on October 21, 1986, the Aero Club of New England and the Associated Industries of Massachusetts (AIM), held a crucial forum on Air Traffic Control at which I was the moderator. FAA administrator Admiral Don Engen participated.

The subject was the FAA's opposition to real life service testing of the Aviation Advisory Commission's air traffic control recommendation, by then 13 years old. After the forum, Engen contracted with United and Piedmont Airlines for service tests. The system in the cockpit, strongly supported by the airline pilot's union (ALPA), is called TCAS, for Traffic Control and Separation. Now used by the airlines, and by many general aviation aircraft, it shows the exact location of the subject airplane and the position in motion of threatening air traffic. The feasibility of using TCAS for allowing direct high altitude point-to-point flights (called "free flight") is presently being service-tested by the FAA and the airlines. It is comforting to know that despite political difficulties, our AAC work was not in vain.

Throughout my career in aviation, I have continued to fly, and to participate in some of the same pastimes that gave variety to my prewar life. In many ways, my life has been shaped by aviation, and I hope that I have, in turn, helped to shape the course of aviation in this country. At the very least, my long experience in the skies has given me a special perspective on the needs of airplanes and their pilots. Many aspects of the aeronautic world could certainly be improved, from the design of modern airports to the methods of air traffic control in use in today's skies. However, imperfect as the system is, air travel has had a tremendous influence on every aspect of modern life. The ability to fly safely and over long distances has made the world smaller, brought people together, facilitated global communication, and created an international economy. Because of this, aviation has made many later inventions and innovations possible. In fact, global air travel was the necessary precursor to the most recent forms of information delivery and commerce such as the Internet and the upcoming world-wide satellite pocket telephone system.

I still have my 1947 Navion, progressively modified with four new engines, each more powerful than the last, and electronics unheard of in 1947. I have flown it over 900,000 miles in all kinds of weather, into major commercial air terminals and tiny landing strips in all the states (except Hawaii), Canada and most of the Caribbean. I keep my plane at home, operating out of a 1620-foot grass landing strip, which the FAA refers to as "Ipswich International Airport." Flying my own plane has given me the hands-on opportunity to learn about the pluses and minuses of personal air transportation; the constantly more complex and sometimes less efficient air traffic control system; and the amazing developments in precise global navigation using signals from satellites. It is certainly a far different kind

of airspace in which I fly today than that in which I got my first taste of flight, back in 1922 when Kick took me up on his Avro's virgin flight.

In the thousands of miles and hours that I have flown, I have covered territory as familiar as my own back yard and as foreign as rural Japan. In all of these flights, I have passed over millions of people and wondered who they were and what kinds of lives they led: So many people all over the world, carrying on their own lives, with their own unique pursuits. Although I will never meet the vast majority of those whose homes I have overflown, I still feel a kind of a kinship to them, simply for having seen their neighborhoods.

Flying for so many years, I have also been able to witness the slow and inexorable evolution of our country from farmland and wilderness punctuated by cities, to a vast, continuous, urban and suburban corridor along both our Atlantic and Pacific coasts. From the air, the areas from Boston to Washington and from San Francisco to San Diego, once varied and pastoral scenes, appear

(above) The Aviation Advisory Committee in Washington, D.C. Left to right: Leslie Barnes (President of Allegheny), James McDonnell (Chairman of the Board, McDonnell Douglas), Tom Sullivan (Executive Director Dallas/Fort Worth Regional Airport Board), Gerald Grinstein (attorney), John Volpe (Secretary of Transportation), Ray Okamota (architect), Loretta Foy (Chief Pilot, Southland Helicopters), Willard Plentl (Virginia's Director of Aeronautics), Crocker Snow, Elvis Stahr (President, National Audubon Society), and John Shaffer (Guest FAA Administrator).

as large continuous cities, with buildings spread thinly in some areas, and more thickly in others. I remember flying at night before the war, when an occasional car on the road was a cheering sight, its solitary lights illuminating a tiny glow in the darkness below. Now, flying over the same area in the evening, (particularly in the winter, when night falls with rush hour) a long procession of cars, as far as the eye can see, snakes through the concrete jungle, white lights moving slowly forward, while the red tail lights form an unbroken, undulating line. Still more frequently, flying today means skimming along in or over the clouds, unable to see the ground or any landmarks, guided instead by sophisticated positioning instruments and the disembodied voices of controllers and other pilots over the radio.

Although the great expectations of the immediate postwar aviation boom have yet to be realized, I know that, at least for me, flying has been a passport to another dimension. A large part of my life's work has been to improve the safety and accessibility of this dimension for other pilots, whether they fly for pleasure, business, or the protection of our nation.

(right) After the war, I took part in a jet pilot's indoctrination course for senior officers. Here, I am getting into a T-33.

"For me, piloting my plane, time has ceased to run sterile through my fingers. Now, finally, I am installed in my function."

Airman's Odyssey, Antoine de Saint-Exupéry, 1932

INDEX

Page numbers in **bold** refer to illustrations

ABOUT THE AUTHOR

Crocker Snow's professional aviation career started in 1927, when he and two friends formed Skyways, one of the first commercial flying operations at East Boston's airport. For the next decade, he sold and maintained planes; flew passengers, cargo and mail; taught others to fly, and participated in air meets and air shows. In 1939, he wrote the first comprehensive aeronautical law for the Commonwealth of Massachusetts and became director of the newly-created Massachusetts Aeronautics Commission.

In 1941, Snow was called to active duty as commanding officer of the North Atlantic Sector of the Air Corps Ferrying Command (soon to become the Air Transport Command), where he was in charge of building a bridge of airports from the United States to Europe, and operating the route. He commanded and trained a provisional B-17 bomb group which earned the highest rating of any similar unit for tactical efficiency and flying skill. Then he organized the 498th B-29 Bomb Group and went to war himself in the North Pacific. Stationed in Saipan (where he became assistant chief of staff, combat intelligence under General Rosie O'Donnell) he led the 498th on the first B-29 bombing raid against Tokyo and took part in numerous bombing and propaganda missions against the Japanese mainland. A Citation for Meritorious Service from the 20th Air Force commended his outstanding flying ability, resourcefulness and energy, saying that "his example has been an inspiration to his subordinates and superiors and reflects great credit on himself and the Army Air Forces."

After the war, Snow returned to his job as Massachusetts Director of Aeronautics where he stayed until his retirement in 1976. Always active in furthering the cause of aviation, he was appointed chairman of the President's Aviation Advisory Commission in 1972. He has also served as president of the National Association of State Aviation Officials and the Harvard Aviation Foundation; director of the National Pilot's Association; chairman of the Conference of National Aviation Organizations and the New England Council Committee on Air Transportation; and a U.S. delegate to the Fédération Aeronautique Intérnationale. He has won numerous awards, among them the Aero Club of New England's Godfrey Lowell Cabot award for outstanding contributions to the science of aerospace, the designation of Elder Statesman of Aviation by the National Aeronautics Association, and the first award from the Massachusetts Aviation Historical Society.

Since his retirement, Snow has stayed involved as a pilot, a consultant, and a lobbiest for the diminishing rights of private aircraft in the rapidly expanding world of commercial air transportation. He lives on Boston's North Shore with his wife of almost 60 years and flies his modified 1947 Navion out of his own backyard airstrip, which FAA refers to as "Ipswich International Airport."